MW01491453

Bird Dog 757

Bird Dog 757
Operation Rabbit Hole

DAVID POIRY

MOLLY:
ENJOY THE
READ !! :

David Poiry

AKA RABBIT

Copyright © 2017 by David Poiry

All rights reserved. No part of this book may be used or reproduced in any manner whatsoever without prior written consent of the publisher except in the case of brief quotations embodied in critical articles and reviews. Special book excerpts or customized printings can be created to fit specific needs.

Although based on a true story, some names have been changed.

Published by: Redwood Publishing, LLC
info@redwooddigitalpublishing.com

ISBN Hardcover: 978-0-692-43718-6
ISBN eBook: 978-0-692-43719-3

Library of Congress Control Number: 2015906501

Interior design by Chad McClung

Third Edition

Author's Note

The reasons for writing this book are many, not the least of which is to share this experience with other young, dedicated officers who might be called upon to embark on a similar deep cover operation. There is no other assignment in the police world that even remotely comes close to a covert investigation of this nature. It is an honor to be selected for such an assignment, but that honor comes with a very high risk. Hopefully this book will be useful to those who are contemplating such an assignment, which will likely subject them to danger, loneliness, and extreme demands.

The choice will have enormous ramifications and will most certainly carry a high personal price. It is incumbent upon the operative to closely analyze the known facts, believe in the objective, and have an absolute, clear understanding of the legal parameters and of the defined objectives of the assignment. Failure to do so, in the end, will raise the question:

"Was it worth it?"

Prologue

Los Angeles, California

There was a time when a young Los Angeles Police Officer was referred to as the "twenty-fifth man." Only one in twenty-five aspirants ever got to call himself a Los Angeles Police Officer. This was before consent decrees and catchphrases such as Affirmative Action became commonplace. It is probably politically incorrect even to reference a society in which false interpretations of equality were non-existent. It was a time when people competed on an equal basis for positions in the workforce and earned their reputations through hard work, dedication, and sheer merit.

Applicants first were held to height and weight standards, and then their intelligence, strength, agility, psychological fitness, personality, and overall physical fitness were determined through a variety of tests.

Los Angeles has traditionally had the smallest ratio of police officers to population of any major metropolitan area in the United States, even excluding the illegal alien population and the semi-permanent employees of the movie industry. When all things are considered, the ratio becomes ridiculous.

As a result, it was necessary to employ young men who had a military bearing and a commanding presence. Thanks to the efforts of such men as the revered LAPD Chief William Parker, corruption was virtually eliminated, and honesty became a byword.

Selection was followed by a rigorous training program, which was modeled after the US Marine Corps basic training program. The purpose of this program was to mold young men into self-sufficient law enforcement officers dedicated to community service and the protection of everything that walked—be it man, woman, child, or beast. A camaraderie developed among officers, and each man pledged his allegiance to the flag of the United States, the City of Los Angeles, and his fellow officers.

Somewhere along the line, it became apparent to each young man that he was something very special. He was a Los Angeles Police Officer. It wasn't a job; it was a vocation. No one could imagine what life would be like without the Department. If you couldn't become a Los Angeles Police Officer, you could always go back to school and choose a lesser profession in medicine, science, or, of course, the law. It was impossible to imagine leaving the Department for any reason. That would be tantamount to failure, the worst thing that could happen to a policeman—except, of course, to be removed.

This is the story about one of those policemen. In time, he would be selected to work the secretive Public Disorder Intelligence Division, aka PDID. He would be assigned to a deep undercover assignment known as "Operation Rabbit Hole." In PDID parlance, he would be a "Bird Dog," a code name for a police spy, source number 757.

Contents

Acknowledgments

This book would not have been written had it not been for the dogged persistence of my great friend and mentor Captain James (Doc) Docherty, who by any measure was the greatest Captain ever to serve on the Los Angeles Police Department.

For many years, he prodded me to write this book, expounding that this is a story that must be told. He was a very close friend of Chief Gates, and he was highly respected by everyone.

Captain Docherty was astonished to learn the story of this incredible four-year investigation conducted by Public Disorder Intelligence Division. It was his firm belief that the chief could not have been aware of the extreme and constant danger to which his undercover officer had been exposed, nor of the depth and reach of this investigation, which clearly belonged to the federal authorities.

Captain Docherty fully understood the mechanisms of the chief's staff meetings, having spent many years in the chief's inner circle. This personal knowledge enabled him to provide insight into the inner workings and mindset of some of the high command. Captain Docherty felt that telling this story would serve many useful purposes, and that it might have positive effects both inside and outside the Los Angeles Police Department.

Rabbit, the undercover officer whose investigations are described in this book, was finally persuaded to tell the story when Captain

Docherty asked, "What is the last thing you remember doing as a policeman?" Rabbit knew exactly what it was. He was leaving his pension hearing with a broken spirit, and upon seeing Billy Harris, his control officer for the entire undercover operation, gave him a deeply emotional hug, and then asked him a question:

"Billy," he said, "before we part, I need you to answer the most important question of my life, a question that only you can answer. A simple yes or no: was the investigation worth it?"

Harris replied, "By the very nature of covert operations, it is always—"

Rabbit stopped him right there. He knew Harris could not or would not answer the question.

Captain Docherty told Rabbit, "Write the story, and when you are finished, you will have your answer."

Captain Docherty, thank you.

Chapter 1
Rabbit

A high-performance black-and-chrome Harley Davidson rumbled north on the Harbor Freeway and approached Downtown Los Angeles, the hub of the sprawling metropolis that has given birth to so many cinematic miracles—a city that has been destroyed a hundred different ways in imaginatively staged disasters on the silver screen.

The driver failed to notice the spectacle in front of him. The first time he'd traveled this route, the tallest building in Los Angeles had been the towering City Hall, which was now dwarfed by an ever-growing number of skyscrapers, giving Downtown the appearance of a concrete and glass rain forest. How could this have happened? The landmark City Hall building, once an icon of this city, could now hardly be seen. The First Interstate building, at that time the tallest building west of the Mississippi, somehow seemed to lack the romantic appeal that City Hall had once given the great city of Los Angeles.

Instinctively the rider deftly steered the Harley Davidson from the fast lane over to the transition to the northbound Hollywood Freeway in a manner that would have been a suicidal attempt in another city at another time. Afternoon traffic was moving at

approximately twenty miles per hour faster than the speed limit.
The Harley Davidson slid onto the ramp for the northbound
Hollywood Freeway. Traffic eased up and he accelerated. It was a
perfect day for a motorcycle ride—eighty degrees, blue sky, and
lots of sunshine. This was the good life by any measure.

The rider, dressed in torn, faded jeans and a black Che Guevara
T-shirt, his long hair beyond shoulder length and blowing in the
breeze, his black beard wildly unkempt, was a thirty-year-old Los
Angeles police officer with a taste for adventure and an insatiable
appetite for living on the edge. His street name was Rabbit. He
worked in the Bureau of Special Investigations, and he had been
assigned to infiltrate the motorcycle gangs of Los Angeles, live
with them undercover, and obtain information on gang homicides.

As Rabbit continued streaking along the Hollywood Freeway,
he passed over the apartment on North Kenmore Avenue, where
he'd first lived after arriving in Los Angeles. He'd been just thirteen years old back then. The place now was a derelict, run-down,
shabby building that had been taken over by junkies, prostitutes,
and illegals.

As he continued motoring north, he thought back to the beginning. At least, the beginning of his life in Southern California.
When his family had first moved to Los Angeles from Indiana,
Rabbit's mom and dad had ridden the train with their youngest
sons. Rabbit had followed, keeping his older brother company
while he drove the family car, which was loaded with the family's
possessions. To save precious dollars they didn't have, the boys slept
in the car along the way. To young Rabbit, this was the height of
adventure. As they tooled along historic Route 66 looking little

better than characters from *The Grapes of Wrath*, he felt like he'd been transformed into Huck Finn. It couldn't get much better than this, he thought. When his brother finally got off of the San Bernardino Freeway, the brothers found themselves on surface streets in downtown Los Angeles.

Los Angeles at that time did not have, by any definition, a skyline. The only tall building was City Hall, except for an AT&T structure that appeared to be tall because it sat high on a hill. Bunker Hill was just that, a hill with a few single-family residences and rundown hotels. The aging funicular railway known as Angel's Flight, which resembled a miniature tram, was nearing extinction.

He remembered how, as they pulled up to a stoplight, he had looked out the passenger window and stared in awe at the figure next to him. A Los Angeles police motorcycle officer sat astride a huge black and white Harley Davidson motorcycle. The tough, tanned features of this seeming giant were all the heroes he could conjure up rolled into one. All he knew about the Los Angeles Police Department was what he'd learned from Sergeant Joe Friday on *Dragnet*. He had always been impressed with their regal appearance. Unlike in other police departments, there were no overweight or sloppy officers. Each uniform was tailored. Every piece of leather was spit and polished. These were the Adonises of Law Enforcement. The appearance of this motor officer only enhanced his opinion of them. It left the impressionable youngster with two driving ambitions: the first to become one of these modern-day dragon slayers dressed in blue, and the other, to ride a Harley Davidson police motorcycle.

He thought of his Mom and Dad, who were the salt of the earth—caring, loving, devoutly religious parents who had made the move to this land of milk and honey in hopes of finding a better life for their children. Rabbit had been a wild, fun-loving, young boy who had kept his parents on the edge of their seats for most of his adolescence. It would take four different high schools and several trips to the police station before he realized how he had wasted precious time, and now he was determined to make up for his errant ways and make his parents proud.

He was going to become a Los Angeles police officer. His father had tried everything he could think of to persuade his boy to become a priest instead, but Rabbit had his sights set on becoming a police officer. He told his father that with a career in law enforcement, he could accomplish meaningful goals, just like a priest, only in a different capacity. The bottom line was that his vocation would be helping those who couldn't help themselves. His father, although disappointed, supported his son's decision.

Three years later at age twenty-one, Rabbit entered the Los Angeles Police Academy. Unlike a great many large metropolitan police departments, Los Angeles required candidates to compete for admission to the Academy, not merely to pass written and oral exams administered by a member of the community and a member of the Police Department. These exams were followed by a thorough medical exam, a grueling physical agility test, and rigorous psychological testing. The academy itself was more than a training ground; it was designed to examine each individual for any possible flaws or weaknesses and then to weed out those who could not meet the Department's high standards. Rabbit felt a great sense of accomplishment at graduation. "Someday," he'd promised himself, "I will be a sergeant or detective." Being an overly optimistic young officer, he'd had no idea what the future would bring.

He left the academy a well-trained, aggressive street cop. He started out working Harbor Division, which operated as its own police department. It was filled with old-timers who were in semi-retirement and not looking to make waves. The Harbor Division covered the San Pedro docks, which were frequented by tough longshoremen and merchant seamen. The old-timers taught him to use the "stick" quickly, and not to give these big, burly guys a chance to get their feet planted. Practicing what he had been taught, the young officer broke the leg of a good friend of his commanding officer.

After a short suspension, he found himself working the mean streets of the toughest police division of the city, the 77th Street division. He quickly established a reputation as a trusted, tough street cop. Rabbit was proud to work 77th Street. This division was the real deal in the cop world, and so were the policemen who worked there. There was nothing Mickey Mouse about it—no other division could match its rich history. It was the City's battlefield, a place to test one's mettle. The 77th policed the heart and soul of the Los Angeles ghetto, the concentration point of the city's highest crime and violence statistics. It was the busiest shop in the city, and it formed tough, no-nonsense street cops—they were in every way modern-day *Impavidus Bellatori*—a Latin phrase used by the Romans to describe Fearless Warriors—and he was proud to be a part of that elite group.

After five shootings, a couple of mini riots, and twenty-one disciplinary complaints, Rabbit began to feel he would probably never fulfill the promise he'd made to himself on graduation day. After a long, difficult road working under tight scrutiny, and after showing much contrition, he caught a huge break: his old field sergeant, Douglas Nelson, was put in charge of the vice unit at Venice Division. Doug knew Rabbit and recognized the potential of this wild, young street cop, and he knew that with some direction, Rabbit could be developed into a top-notch, freewheeling undercover vice cop.

Very few officers have the qualities necessary to carry off an undercover assignment with complete success. It requires an unparalleled acting ability, coupled with imagination, daring, and dedication. This was right up Rabbit's alley. He got the job and loved it. He grew a beard and dressed like the free-spirited person that he was.

Long hours and unpredictable work schedules, along with the ever-present smell of cheap perfume from late-night arrests, brought about the dissolution of a short marriage. His wife had grown up with the LAPD. She was the daughter of Detective Lieutenant Ralph Weyant, who had spent his distinguished career working homicide, but she never knew the machinations of a Vice Unit.

Rabbit excelled in this assignment. His arrest recap was the highest in the division. Often he was loaned out to other areas of the city to work on complicated vice cases that were beyond the capabilities of most ordinary vice cops. On several occasions, he assisted in narcotic cases and other special operations. It was all good. His mentor was eventually selected to become a member of the elite Administrative Vice division, and a whole new vista was opened for Rabbit.

##

Without warning, freeway traffic stopped. Rabbit had become transfixed in his trip down memory lane. He was lost in his daydream and in the hypnotic rumble of his Harley Davidson. He swerved hard left to avoid crashing into the stopped vehicles in front of him. In doing so, he nearly crashed into the center divider. In addition to the near accident, he realized he had missed the Sunset Boulevard off-ramp. It was two miles behind him, and he was already 30 minutes late for an intelligence briefing with his sergeant and a Special Operations lieutenant. The lieutenant was tasked with personally selecting undercover operators to work the upcoming Pink Floyd rock concert. It would be a very sensitive police undercover operation, and it would be subject to much after-the-fact scrutiny—and the chief would not tolerate any screw-ups.

This would be one of those make-or-break moments in the lieutenant's career. If there were no problems, it would be a feather in his cap. On the other hand, a faux pas on his part would send him directly to the basement to be put in charge of the Property Division.

Rabbit did not want to be a part of this operation, but of course there was no option. It was obvious that "those in charge"—whoever "they" were—didn't want this concert or any further concerts. The tactic would be to make lots of dope arrests and then "they" could demonstrate the inherent evil of rock concerts. Rabbit had tried to excuse himself from the operation, but the lieutenant wouldn't consider the request.

The task force would be made up of seasoned undercover operators, and Rabbit would be one of them. It would be a one-day operation. Rabbit argued that he was presently working an investigation gathering information on guns and homicides, and it made no sense to become involved in low-level drug arrests and subsequently be subpoenaed to testify in open court and risk compromising his identity. It would obviously jeopardize a major investigation. Rabbit told them that the best way to police the event was to deploy uniformed officers. The lieutenant didn't care what Rabbit's opinion was, he just wanted qualified operators, and he gave Rabbit a paper with a date, time, and location to report for the concert. With that, the meeting abruptly ended. Rabbit mumbled, "Another dumb-ass operation by the school boys downtown."

Chapter 2
Rock Concert

The City of Los Angeles had a strict prohibition against rock concerts. By the mid-seventies, however, it had become apparent that this entertainment problem could no longer be avoided. A test run was planned with a Pink Floyd concert at the Los Angeles Sports Arena. Because of the proliferation of drugs among the attendees of rock concerts and the attendant violence that had occurred in other cities, major plans were made to closely police the event. High-level meetings were held involving the various department entities that would be involved. It was determined that a task force would be formed with a large contingent of undercover officers.

On the day of the concert, the police cast was assembled and two roll calls were held. The first, which was held at a remote location away from the Sports Arena, involved the undercover officers, their supervisors, and the backup teams. Strict guidelines were laid down by the grizzly old lieutenant, who was unmistakably a cop in spite of the plain clothes he wore.

"You're gonna see a lot of assholes out there, but you can't touch them. There's no law against being an asshole. If there were, we wouldn't have any defense attorneys. We don't want to burn your cover; so don't get involved in just any arrest. If you see any kind of

major violation, or if you make a dope buy, just give the prearranged
signal. A backup team will take the violators down." There was a lot
of murmuring by some of the younger, less experienced undercover
cops, who wanted to make the physical arrests themselves.

The lieutenant in charge was very patient. "If you make a physical arrest, you're burned. There will be more dope sales out there
than popcorn sales at the movies. One of the detectives will grab
you when it's time to come in for reports. They'll make it look like
an arrest. Any questions?"

"Hey, Lieutenant, what if we see someone blowin' a joint, but
not selling?"

"You think we have enough manpower to arrest 100,000 people?"

When the giggling subsided, the lieutenant continued. "We're
only interested in the dealers. There's going to be a judge and some
people from the DA's office checking on the arrests to make sure
we don't go overboard. No humbugs. No entrapment. If you don't
have a dead-bang case, let it go! This is a major police operation.
Everyone in the Council will be watching, and the brass wants us
to look good."

The lieutenant then had all the undercover officers stand up and
face one another. "Make sure you remember these guys. Contrary
to the way they look, they are not assholes." He looked them over
for a bit and then continued, "Well, not all of them." That drew a
laugh. "Okay, guys, let's hit it."

The young operators left the room quickly, eager to assume
their roles. The seasoned operators talked and played grab-ass as
they slowly made their way out of the assembly. For them, it was
just another humdrum day at the office.

The Sports Arena was rocking long before the main event. It seemed as though every young person in California had made it to Los Angeles for the concert. Angelenos are accustomed to smog, but the interior of the coliseum looked like a third-stage alert. There was enough grass being burned to dry up Humboldt County. By the goofy looks on a lot of those kids, some labs had been working overtime to pump out LSD, Quaaludes, and a wide variety of other mind-altering drugs.

In less than a half hour, Rabbit had the first three arrests. Back in the command post there were some very nervous people. The judge and the prosecutors were skeptical about the ease and rapidity of Rabbit's arrests, especially since no one else had scored their first arrest yet. The judge turned to the field commander and said, "I thought we agreed there would be no manufactured cases."

The captain was at once nervous and angry. "We'll look into it right away, Your Honor."

He then turned to one of the detectives, "What the hell is this Rabbit fool doing? Didn't you tell him there would be no humbugs?" The detective was a little pissed at the captain's attitude, but told him he would bring Rabbit in.

A short time later, Rabbit entered the CP with the detective who had been sent to get him. "This is Rabbit, sir." The group of dignitaries and the field commander tore themselves away from the coffee machine and turned toward the voice.

The judge broke into laughter when he saw Rabbit in all his glory. He had a natural full beard which ran halfway down his chest. His shoulder-length black hair was stringy and matted and looked like he had shampooed it with used motor oil. A filthy black

T-shirt extolled the virtues of marijuana, and his jeans gave new meaning to the derelict look of the day.

"Are you seriously a police officer, son?" Rabbit politely nodded in agreement. The judge shook his head, still laughing. "I'm sure these arrests haven't been manufactured, but I'm not so sure that a defense of entrapment wouldn't be appropriate." Everyone in the room broke up with laughter, including the Judge.

Quickly Rabbit became a fair-haired boy with the Command staff. He made many more good, solid arrests that night, and confiscated a lot of dope before retiring to the command post to prepare voluminous reports.

The next day, his sergeant, Doug Nelson, thought the time was perfect to approach his commanding officer and suggested that Rabbit would be a hell of an asset to the Division. After some discussion, the captain agreed to take a close look at him.

Several days later, Captain Green summoned Nelson into his office. The office was a perfect extension of the man who occupied it. Autographed pictures of various dignitaries adorned the walls, which were painted a different color than any of the other offices. Decorations that had been tastefully prepared by his wife, who was an interior decorator, paid tribute to his arrogance. His wardrobe blended with the soft pastels, and each accessory was in perfect harmony with the colors of his office. He constantly held a filtered cigarette in his clenched teeth, much like FDR and various matinée idols of an earlier time.

Nelson knocked gently on the door frame. He felt as though he should remove his shoes prior to entering.

"You sent for me, sir?"

The captain threw a very thick dossier at him.

"Take a look at that shit."

Nelson glanced through it and saw it was Rabbit's rough, handwritten resumé. "Uh-huh," he said.

The captain was incredulous.

"Uh-huh? That's all you have to say? I thought you knew this fool from when he worked for you in Venice."

Nelson handed the dossier back to the captain.

"I did! He's the best undercover operator I've ever seen, Captain. You saw what he did at the Pink Floyd concert."

The captain's patience was beginning to wear thin.

"Nelson, this is one of the most elite divisions in the Department. Officers in here are given perks that other officers and detectives can't even begin to imagine. There is a waiting list to get in. We take only the crème de la crème."

"But sir, he is the best at what—"

The captain exploded. "The best? Have you lost your goddamned mind, Nelson? He's a loose cannon. This madman has been involved in five shootings, has twenty-one personnel complaints in his package, and to top off his stellar record, he has been to a Department Trial Board personally ordered by the chief for excessive force. He should have a team of Internal Affairs investigators assigned to him full time."

Nelson maintained his calm. "He's probably the best vice cop in the city. We've loaned him out for several major cases. All that stuff in his package happened years ago, when he was running wild in a black-and-white with his pants on fire. He hasn't had a beef since he started working Vice."

The two stared at each other for a moment, and Nelson threw in the kicker. "Narcotics knows all about his package, and I know for a fact they are trying to recruit him right now."

Nelson knew there was no way the captain would let another division beat him to an exceptional, experienced operator. He knew that at the next intelligence briefing with the Chief of Police, the commanding officer from Administrative Narcotics Division would make some remark about recruiting Rabbit before anyone else even had a shot at him.

"I'll think about it, Nelson. But let me warn you, if I do take him in—and I'm not telling you that is a given—he'd better not screw up. Because, if he does, it won't only be his ass that I'll have; it will be yours, too."

Nelson had to suppress a smile. He knew the old man wanted Rabbit, especially after all the back-slapping he'd gotten from the concert. Nelson had hit him between eyes with a *coup de grâce*. Green just wanted to cover his own ass in case Rabbit ever did screw up.

"Yes, sir, I'll take that chance."

Chapter 3
Prostitution Unit

When Rabbit reported for duty with the Administrative Vice Division, he was assigned to the night watch prostitution section. All the special operations people salivated when they saw him. Even though he had joined the "elite," he was told to keep his appearance the same. It seemed as though everyone in the division had a special little problem that could easily be solved if they could use Rabbit. A lot of police officers wear unique disguises, but Rabbit stood alone. He had a wild look in his eyes to go along with his unusual appearance.

Danny Shih was Rabbit's lieutenant, and he soon became annoyed with all the requests.

"Boss, we just need him to sit in a bar for a few days to pick up some conversation."

"Just one week! He makes a couple porno connections and he's done."

"We've got some hardcore assholes on Melrose who are operating a slave market. A few days and we'll have him back."

Shih knew better. He had been in specialized assignments for too long to be stroked by other units. He knew that little loans usually dragged out, and then there would be the constant interruption of court testimony. Shih had his own problems and cases to be solved, which made him more than a little reluctant to lend Rabbit out to other units. Shih was a seasoned detective and street-smart cop. He knew that Rabbit's value was in his acting talents and vivid imagination. Shih wanted to keep Rabbit focused on the cases at hand.

These were good days for Rabbit. With Nelson at his side or providing cover, he got to roam the city doing his thing. He could clean himself up and look like either an eccentric, hip, well-to-do person, or a street bum. He operated in the best hotels in Beverly Hills and the West Side with the same ease that he operated among the low life on the side streets of downtown LA and Hollywood. In his inimitable way, his role-playing into criminal activities included all walks of life. He worked anything and everything—pimps, businessmen, drug addicts, bikers—it didn't matter. He was beyond typecasting.

In one operation, a major pimp in the Hollywood area was the target. Lamar Jefferson was a tough, streetwise guy who had grown up in South Central Los Angeles. When he decided to major in pimping whores, he kept his minor in stolen property with a specialization in credit cards. Administrative Vice had targeted Jefferson about a year earlier, but he was invincible.

A big break finally came when Jefferson battered one of his girls one time too many. She decided to roll over on him. The only problem was that Jefferson always wanted to "test the new material" before putting her into his stable. That precluded any possibility of using an undercover female officer as an operator.

Rabbit and other detectives brainstormed the problem over beers at a local watering hole one night after work and came up with an idea. They would have the unhappy hooker introduce Rabbit to Jefferson as a gay man who happened to be an expert in forgery and credit card scams.

The first meeting was at a bar on Sunset, a notorious pimp hangout. Jefferson, lacking any sort of sophistication or tolerance, was slightly amused and somewhat disgusted at having to deal with a gay forger, but had to admit that Rabbit had potential. Because his persona was so outrageous, Rabbit knew he had no reason to worry that Jefferson would frisk him for a body wire or weapons.

After a few meetings, Rabbit had gained Jefferson's confidence, and he was invited to come to Jefferson's home at the top of Mount Washington, a wealthy, fashionable section of Hollywood. The home was not especially grand for the neighborhood, but it sat on top of a very high hill and had a commanding view of the entire city.

The inside of Jefferson's house was furnished expensively, but with very little taste. It was as though he had purchased everything he'd dreamed of as a disadvantaged youth and stuck it wherever it physically fit. The colors were garish to the point of hurting the eye. The "mansion," as Jefferson referred to it, was a heavily armed fortress that always housed at least one of his armed lieutenants. The reason for Rabbit's visit was ostensibly for him to learn the intricacies of Jefferson's operation.

Rabbit was fitted with a body wire that today would be considered very unsophisticated, but it was the best available at that time. The "Fargo Unit," as it was called, had a limited life span, and the battery pack was worn inside the waistband and next to the skin. As it began to wear down, the battery became hotter and hotter and eventually caused severe burns.

Prior to the operation, a plan was developed: Rabbit would get Jefferson to perform some act involving a credit card scam so that the police would have Jefferson dead-bang on a conspiracy case. The body wire would serve as a protection for Rabbit and also alert the waiting troops when the necessary evidence had been collected, enabling them to spring into action and take the operation down.

Murphy's Law works overtime during undercover police investigations. This day was no exception. Jefferson sat down with Rabbit and gave him some sample signatures to forge. When Jefferson was satisfied, he would produce the necessary ID and they would go out and commit some crimes. Just as Rabbit started to practice his forgery, one of Jefferson's girls entered seductively, and Jefferson decided to sample his own merchandise. As Rabbit labored at the desk, Jefferson stood several feet away caressing the young hooker and salivating all over her. She went into her ecstasy act and began to moan and groan due to the pleasure that was overcoming her. The more she moaned, the more Jefferson got into what he was doing. Pretty soon he too was moaning and groaning, each trying to outdo the other.

On the other end of the wire, detectives were straining to hear what was going on. They were unable to make out what the groaning was all about. They were getting nervous. After a while, Jefferson lay on the floor, rolling over and over with his pants and shorts off; the girl was now completely naked. The two of them got wildly involved in their sex escapades, both screaming and hollering.

By now the dying wire was starting to transmit a lot of static. It was also starting to burn Rabbit, which caused him to wince and grunt a few times.

That was all it took for his backup teams. They were sure Rabbit was in trouble. They decided to assault the castle. Several of the detectives were past the prime of their lives and a little overweight. Their arduous trek up the steep hill caused a lot of noise, which alerted Jefferson's lieutenant. At first Jefferson and his bodyguard were going to shoot it out, but they quickly decided that the odds were not in their favor, so they split. As soon as they hit the hill on the other side of the house, Rabbit tackled Jefferson. The two of them bowled over the pimp's lieutenant and the naked whore. All four tumbled halfway down the hillside before coming to a rest. Before they could gather their wits about them, several younger, uniformed officers who were along for the raid appeared from nowhere and had the cuffs on all concerned.

Prosecution was not as easy as it could have been if the investigation had not ended prematurely, but it was successful nevertheless.

About this time, the lure of the job and the long hours created another personal problem with Rabbit. The Playboy Bunny with whom he had been living for the past two years became tired of dealing with the unpredictable hours and secretive nature of undercover assignments. After many attempts to reconcile herself with these issues, she packed her things and moved out. Rabbit didn't realize how much she meant to him until she was gone. He got down in the dumps about his love life, and it started to affect his concentration and work. He needed time away from work to refocus; so he went down to Cabo for a week of fishing, tequila, and introspection at the Cabo Wabo. The self-prescribed therapy worked wonders. He wanted to stay forever, but he had court cases stacked up that he needed to handle back in Los Angeles.

On his first day back to work, Rabbit walked into the squad room feeling like a new man. It didn't last long. Nelson had been assigned to a desk job, and Rabbit was assigned to another partner.

"Doug, what happened, man?" Rabbit asked. "You look like shit."

"What happened? I'll tell you what happened. My fucking brother-in-law had a dope lab in the back of my garage. He was cooking up dope and blew it up. Too bad it didn't kill the little bastard. The garage burned down, and he now looks like a mummy. Narcotics took me out to the house and turned the dope dogs loose inside, looking for more drugs. They found none—zip; zero—and then they put me on the polygraph to see if I knew anything about the dope in my garage. Then they assigned me to an inside desk job until they figure out if I'm the French Connection in Los Angeles."

"It's just fucking perfect," he added. "I wouldn't have it any other way. It will give me something interesting to talk about at my upcoming oral board for my promotion to lieutenant."

By the time Internal Affairs completed their investigation, which completely exonerated Nelson, Rabbit was deep into an investigation with his new partner, Detective Sergeant John Paul Dodaine.

John Paul was an old-school detective, set in his ways, and didn't like working with a partner—especially some young kid like Rabbit. It was a difficult situation for both of them, as Rabbit didn't want to work with an old man like John Paul, either.

Nelson gave Rabbit a pep talk and told him how the new program was going to run and not to bitch: this was a non-optional deal for everyone. The lieutenant had said this was how it's going to be, and that was that.

Nelson said, "John Paul is really good at what he does. His cases are always complicated and airtight."

John Paul had come over from Intelligence, where he had worked for a number of years before something bad went down and he was out of there. No one in Administrative Vice knew what it was, just that it had to have been bad. The people over in Intelligence never shared anything.

"Anyway," Nelson said, "John Paul is definitely a product of the old spy school. There is a lot to be learned from him. Who knows, maybe you can even get the old guy to loosen up a little."

From that night on, John Paul Dodaine and Rabbit became Administrative Vice, night watch prostitution team 6Y52.

Chapter 4
The Stripper

It had been one of those perfect postcard summer days of August in Manhattan Beach—a blue sky, a slight ocean breeze, and eighty-two degrees. Rabbit and his shepherd dog did their ritual five-mile run on the beach and then finished with the six-block walk up over Sand Dune Park and down into the tree section, where just the two of them were living since the recent departure of the Playboy Bunny. Rabbit loved living the beach life. The little small-town atmosphere made it a storybook place. It was laid-back, and full of fun, hot beach babes, and peaceful times.

On the other hand, the place he chose to work was the city of Los Angeles, which was a whole different planet. On this August day, as he drove north on the Harbor Freeway toward police headquarters, the traffic was much worse than normal stop-and-go. He took the Florence off-ramp, went eastbound to Broadway, and then turned north again. Now he was back on the streets of the 77th Street Division, generally referred to as Watts. He looked at the people and the police cars racing up and down the streets and thought nothing had changed in the five years since he had transferred out, except that traffic was worse.

He entered Parker Center, took the elevator to the fifth floor, and walked into the Administrative Vice squad room thirty-five minutes late. As he passed the lieutenant's desk, he heard the old lieutenant, who hadn't done an honest day's work in years, mutter, "Glad you could make it." Rabbit thought to himself, *I should have called in sick and stayed on the beach.* Detective Sergeant John Paul told Rabbit to square his stuff away, after he had completed his routine paperwork and phone calls. They were going to take a ride to the south end. He had set up a meeting with a dancer at a strip club.

The stripper's name was Charlie. She was a runaway child from Possum Grape, Arkansas who'd found herself working in a sleazy South Los Angeles strip joint. This wasn't what she had intended to do with her life; like so many girls in her circumstances, she did it out of necessity. She was young and beautiful, and she had a charming personality. In addition to those attributes, she was very smart and ambitious. In a short time, she'd made a lot of money as a dancer and eventually bought a small bar in a working class neighborhood, a suburb just outside the south end of Los Angeles. She ran the bar in the daytime and worked as a stripper at night. Dancing was far more lucrative than her bar business.

One afternoon a tall, handsome, well-dressed man entered her bar and walked directly to the rear booth, where he took a seat next to a sleazy black pimp named "Popsickle." The man looked so out of place, she could not imagine what business he had with the pimp. She went to the table to take his order, and in a heavy French accent he asked for a Southern Comfort on the rocks with only one ice cube. This was how Charlie first met Detective Sergeant John Paul Dodaine of the Los Angeles Police Department, Administrative Vice squad.

John Paul had selected this out-of-the-way bar to meet his informants. It was an ideal location, and he knew the chances that he would ever be seen by anyone involved in his criminal investigations were nil. In addition to that, John Paul enjoyed the bar, as it was a place where he could relax and enjoy a drink.

Over time Charlie began to find John Paul to be very interesting. She thought about how nice it would be to have a man like him in her life, but she knew he wasn't the one, as he was over twice her age and happily married. None of that stopped her from developing a close friendship with him. She loved his French accent and enjoyed listening to stories of his childhood growing up in Provence in a little village in the south of France. He'd lived there until he was 14 and then moved with his family to New Orleans, where his father had taken a job working for a US government intelligence organization. Charlie always loved hearing about Provence and dreamed of one day being able to go there. Being a stripper, she thought it most likely that the closest she would ever get to Provence would be John Paul's stories.

John Paul was well aware of Charlie's feelings, but knew he could never get involved in a relationship with her—not that he wouldn't like to. It would just never work. His young partner, on the other hand, might be a great match for her. Rabbit had his own travel stories, and if it worked out, one day Rabbit could take her to Provence.

John Paul and Rabbit pulled into the topless bar's parking lot. The cars all looked like they belonged in the junkyards of east Wilmington or an impound lot in South Central. At the front of the building they pulled open an ill-fitting, old, thick, wooden front door that was covered with metal and had several bullet holes in it. They entered through the door and into a heavy cloud of cigarette smoke. They were facing a one-way mirror with a round speaker hole in the middle. The mirror was protected with ornate wrought iron covered with a steel mesh. A deep male voice behind the mirror said it was five dollars each for admission.

The two cops paid the cover and pushed back the dirty, heavy, red stage curtain covering the entrance to the room. The doorman pushed a button and the turnstile buzzed, indicating they could pass through. The bar reeked, the same as every sleazy ghetto bar. The carpet, what was left of it, was a filthy red color that was sticky to walk on from years of spilled drinks. The inside of the place looked like a cheap, B-grade movie set.

The customers were all loud, trash-talking play gangsters and a few lightweight, wannabe pimps. One thing they all had was cash, and a lot of it. There was a row of red plastic covered chairs at a small countertop connected to the stage, separated from it by a wrought iron rail. All the chairs were occupied. The handrail was lined with five-, ten-, and twenty-dollar bills.

The music was blasting through cheap, worn-out speakers. Red, blue, and amber flashing lights attached to the ceiling reflected off the mirrored stage walls, illuminating the room with a warm glow of color, like you would find in a cathouse.

There in the center of the stage was a beautiful young woman who moved sensually, yet gracefully, in perfect rhythm with the music. She was wearing a two-piece green sequined costume that sparkled in the rotating lights as she spun, twirled, and danced like a butterfly. In a slow, seamless move, she slid her hand across the top of her costume and it magically fell to the floor, exposing her perfectly-shaped voluptuous breasts. The customers went wild, yelling and screaming and throwing handfuls of money on the stage like madmen.

This obviously was the star performer. She was one of the most beautiful women Rabbit had ever seen. At five-foot-six and 125 pounds, she was perfectly proportioned, with long, thick, flowing brown hair and large, deep-brown eyes. She exuded a personality that drove men to frenzy. This was Charlie, dancer by night and entrepreneur by day.

When she took her break from dancing, Charlie joined Rabbit and John Paul. Rabbit remembers being introduced and also remembers being unable to speak lucidly. He was at a loss for words. Charlie, who was going through the pangs of a recent romantic breakup herself, was attracted to Rabbit immediately. She misconstrued his momentary inability to communicate as shyness and found it to be cute. It was the beginning of a long and beautiful love affair that would transcend all the natural obstacles that were in their paths. One date led to another, and day by day their love grew stronger and deeper. Eventually they moved in together and began to dream of the time when they could marry and raise a family.

Charlie's and Rabbit's hopes of reaching nirvana had to be put on hold, however. Somewhere along the line, the command staff made a connection between vice crimes and all other crimes, especially in the Hollywood area. The once-glamorous Mecca of the entertainment industry had fallen into decay. Prostitutes, drug dealers, muggers, and thieves had taken over the streets that had once been graced by beautiful young hopefuls and well-known stars of the stage and screen.

The transformation is as old as man. Once hookers begin to ply their street trade, they are followed quickly by the dope dealers who supply the hookers and their pimps. Other drug users follow the source and look for an income to satisfy their cravings. Income is often provided by trick rolls of the hookers' customers. The tricks are usually married, and therefore, more often than not, unwilling to make a crime report when victimized.

Fences move in to compete for the trade of stolen property. Eventually, there are not enough street victims to satisfy the growing number of thieves, and the residents of surrounding neighborhoods become prey. Total chaos sets in.

An ambitious and eventually enormously successful sting operation designed and orchestrated by Detective Sergeant John Paul was activated in the Hollywood area. Phony undercover fencing operations were put in place, along with make-believe crooks.

A key group among the undesirables in Hollywood was the motorcycle crowd. Rabbit's job was to buddy up with members of Hell's Angels, Vagos, Straight Satans, Wheelmen, and other outlaws. His assignment during this Special Operations Task Force was to penetrate the gang culture in order to disrupt their various criminal enterprises involving guns, drugs, and motorcycle thefts. He was ordered to gather criminal intelligence, and he was given wide latitude to operate anywhere in Hollywood and the Valley.

He was happy for the change. He had grown tired of the structured daily routine of all the paperwork associated with the Administrative Vice assignment. He could think of nothing he would rather do than ride his Harley for a living, by himself and away from John Paul. In essence, he was in hog heaven.

Rabbit had operated as a biker for a while in the past. He knew what he would have to do. He'd never forgotten the first time he had tried to operate in a biker bar years earlier in the Venice area. He had walked straight over to the bar, ordered a beer and a double shot of Jack Daniel's, and tried to keep from shaking out of his skin. After a brief encounter with some of the patrons, he came down with a severe case of "burn fever." That's when an undercover operator is convinced that their cover is burned. He felt like he was wearing his uniform. He just knew that everyone in the bar had made him for the heat. It wasn't the case, of course, and in time he learned that many of the bikers were just ordinary guys who happened to live a different lifestyle. His key to success was adopting a similar lifestyle, which came easily to him. All he needed to do to fit in was talk up mutual areas of interest. His knowledge of motorcycles, especially Harley Davidsons, gave him a decided edge.

When Rabbit finally hit the streets, he made a beeline to the International Hot Dog Stand on Hollywood Boulevard. That was not by accident. The stand boasted that it sold hot dogs from all over the world with an array of condiments and various accoutrements. This ultimate hot dog experience was just a stone's throw from one of the biggest tourist attractions in Tinseltown, Grauman's Chinese Theater, where people came from all over the world just to put their feet in the footprints of the matinée idols of yesteryear. Yet it was light years away in terms of culture. The path of stars honoring entertainment luminaries covered the sidewalks that ran past the hot dog stand, but all similarities of fame and glamour ended there.

In the darkened lot behind the stand, penny-ante dope deals were consummated, and connections were made for many other criminal activities. These were not high rollers by any stretch of the imagination.

On a smoggy late afternoon, Rabbit rolled up and parked his bike next to the other bikes along the curb. He remained seated for a while, just trying to look cool. The evening commute had started, and the streets were crowded with Angelenos going home from a variety of occupations, most of which would be similar to those of people working in any other town anywhere in the country. They sat patiently in air-conditioned cars taking the traffic gridlock in stride. On the sidewalks, the tourists passed by in droves, groups of Asians in clusters with cameras hanging from their necks. Middle-class Americans from Middle America, dressed in Bermuda shorts, loud Hawaiian shirts, and black, knee-length socks and sandals, strolled by and stared at the gathering of misfits as though they were part of a movie set. You could see them looking for their cameras and waiting for a director to begin barking, "Action."

Rabbit dismounted his Harley Davidson ceremoniously, as though he were John Wayne getting off a horse. He swaggered over to the stand and ordered a plain dog, as though he were familiar with all the other varieties without reading the posted menu. He needed something bland to go along with the god-awful Boone's Farm strawberry wine he would sip from a plain brown paper bag after he walked back and lounged comfortably on his parked motor. The reason for that choice of beverage was to avoid having to share it with any of the local assholes who might want a sip. Nobody wanted this stuff. It was only marginally fit for human consumption.

This was to be a waiting game, because strangers were eyed with a great deal of suspicion. The only conversation he engaged in was flirting with passing females who looked as though they belonged in that particular crowd. This became a nightly ritual until he finally scored a bag of weed from one of the local babes named Angie. Even hard living failed to make her look much older than her seventeen years. She was like so many of the young people who had fled to Hollywood to escape their oppressive home lives or battered existences, or who were just antisocial youngsters seeking fame and glory. Usually, they only found misery, loneliness, and despair. Their lives turned into prostitution, theft, and drugs.

Angie wore the standard uniform, which consisted of worn-out jeans (with holes strategically placed to show some skin around her butt) and a faded tank top that showed off what could have been the breasts of either a high-fashion model, or just another young junkie street whore. She introduced Rabbit to a few of her friends, who introduced him to others. The histrionics of this rite are unique. No one is open in front of a new face. Newcomers are usually introduced as someone who has been known for a long time. Once he became known, Rabbit was free to visit other hangouts and able to fit in with any of the local habitudes.

When his newfound friends became relaxed, they spoke openly about their recent capers and invited Rabbit to join in. He usually had a reasonable excuse for why he couldn't participate at the time, but he always offered the name of the fence he used. The thieves were thrilled to be able to use Rabbit as a reference with the best-paying fence in town. This fence was actually an organization located in a musty office off Sunset Boulevard and run by two equally great undercover detectives from Ad Vice who had a different specialty. They were Terry Silva and Steve Martinez. They worked major cases and were the best at what they did.

Silva's persona was low-key. He presented himself as affiliated with organized crime. He maintained the commanding presence of an overlord. His partner Martinez, who played his right-hand man, was the total opposite.

Martinez had grown up in East Los Angeles, in a tough Mexican neighborhood that was home to gangsters, drug dealers, and illegals. It was apparent he was the muscle of the enterprise. Somehow, he managed to escape the barrio unscathed and became a policeman. His background investigator for the job must have been a relative, but his history with the Eastside gangs served him well. He had the gangster flash down perfect. He talked the talk and walked the walk. In fact, his entire look—shaved head, black goatee, muscular build with Popeye forearms, ever-present black wrap-around sunglasses, diamond-studded gold Rolex, and what looked like a two-pound gold cross on a heavy gold chain around his neck—made some cops wonder if he was playacting or just a badass street gangster with a gun issued by the Department.

It didn't matter. Silva and Martinez were a perfect team for what they did. And most importantly, they did it flawlessly. Rabbit provided them with a steady flow of customers, and everyone was pleased, most of all Rabbit. He started to think this operation would go on forever.

These two high rollers couldn't afford to take any chances on being burned by the cops, so it was reasonable for them to demand some kind of ID before doing business, even with a recommendation from a biker named Rabbit. Unknowingly, the thieves were videotaped and photographed.

Rabbit's success rate exceeded even his own expectations. He could not believe he was getting paid to do this. He wasn't totally undercover. He carried a false ID, but was able to resume his own life during the off hours.

As the investigation continued successfully, one of the many ongoing audits noted that Rabbit had not attended narcotics training for undercover operations. An analyst duly noted that in his report. Subsequently, Rabbit was ordered to the Academy for training in the department policy regarding smoking marijuana in the course of an undercover assignment. The training was to include the technique for pretending to smoke marijuana, although the time for such training had already come and passed.

The narcotics-training sergeant, upon seeing Rabbit with his chest-length beard and long hair, quipped, "I think this training class is probably way too late." The sergeant began the instruction by showing Rabbit how to clean the marijuana and how to roll a joint in Zig-Zag papers. The training was quite basic and ridiculous. Finally, they got to the part where the joint was lit.

The Detective had a glass pipe contraption which enabled him to light the joint without having to put it in his mouth—and of course, without smoking it. He demonstrated how to deeply inhale the smoke and what the body would look like when this happened. It was quite a silly demonstration.

He then explained, "The only way a glow will appear is if you pull in a little and blow through the joint. You will have to take some of the smoke into your mouth to be able to blow it out eventually.

However, under no circumstances are you to inhale the smoke. I cannot emphasize that enough—under no circumstances are you to actually inhale the smoke. Just throw your chest out as though you were really inhaling deeply. You got that?"

Rabbit looked at him as though he were crazy. This whole training session was silly. He tried it several times, but was not a bit convincing. Finally, he quit playing around. He took a hit and inhaled it. Rabbit smiled broadly, "Hey, that's good weed."

The Detective blew his top. "Are you out of your mind? You're actually smoking dope here at the Police Academy."

"Sorry! It was an accident."

They tried several more times, and finally the Detective said that it was just about as good as it was going to get. But he repeated his admonishment never, never to inhale marijuana smoke.

Rabbit got the big picture. His bosses were doing just as they were expected to do. They were covering their asses. He knew full well this was just more department nonsense.

The operation continued to produce a high recovery rate of stolen property, suspects identified, and cases solved, and Rabbit was receiving exceptional outstanding rating reports for his participation in bringing the criminals into the sting operation. The only downside to it was the effect it was having on Charlie. She especially didn't like the change she saw in Rabbit's demeanor and appearance. He was not the same man she had fallen in love with.

Chapter 5
Motorcycle Gang Ops

Everything was proceeding according to plan. Rabbit worked the bikers, riding his Harley Davidson undercover, and for the very first time, with the full knowledge and approval of the high command of the Los Angeles Police Department. This was nothing short of a modern-day miracle. Rabbit even went as far as to request the ten percent hazard pay that is accorded to uniformed ticket-writing motor cops. His request was promptly denied. It was okay. He'd never expected it anyway.

Rabbit's routine took him in and out of all the biker bars and strip joints in the Valley. In time, he and a biker named Grasshopper started hanging out together. Grasshopper was a great source for Rabbit. He knew all the bikers and all the chop shops in the San Fernando Valley. Grasshopper and Rabbit became close buddies. Rabbit soon became trusted and was part of the circuit. The bikers all had different stories to tell. A lot of them were former military who had been in Vietnam. They had become disenchanted with the system and simply dropped out. Some of them were regular guys like those Rabbit had grown up with—cut their hair and beards, put them in Hawaiian shirts and Bermuda shorts, and any one of them could be just another nondescript neighbor in suburbia.

But they'd opted out and taken playful names like Roller, Bear, Stretch, Hillbilly, Snake, and Crash.

They were all interesting characters. Some, of course, were more interesting than others. One of the craziest was known as Snake. He stood six-foot-four and weighed 275 pounds, and he had a three-foot ponytail. He'd been born in Texas, in a wasteland near the Mexican border. As he told the story, his Mom had been a whore and his father a drunken abuser in every way. Snake had eight brothers, and they had nothing. They'd gotten by any way they could. As he was growing up, for both sport and money, he and his brothers would catch rattlesnakes and sell them to a nearby reptile farm. The ones they didn't sell ended up on the family barbecue.

He had no fear of vipers, and his fascination with them had followed him into adulthood. He had rattlesnake tattoos all over his body. One was a diamondback coiled around his neck in a fierce strike position, with the reptile's head emerging from under his beard, mouth opened, fangs in a fierce strike position. This obsession extended to the paint job of his chopped Harley Davidson. The small, six-inch square pad on his motorcycle that he called a seat was covered in snakeskin. Everything was about the snake.

For macabre entertainment, he carried a large leather bag over his shoulder that resembled a mail carrier bag with a heavy flap and a rattlesnake inside the bag. He thought it was great fun to toss the snake on the shop floor while everyone was hanging around having beers and smoking joints. Most people found it very unsettling to see a coiled, pissed off rattlesnake a few feet away. It always ended in pandemonium. Only Snake saw the humor in the insanity. That is, until one day the snake bit him, and the ensuing infection required his thumb to be amputated.

Rabbit continued to gather information, as was expected. Consequently, the detectives downtown were able to clear several cold case homicides of bikers whose bodies had been tossed into the Hansen Dam. Of course, there were other, lesser crimes cleared as well, all of which helped keep the operation in business—it was always about the numbers.

Everyone involved in the sting operation was well pleased with its progress. In time, Rabbit became a big brother to Grasshopper. At one point, Grasshopper blew up the transmission on his Harley. Hard pressed for the money to repair it, he asked Rabbit if he would help him steal a motorcycle to strip down for the transmission and make a few extra bucks selling off the other parts. Rabbit talked him out of it by giving him a slightly used transmission. Grasshopper was touched. Rabbit didn't tell him he had appropriated it from the Los Angeles Police salvage yard.

Without even realizing it, Rabbit had begun to drift away from the normal world he knew. Normal had become Jack Daniel's, young biker party babes, weed, and needless bar fights to establish alpha dominance. Of course, living this life, what else would one expect? He continued turning in information. That was what counted.

Marijuana was a common staple in the biker world. It wasn't any different from having a beer, and contrary to the popular belief among staff officers of the Department, smoking weed could not be faked. Getting caught by a gang of bikers in the back of a chop shop trying to do something as stupid as fake smoking a joint would have dire consequences, with the possibility of a trip to the morgue.

That would be far worse than any punishment the Department or the court could hand out. This was just part of the job, and one more needless, nonsensical aspect of the assignment. One thing Rabbit did discover was that the movie that he had grown up with, *Reefer Madness*, was a real stretch of the imagination.

One hot August afternoon, Grasshopper and Rabbit were at the Purple Haze, a custom paint shop in Van Nuys. They swirled down a few beers watching Stretch, who was a master painter, finish reinstalling the gas tank on Grasshopper's motorcycle. Grasshopper had Stretch paint dark blue ghost flames over the black painted gas tank. The job required skill rivaling the talent required to paint the Sistine Chapel. Grasshopper decided he wanted to do a canyon ride with his new paint job when the rush hour traffic was over, and he wanted Rabbit to make the run with him. Meanwhile, he and Rabbit continued getting buzzed up. Grasshopper said he was going to pay Rabbit back for the transmission Rabbit had given him. He had a buddy who was the number-one amphetamine dealer in the Valley who needed some dudes with guns to accompany him on a drug deal to meet his Mexican supplier. It would happen in the next couple of weeks.

While Stretch was finishing bolting the gas tank onto the frame, two young biker babes were in the shop hanging out and getting high. They wanted to go on the canyon run with Grasshopper and Rabbit. For biker babes, they were nice looking, and they actually appeared clean. One of them had exceptionally large breasts, and she knew it. She wore a T-shirt with the neckline cut low, barely holding her breasts in. Rabbit didn't know how old these girls were, but they sure didn't look old enough. Rabbit could see big trouble, so he said he didn't want to run the canyon with a passenger, being that he was buzzed up. Big Boobs said if the girls could ride along, they would take them to an awesome party house.

Soon, both Harley Davidsons were headed into Topanga Canyon with the two hot babes riding on the backs. As they made their way up through the country-like roads that wind through the mountains that separate the San Fernando Valley from the rest of Los Angeles, it was like riding into another world. The Topanga Canyon area is a peaceful, bucolic setting with great attention paid to naturalness. The people who inhabit this rustic setting so far removed from the glitter and glamour of the big city are private and peace-loving. Whether wealthy or poor, they tend to be less judgmental than most other residents of the city. However, even they have a breaking point. The little hamlet made up of quaint shops is not an ideal setting for a motorcycle horde, but up the dead-end canyons, it's perfect.

Grasshopper, Rabbit, and the babes motored up one of those roads to a ramshackle house that was little more than a broken-down log cabin with an oversized Doughboy pool. Motorcycles lined the narrow road adjacent to the location. They were parked with meticulous precision, belying the rough appearance of the miscreants who had parked them.

In the back yard, card tables and folding chairs were placed haphazardly. Kegs of beer adorned the tables, and buckets of ice contained long-neck beer bottles, wine, and jugs of Jack Daniel's. Any kind of dope you wanted was also available. There was much whooping and howling as the evening set in.

Rabbit had seen a lot of wild things in his undercover world, but nothing like this. It was Sodom and Gomorrah in real time.

The pool was filled with naked bodies, laughing and drinking, smoking dope and having wild sex. Others were lying on the chaise lounges or on the ground having sex. Some were passed out. One young female was posed in a teaching Buddha position, chanting. Two males were urinating where they stood, chatting like they were waiting for a taxi. Age meant nothing. Old guys were with young babes. Girls were having sex with girls. It was absolutely sordid. If Yahweh knew about this place, surely he would rain down burning sulfur upon it. It looked like they were about to start filming a Roman orgy scene for a porn movie.

Grasshopper wasted no time stripping down and jumping into the pool with the girls who had ridden up with him and Rabbit. In less than a heartbeat he and Big Boobs were having sex like two dogs in heat. This place was beyond the pale.

Rabbit moved about with his Jack Daniel's, looking for anything that might have something to do with his police investigation. He saw a few bikers he knew, but they were all too wasted to talk. He made some small talk with the guests and moved on. He observed three exceptionally bad actors he had not seen before. Definite ex-cons. One had the towers of San Quentin prison tattooed on his forearms. All three had the prison stare. The worst part was that they were looking directly at Rabbit. He felt uncomfortable for the first time in many years. There was no way he was burned; maybe it seemed weird that he was not participating in the debauchery.

Grasshopper was now out of the pool, bare-ass naked, pouring Jack Daniel's into a plastic cup. Rabbit told Grasshopper he was going down to Venice to see his old lady, who had a crash pad in the canals. Grasshopper told Rabbit how good the sex was with

Big Boobs and Rabbit ought to grab some before he split. He told Grasshopper he would pass, she was all his. He didn't want his dick to fall off.

Rabbit noticed that the three ex-cons were now watching the sex show in the pool. He asked Grasshopper if he knew them. Grasshopper said the one with the San Quentin watch towers tattoos was Shank, an associate of Grasshopper's dealer buddy. Shank handled the dope trade in Sunland and Tujunga. The other two had just been released from prison, but he didn't know them.

Rabbit finished his drink and left, never looking back. He didn't want to chance suffering the same fate as Lot's wife.

He hid out at the beach for a few days. He needed a break from all this insanity. He wondered whether he should consider getting back into the mainstream and becoming a regular detective, investigating crimes like malicious mischief and stolen bicycles. But he knew that really wasn't a viable option—he would die of boredom.

Three days later he was back at the Purple Haze custom paint shop. Grasshopper had his Harley back for repair. The night of the party he'd taken some LSD and tried to ride his motorcycle, but before he'd gotten the kickstand up, the bike had fallen over and flattened the right side of the gas tank, destroying the new paint job with the ghost flames. He was depressed and pissed off.

Now Grasshopper was in serious need of money. He called his buddy, the amphetamine dealer, and asked about the job that the dealer needed armed backup for. His buddy told him in two weeks the deal was going down, and that was when he would need ten bikers with guns to ride out with him to the Four Corners, the famous spot where Utah, Colorado, Arizona, and New Mexico border one another. He was buying $50,000 in amphetamines from his Mexican supplier at a prearranged time and place. Even though they had done business before, there was no guarantee that this time it wouldn't be an attempted rip off. He and the Mexicans had agreed, as before, that each side would have ten armed men, and that the meeting would take place in an open, flat area so there would be no chance for any surprises from either side.

If the buyer has the money and the seller has the drugs, no problem. The pay for each of the armed security would be $500. Grasshopper committed himself and Rabbit to be two of the security detail.

Rabbit was more than a little apprehensive about the size and scope of this plan. Narcotics were not Rabbit's forte. Grasshopper convinced him this was a good deal and easy money and there wasn't any need to worry; he'd known the dealer for a long time and had done a lot of business with him. He wasn't the least bit concerned about the deal going wrong. The guns were just an insurance policy for both sides.

Rabbit still wasn't sold on the idea. This deal wasn't his call. He would inform his boss, who had worked narcotics prior to being assigned to the Special Operations Task Force. This was way outside Rabbit's area of expertise.

When Rabbit reported the large pending drug transaction to his boss, the officer in charge of the sting operation, and the entire team, everyone was ecstatic. This would be a major bust—possibly thirty arrests, $50,000 in cash, $50,000 worth of amphetamines, twenty or more guns, plus the conspiracy. Two weeks to get everything set up was more than enough time.

Right about this time, it occurred to someone in the chain of command that Rabbit had never gone through the department's official motorcycle school, and as a result was not certified to ride a motorcycle on duty. There was no way he would be allowed to ride a motorcycle to Four Corners without attending motor school.

It was argued that a lengthy delay in the investigation was not possible. The powers that be decided he could circumvent the requirement for school if he could pass the riding test required of motorcycle officers. A test was arranged. Rabbit reported at the appointed time at the bottom of the dry, concrete LA River. He was met by a grizzly, twenty-five-year veteran motorcycle sergeant who was obviously disgusted by the sight of this long haired, bearded, hippie freak.

There was no way in hell that this asshole on a chopper could be a Los Angeles Police officer. Grudgingly, the old sergeant proceeded with the test.

"Where's your helmet?"

"Don't have one."

"No helmet, no test."

Rabbit didn't want to take the test anyway. So he rode off. His control sergeant told him he would have to return to take the test. Rabbit said that bikers don't wear helmets and he didn't own one.

It took almost an act of Congress to get the helmet issue waived, but finally it happened. He conscientiously went through all the phases of the test. He did figure eights and circles while keeping his feet on the pegs. He successfully completed all the acceleration and braking tests. Finally the old sergeant instructed him to lay his bike down while traveling at a slow speed in the deep sand of the dry river.

"Sergeant, I'm not sure if you're serious, or just fucking with me," Rabbit said, "but whatever the case, I'm not laying my motor down. One thing I know for sure, any fool can crash."

The old sergeant would not budge on that one. His captain finally ordered the sergeant to put the results of the various tests on the appropriate form and let Rabbit go his merry way.

The sergeant acquiesced and gave Rabbit a passing grade on the driving test. However, he dutifully noted the mechanical violations he observed on Rabbit's motorcycle. As the sergeant mounted his motor to leave, he wondered what had happened to his cherished Los Angeles Police Department.

Chapter 6
The Mouse Trap Saloon

The most important thing Rabbit took away from his private motor school test with the cranky old sergeant was the realization that he really didn't fit into the conventional and rigid police world, which was so filled with nonsensical rules and regulations.

Back on the street the following day, he was instructed to meet with Sergeant Allen, who would be his new supervisor. Temporarily on loan to the task force, Sergeant Allen was assigned to Homicide Division, cold cases. For several years, he had been investigating motorcycle gang homicides in the Los Angeles Police Foothill Division. Foothill had a serious gang problem. Murders had increased sharply over the past five years, and there had been few arrests, due to the tendency of gang members to be tight-lipped, like the mafia, and settle homicide matters on their own. His top priority case was one in which an Illinois narcotics officer had been killed in a drug deal that had turned out to be a robbery. During the shootout that occurred and the ensuing mayhem, the suspect known as Shank escaped and fled to the Los Angeles area. There was unconfirmed information that he'd worked as a part-time bartender at the Mouse Trap Saloon in the Sunland/Tujunga area, in the far northeastern part of the San Fernando Valley.

When the sergeant became aware of Rabbit's close connection to the San Fernando Valley gangs, he approached the commanding officer of the task force and persuaded him to allow Rabbit to work the Sunland area for one week, maybe two, to see if he could learn information that would help locate the suspect Shank.

Sergeant Allen had plans to use this current special assignment as a springboard for a promotion to lieutenant. Generic cases weren't going to be enough; he needed a headliner. He wanted to put together something big, and making an arrest in this cold case homicide would bring him that recognition.

The sergeant was aware of the pending amphetamine bust Rabbit was involved in at Four Corners, and he knew that as soon as that went down, Rabbit would be pulled out of the undercover operation. The sergeant knew if he wanted a chance to arrest Shank, he had to have Rabbit start working the information immediately.

Allen told Rabbit what information he had on Shank and what information he was after.

Rabbit recalled the name Shank. He was one of the three ex-cons at the bacchanal in Topanga Canyon that he and Grasshopper had gone to with the young babes. Shank was the one who had the watchtowers of San Quentin tattooed on his forearms. He looked to be a serious badass. As an ex-con, he probably had the innate ability to feel the presence of a cop a mile away. Rabbit hoped this Shank that Allen was interested in was not the same asshole.

Rabbit's contacts and hangouts were all in the San Fernando Valley. The place Allen was talking about sending Rabbit into was on the outside of the eastern edge. It was a whole different ball game with different players out there. It was at the end of the known world, located in the foothills of the San Gabriel Mountains just a few miles from the Hansen Dam, which had been used on occasion as a watery graveyard for murdered bikers.

The community was an isolated part of the City of Los Angeles that was policed by Foothill Division. It was like an alien nation. The place was referred to as The Rock. It was Sunland and Tujunga, two small towns that had merged together and been annexed into greater Los Angeles in the late 1920s and then been forgotten like abandoned stepchildren. Now it was a haven for bikers, and all the motorcycle gangs of the city were represented there. Although for the most part they lived in peace, there were some very badass bikers and a lot of hardcore ex-cons. Most of them carried guns.

The Rock probably had the highest concentration of biker bars anywhere. The count was somewhere around forty. The cops kept a low profile and left the location alone. The policing was handled by the bikers themselves.

The most hardcore bar of them all was the Mouse Trap Saloon. That was where Allen told Rabbit the target had been seen. He told Rabbit to go in there within the next few days and get whatever information he could on the suspect. Rabbit's knowledge of the biker world told him not to attempt this operation on his own. Everything about it was wrong.

Although it would have some downside, he tried to get Grasshopper to accompany him. Having Grasshopper was better than having no help at all. Two unknown bikers entering a tight-knit biker bar like the Mouse Trap might just be there for a beer. On the other hand, a lone rider had to be looking for someone or something.

Grasshopper had no interest in riding out to The Rock. Rabbit tried to get his interest up by suggesting they could maybe hook up with Shank and try to develop a source for them to score amphetamines that Rabbit could deal out in Venice. Grasshopper wanted no part of that. He told Rabbit it was a bad idea, and that he couldn't go around his dealer.

Meanwhile, the days were passing, and the drug deal at Four Corners that Grasshopper had committed himself and Rabbit to as backup guns was quickly approaching—and that would end Rabbit's undercover operations in the biker world.

Allen directed Rabbit to get on with the Shank assignment. Reluctantly, Rabbit made his plan to go to the Mouse Trap alone the coming weekend.

Rabbit rolled into the parking lot of the Mouse Trap Saloon as ordered, and knew he was in the right place immediately. The only four-wheeled vehicles in the lot were beat-up old pickup trucks that bore bumper stickers saying, "Kill a biker, go to jail," or the trademark Harley Davidson wings. The lot was small and very dark, and covered by low overhanging trees. A single floodlight was trained on the entrance.

The people in the lot were scary. These were not the bikers with all the studs and flash. These were obvious badass bikers whose long hair was not pulled back in neat ponytails. This was the real thing, and so was the bar.

Rabbit sat on his motor for a while and just took in the scenery, which was not unusual. The more he saw, the more out of place he felt. The place was just about two steps too bad for his blood. The fear flasher inside his head was beating rapidly. It was one thing to ride a Harley and blend in with the Hollywood weirdos and jack around with Valley bikers, but this was a big throw of the dice. *These are all super bad dudes*, he thought. Any one of them could do him in a heartbeat. He thought about the undercover work he'd done at Venice Division and the investigative reports from victims. He thought about the poor fool who'd received two hundred stitches from thirty slash wounds as a result of wandering into the wrong biker bar out of curiosity.

As he pondered the situation, he decided this was a very bad idea and decided to blow off the whole venture. He started his bike and rode off. A quarter of a mile away, he began to think about the possibility that the young sergeant was sitting somewhere in the dark with the bar under surveillance. He had to at least go inside.

Reluctantly, he pulled over to the next bar he came across. This was a typical neighborhood bar in which most of the patrons were on speaking terms with each other. Rabbit felt anything but at home in this place as well. The local blue-collar patrons eyed him suspiciously. He was aware of their concerns, but there was nothing he could do about it. Besides, he didn't care.

Two Jack Daniel's later, the fear flasher started to subside. He got back on his bike and returned to the Mouse Trap Saloon. As he stepped inside, it took a few seconds to become adjusted to his surroundings. Before he could focus his eyes in the low light, he was overcome by the distinct smells of sweat, motorcycle grease, stale beer, cigarette smoke, and the burning bales of marijuana. This was a badass cave.

As he stood in the entryway with a slight smattering of lights dancing around his head, the interior of the bar came slowly into focus. He had arrived. The crowd looked as though it came directly from San Quentin. Wearing a filthy white T-shirt, torn Levis, and a trashed leather jacket, Rabbit hoped his best biker look would be enough to fit in.

Everyone seemed to know everyone. There were no strangers—except for Rabbit. He had never been in a place filled with outlaws like this. This little visit was no Mickey Mouse misdemeanor bar investigation; this was big time. These boys were serious ex-cons, and he could feel he was not ready for it. He could see why this place was off limits to patrol officers. It was a den of wild beasts just waiting to tear the limbs off somebody.

Rabbit could feel the eyes on him as he made his way across the room. He reached the bar and sat down. A gnarly old bartender who resembled Quasimodo limped up to him and stared without speaking, waiting for an order. Rabbit asked for a beer and a double shot of Jack Daniel's. It was produced as if by magic. The bartender waited to be paid. Rabbit laid down a twenty-dollar bill and asked casually if Shank had been around.

At the moment, he thought his inquiry had been nonchalant enough, but the words had no sooner left his mouth when he realized he had committed a grave faux pas. He had never been in this bar and knew no one. In a badass biker bar, you just don't walk in, sit down, order a beer, and start asking questions. He wished he could reach out and pull the words back. The bartender, whose face and body bore the scars of a horrendous collision with a dull hatchet, merely glared at him.

The bartender had the eyes of a tortured soul. He glared at Rabbit with doubt for what seemed like an eternity and then asked him what he wanted with Shank. Rabbit answered that his buddy Grasshopper had said maybe Rabbit could do some business with Shank. That was a lie, but it was the best answer Rabbit had. The bartender produced a pencil and a piece of paper and told Rabbit to write down his name and telephone number. Rabbit did so, and wrote the name of a biker bar in Venice where he hung out and was known. The bartender picked up the paper and ambled to the phone at the far end of the bar. He looked back at Rabbit as he made a call.

Once more fear gripped Rabbit by the throat, but he knew he couldn't run. He had to sit and wait for an opportunity to make a casual retreat. His exit plan was to finish his drink, go to the head, and then leave.

He sat quietly and looked around with mild curiosity, in keeping with the code. This was a crowd like no other that he had ever been with before. Those without shirtsleeves bore the unmistakable tattoos that are acquired in the joint. San Quentin, Folsom, and all the others have a style all their own, with no variation of colors. He had been warned that this crowd was made up almost exclusively of ex-cons, but this was beyond his wildest expectations. These were not petty thieves or small-time dope dealers. These were heavy-duty hard cases with violence in their backgrounds.

Rabbit had had enough. It was way past time to leave. As he'd planned, he walked to the bathroom. It had the look and smell of a public toilet in the worst slum of India. As he finished his business and turned to leave the cramped little space, three behemoths appeared. In an instant he was grabbed by the right arm and slammed into the wall. As he tried to pull free, he was punched

in the side of the head. A second shot to the chest felt like he had
been hit with a sledgehammer. Rabbit tried to punch back with
his left fist, but it was futile. It was too little too late. The trap door
was closed, and he was in the center of a firestorm. Then came a
flurry of punches. Everything lost color; it was all a blur. He felt
his knees buckle, and he battled to stay on his feet. Then came
a powerful blow to the stomach, and as he doubled over, a blunt
object smashed into the back of his head and sent him crashing
to the floor. He wrenched trying to breathe. He struggled not to
lose consciousness, but he was totally disoriented. He could feel no
pain as he lay there, numb and motionless. One biker stood with
a foot on Rabbit's neck, pinning him to the floor, while another
pulled up his jacket and shirt and searched him.

Rabbit heard the second assailant say he didn't have a gun
and wasn't wearing a wire. One biker then took his wallet and
went through it, finding a fictitious driver's license; motorcycle
registration matching the license; an old, wrinkled, past-due traffic
citation for loud exhaust pipes; a small plastic pill bag with a few
marijuana seeds and enough weed for half a pin joint; and a few
crumpled Zig-Zags. One of the bikers asked if there was a badge.
The answer was no.

The biker with his foot on Rabbit's neck asked, "Should I off
him?"

The guy who was obviously in charge said, "No, he's not a cop.
Fuck 'im, let's go." The three bikers walked back out to the bar.

Rabbit lay motionless on the cold, unpainted cement floor,
which reeked of urine, vomit, and Pine-Sol. His right eye was
swollen shut from the punch, and it felt like it was going to explode.

What vision he had left was blurred. He managed to push himself up to a sitting position with his back leaning against the wall. He couldn't stand. He was dizzy, and his stomach and chest felt like he had been hit with an iron fist.

He was bleeding profusely from his nose and mouth, and though his lips were numb, he could feel that his two front teeth were broken. Only semiconscious and barely able to breathe from the punch to the stomach, he longed for his police partners and his pistol. He wanted to go out into the bar and shoot the bastards dead, all of them. But that wasn't going to happen. He was all alone. What he now needed was somehow to regain enough strength to stand up and stay balanced.

Finally, he struggled to his feet and leaned on the wall. Slowly, he made it over to the sink. It only had a cold water handle, but it at least supplied fresh water and helped get rid of some of the cobwebs. He hurt real bad.

At one time, there had been a mirror on the wall above the sink, but that had evidently been smashed on another happy occasion. With no mirror, he couldn't assess the damage to his head and face, not that it mattered at this point. He got himself somewhat together and managed to pick up his wallet and its contents from the floor, making sure he had everything he needed. He knew if he could get out of this hellhole, he was not coming back, ever.

Slowly he pushed the bathroom door open and walked back into the bar. It was just as he had left it before he went to the bathroom. It was like the *Twilight Zone*—exactly the same as before, as if everyone had been frozen in place. No one, not one person looked at him. He looked around, struggled to focus with his one good eye, and tried to recognize the assholes who had just beaten his ass. It was impossible. They all looked the same. He wished he had a stick of dynamite. He would have done the civilized world a big favor and blown the place up along with everyone in it.

Without incident he made it outside and limped to his motorcycle. He was elated to find it had not been trashed, stolen, or set on fire. It took every ounce of energy he could muster to kick-start his motor, put it in gear, and ride out of the parking lot onto the highway, leaving the rat hole from hell behind him.

As Rabbit made the long, cold ride down the Harbor Freeway, the frigid night air stung the open wounds on his face like salt in an open gash. He wanted to try to forget the beating he had just received at the Mouse Trap. He hoped when he got to his little beach house in Manhattan Beach, Charlie would be there and the two of them could take a long therapeutic soak in the wooden hot tub, and maybe Charlie could apply her magical caress and make him feel better.

When he finally arrived at the house, there was no Charlie. She was lonely and had gotten tired of waiting for him. Her patience with Rabbit and his motorcycle assignment was wearing thin, and she was starting to drift away.

The next morning Rabbit awoke, feeling like he had been thrown from a speeding truck and run over by a freight train. As a young policeman he had been involved in altercations in Watts, but nothing like this. This time he'd lost, and lost bad. He vowed it would never happen again.

The physical damage to Rabbit from the beating was mostly obscured by his hair, beard, and clothes. The most visible injury was to his right eye. It was swollen and blackened, and there was a cut on his eyebrow. His nose, although not broken, was puffed up, but the damage to his mouth was all on the inside. His neck was stiff, but there was no visible damage to it. He could feel a depression at the back of his head, but that was covered by his long hair. The bruises on his back and stomach were just soft tissue damage, and they would heal on their own. Rabbit was thankful that it wasn't worse. He could easily have ended up in the Los Angeles County morgue.

The following day he had a meeting with that dimwit Sergeant Allen for a debriefing on his investigation at the Mouse Trap Saloon. He couldn't make it, so he called and told the sergeant he wanted a few days off.

Five days later they met. Sergeant Allen took one look at Rabbit and asked, "What the fuck happened to you?"

"Let's see," Rabbit responded, "I was directed by a sergeant, who apparently doesn't know shit, to ride out to The Rock in Sunland/Tujunga, and unbeknownst to me, walk my ass into the worst, baddest biker bar in Los Angeles, with no gun and no backup cover, to get some information on an outlaw who had already killed an undercover cop. As a result I got my ass beat like never before, and luckily, didn't end up in the county morgue."

Of course, the sergeant wanted Rabbit to fill out a formal crime report describing the event and the suspects. Rabbit knew that to be a complete waste of time. Besides, the only description he could give of the assholes was that they looked like three oversized gorillas with big long beards.

When news of Rabbit's injury finally made its way to his commanding officer, both the sergeant and Rabbit were immediately called into his office. The captain wanted a full account in detail, and Rabbit relayed the events that took place at the Mouse Trap Saloon.

The captain then asked the idiot Sergeant Allen if this operation had gone as Rabbit described. The sergeant acknowledged that it had. It was apparent that the captain was having a difficult time controlling his anger over what had taken place. This was about as bad an error of judgment as the captain had ever seen anyone make in his thirty-one years with the Department. It was inexcusable. He could easily have lost a policeman.

The captain informed the sergeant that he was finished using Rabbit or any other undercover officer for any more of his ill-conceived, poorly-executed, foolhardy investigations. Sending an operator into an environment like that without a clear, well-thought-out plan and adequate cover for the officer's safety made as much sense as assigning a young, uniformed patrolman to walk a nighttime foot beat by himself in the housing projects of Watts without a gun, stick, or radio.

The captain told Rabbit that the motorcycle gang investigation was over, effective immediately. He directed Rabbit to take a week off and give his face some time to recover. He added that Rabbit looked like he'd kissed a speeding freight train, and that was "not the image we want to project around here." The captain further instructed Rabbit to be back in his office the following Monday at 9:00 a.m. with the beard gone and wearing a suit and tie.

The first call Rabbit made upon leaving the captain's office was to Charlie. He couldn't wait to share the good news with her. She was ecstatic to hear that the biker assignment was over and that the beard would soon be gone. Now, just maybe, they could have time to get reacquainted and finally make plans to live an uncluttered lifestyle like normal people. The week was heavenly. Rabbit thought all that crazy undercover stuff was now very much a thing of the past. He was finished with it forever.

It seemed weird that he would never see his buddy Grasshopper again. Rabbit had actually begun to like him, and he had been a big help. He smiled—too bad he couldn't write Grasshopper a Department commendation for his help in making the police operation so successful. He wondered if the dope deal had happened at Four Corners, and if poor old Grasshopper had gotten paid his five hundred bucks that he so sorely needed.

Chapter 7
Detective School

As ordered, one week later Rabbit was sitting outside the captain's office an hour before the scheduled appointment. The first thing one learns in the LAPD is never to be late for a meeting with a ranking officer. Rabbit was wearing his suit and tie, accented with a clean-shaven face and standard haircut. It felt weird to be in the straight world. As for his injuries, Rabbit's eye was looking better. The swelling and bruising on his face was quickly healing and was nearly back to normal. Even so, his head didn't look like it belonged on his body, and his beardless face caused a lot of chuckles in the squad room.

Finally the captain arrived, and Rabbit was summoned into his office. The captain recounted the meeting when Detective Nelson had first requested Rabbit to be brought into the division several years earlier, and how shocked he had been when he saw Rabbit's complaint history. Even though he was persuaded to bring him into Administrative Vice, there had always been a lingering apprehension.

However, the depth of Rabbit's investigations and the number of successful prosecutions that had resulted from them had changed his mind. The professional way in which Rabbit had dealt with the investigation and subsequent beat-down at the Mouse Trap Saloon showed the captain that Rabbit had become a seasoned, mature investigator. His outstanding work in Administrative Vice had earned him the captain's recommendation to attend police detective training school at the academy, in preparation for Rabbit to be appointed detective.

The captain concluded by informing Rabbit that he was extremely pleased to have him in his command and that he deserved promotion to Detective. Rabbit was ecstatic. His dream of achieving detective rank was now just around the corner.

Detective School had to wait until Rabbit had completed a ton of paperwork relating to the sting operation. Most of the paperwork had been processed as the operation progressed, but there were debriefings and additional reports generated by previously unknown facts. This was almost like a real job. He came in at nine in the morning, suit and tie ready, and stayed in the office for the entire day answering phone calls, drinking coffee, and doing paperwork. He was serious, like the rest of the detectives in the squad room. He didn't even get to sip a beer or have a double Jack Daniel's during working hours. It was hard to concentrate on the mundane aspects of police work after having worked undercover in the motorcycle world.

As promised by the captain, the assignment to Detective School came through. Thirty days of eight in the morning until five in the evening, Monday through Friday, with different instructors and written tests. Most of the instructors couldn't resist telling war stories about how it was when they had worked the streets. However long ago that was, nobody could remember that far back, and they actually didn't care. The essential material probably could have been completed in half the time. As classroom work went, much of it was very boring. At one point Rabbit asked if there were going to be any classes on undercover operations, hoping to get an automatic "A" in that class. The response: "This school is about detective work, not a grab-ass Hollywood acting school."

The closest the school got to an undercover class was a lecture by Lieutenant Ginelli from Administrative Narcotics. The Lieutenant and Rabbit had been good friends since their time working patrol in Watts together in 1968.

After the class, Lieutenant Ginelli and Rabbit had lunch at the Academy café. Most of the talk was about the old days in the 77th Street Division. The lieutenant wanted to know where Rabbit was going to after he was promoted to Detective. Rabbit admitted that his captain had been good to him, so he would stay in Administrative Vice. The lieutenant said it was no secret in the bureau that Administrative Vice was about to have a major personnel cutback, and there would be no new detective slots. He offered Rabbit a job in Narcotics, on his crew, as an undercover operator.

Rabbit appreciated the offer and would have enjoyed working for his old friend, but he declined. He had decided that he was all through working undercover. It was too demanding and stressful. Besides, he wanted to get married, have a family, and live as normal a life as possible.

Chapter 8
The Secret Division

Rabbit was sitting at his desk in the squad room reading prostitution complaints when John Paul walked over to Rabbit's desk and handed him a piece of paper bearing the name and number of a detective. Everything on the covert side of police operations was hush-hush, and John Paul was the epitome of discretion. He merely whispered to Rabbit, "Call this guy."

"Why, who is he?"

"Just call him."

With that, John Paul was on his way. By now Rabbit had become accustomed to the cloak-and-dagger nature of Administrative Vice. Sometimes the secrecy was merely a habit. Sometimes, as was the case in this instance, it was best for no one else to be aware of the activity.

He shrugged and dialed the number. He wasn't paying too much attention, as the female voice on the other end slurred through a mechanical greeting, announcing the identity of the office he had called. He asked for Detective Billy Harris and was told to hold.

After a brief pause, Harris came on the line, "Detective Harris, may I help you?"

"Detective Harris, this is Rabbit from Administrative Vice. I was told to call you."

"Rabbit, yeah, glad you called. Can we meet somewhere? I'll spring for coffee."

"What is this about?"

"I'll tell you when I see you."

Rabbit was a little skeptical, but curious.

"Okay. How about the cafeteria on the eighth floor?"

"That is not a good idea. How about Denny's on Vignes?"

Rabbit was now intrigued. Who the hell was this guy who wanted to meet away from the police building, and what could he possibly want? His first inclination was to blow him off.

"I'm sorry, I can't do it. I'm buried in paperwork."

"It's in your best interest to meet, believe me!"

Rabbit thought, *what the hell*. He had nothing to lose, so he agreed.

Denny's sits in the shadow of the 101 Freeway where it joins a conglomeration of other freeways in the downtown Los Angeles area known as the Four-Level Interchange. It's a maze of major arteries that probably drove some poor engineer into psychosis.

As Rabbit entered the restaurant, he was immediately greeted by a rotund gentleman who looked like a twin of Jackie Gleason as Minnesota Fats. The gentleman was pleasant and soft-spoken and appeared to be well-seasoned. He invited Rabbit to a secluded booth—that is, as secluded a booth as it is possible to find in a Denny's.

The man introduced himself as Detective Billy Harris of Public Disorder Intelligence Division. He told Rabbit that he, Rabbit, had come highly recommended, and that a thorough search of his package indicated that he was just the man they were looking for. They had a special assignment, and his background and profile were exactly what PDID needed.

"Hell, I don't even know what PDID means," Rabbit said.

"Public Disorder Intelligence Division."

"You mean you want me to go undercover again?"

"Exactly!"

The waitress was just coming to take their order when Rabbit started to get up.

"I'm sorry, my friend, not interested. I no longer work undercover."

Harris grabbed him by the arm, "Rabbit, at least have a listen."

Rabbit thought for a second and sat down. After ordering two cups of coffee, Harris continued.

"Don't be too hasty. With your package it is going to be tough to get a promotion. I can guarantee that if you do a good job for us, a promotion is a lock for you, sergeant or detective."

Rabbit said, "Don't need it. My captain at Administrative Vice is taking care of that."

There was an awkward silence for a few moments as each of the men studied the other. The waitress brought the coffee. As soon as she was beyond earshot, Harris continued.

"Look, we don't need a decision right this minute. I know you are off to Mexico for a two-week vacation. While you're gone, at least think about it. When you get back, let us know."

Rabbit sighed. He wanted desperately to be promoted, but he was tired of undercover operations and the exceptionally weird hours that went with them. Besides, his captain in Administrative Vice was now firmly in his corner. Rabbit had decided he would never go along with another weird assignment. There was no way he would accept this offer, but he agreed to at least think about it.

As he drove back to the police building, he thought it odd that the PDID Sergeant would know about his vacation to Mexico. That information was not even known in his squad.

Rabbit had been to Mexico with bikers more times than he cared to count, and it was always the same hell-raising fracas. This journey, however, would be different than any before. This was to be all about him and Charlie making a lifetime commitment to each other. Their relationship had reached a level of love and devotion that neither had ever experienced. They had decided they didn't need a priest's blessing and that they would make their vows to each other in Mexico and proceed as husband and wife.

The assignment that Rabbit was working made it impossible to plan a conventional wedding at that time. Rabbit promised Charlie that as soon as the current investigation permitted, they would have the grand church wedding that she had always dreamed of having. Their time together in Mexico was beautiful in every way, and neither wanted it to end. They honeymooned, drank margaritas, frolicked on the beach, and devoted all of their time to making each other happy.

They were a million miles away from the world with which they were familiar. Neither mentioned strip joints or police work. They laughed a lot and loved even more. It was as though they were enjoying conjugal bliss for the first time in their lives. The two became one in every way imaginable.

Their two weeks in paradise finally came to an end, and reality set in. As they packed up the truck for the long drive home, Rabbit's thoughts drifted back to the LAPD and the commitment he had made to Harris. In Mexico, he had tasted a lifestyle he had forgotten existed. *This is what men die for*, he thought. This is what life is all about. He was deeply in love and could only think now of starting a family with Charlie. He couldn't help but think of his own father and wonder if he would ever measure up to him. Maybe not, but he was going to give it a try.

He thought back to the assignments he had been doing recently. He felt the loneliness that only a long-time undercover operation can bring on. Police work is all about partners. Whenever tales of heroism, fun, misconduct, or anything else are told, they always involve a partner. In dangerous or stressful assignments, there is always the post-watch visit to a local watering hole for choir practice, which serves as the world's greatest group therapy session. His recent assignments hadn't afforded him the luxury of bullshitting with his pals. He didn't feel like a cop anymore. No way was he going to accept the PDID offer. He was going to work cases like normal detectives do, without going undercover. He just wanted a normal life.

As soon as he and Charlie crossed the border from Tijuana, Rabbit pulled over to make his phone call; he couldn't wait. Thanks, but no thanks, he would tell Harris. It might take a little longer, but he knew he was going to get that promotion to Detective in Administrative Vice.

When Harris answered the phone, Rabbit told him how grateful he was to have been considered for such a prestigious assignment, but his commitment was to Administrative Vice. Harris was understanding, but said he would like to have Rabbit come in to the division to announce his decision. Rabbit challenged the necessity for this. After all, there was no way that he would take the transfer, and it was in everyone's best interest to let it go right now.

Harris reminded him that without extending the courtesy of a personal appearance, it was extremely impolite to tell a captain no. After all, he didn't really want to cut his own throat, did he? An appointment was made for Rabbit to speak with the commanding officer of PDID in two days.

He was wearing a frown when he returned to the vehicle, and Charlie questioned him about it.

"It's nothing really. I was offered a job, but I turned it down."

He broke into a grin, and Charlie relaxed. She put her hand on his lap and her head on his shoulder and dozed off as the truck headed north toward Manhattan Beach.

As he drove in silence, Rabbit couldn't help but reflect on the conversation he'd just had with Harris. For years he had worked hard to overcome the reputation he'd established earlier in his career. The last thing he wanted to do was give some captain the impression that he was telling him to get screwed, even if that was the case.

Harris was waiting when the elevator doors opened on the seventh floor of Parker Center. He greeted Rabbit as though they were old war buddies. Rabbit was a little taken back at this display of friendship by someone with whom he'd had only one brief meeting and a terse phone call. Harris put his beefy arms around Rabbit's shoulders and guided him toward a nearby office.

"Well, guy, how was Mexico?"

"Great. Just great. I just wish it could have been for a whole lot longer."

"Vacations are always too short, unless you have your mother-in-law along."

Harris opened the doors to PDID and introduced Rabbit to the secretary, Carol, and told her that the captain was waiting to see them. With an official air and serious focus, she called the captain on the intercom and announced the visitors. As she hung up the phone, she said, "You can go in."

Rabbit thought to himself, *if she is happy with her job, she should tell her face about it.*

As they entered the small, modest office, Rabbit noticed the various degrees from East LA College and Pepperdine University that were hung on the wall. A few pictures also graced the walls, each one a testimony to how many important asses this guy had kissed.

The captain came around from behind the metal desk that is traditionally occupied by officers below the rank of Commander. He had a look of someone who had forgotten completely about physical activity and had been concentrating on the social aspects of life. He could probably get by in a uniform, but he looked awfully soft and pale.

He shook Rabbit's hand and motioned for him to have a seat. Looking at this guy, Rabbit had the feeling he was dealing with a car salesman, and he got ready for the inevitable dissertation about how lucky he was to have been chosen for this opportunity. Then the captain gave Harris a directive nod of his head, and Harris disappeared.

"So, tell me, Officer—or do you prefer to be called Rabbit?"

Rabbit thought this was first time he'd ever had a captain ask his permission for anything.

"Rabbit would be fine, sir."

"Well, then, Rabbit, what do you think of our little organization?"

"To tell the truth, sir, I don't know anything about it. I mean, since I don't plan on coming here, I didn't think it was necessary to learn about it."

The captain looked generally surprised. "Not coming here? Surely someone has briefed you."

A frown crossed Rabbit's face. "Uh, excuse me, sir—briefed me about what?"

The captain smiled benignly. "Hasn't your captain told you about the cutbacks at Administrative Vice?"

"What cutbacks, sir?" Rabbit did not like hearing this. It was the second time in several weeks he had heard that Ad Vice was about to experience a cutback.

"Administrative Vice is being cut back by about one-third. You are one of the people scheduled to return to uniform, but at a reduced rank. You will be going back as a Policeman Two."

Rabbit was visibly shaken by this.

"Sir, that is not possible. My captain just sent me to detective school in anticipation of promotion to Detective."

The captain quickly continued, "Well, sadly, that is not so. Administrative Vice has no control over the cutbacks. That's why we picked you up. You have a natural talent for operating undercover, and we figured it would be a waste for you to go back to an obvious dead end."

Rabbit shook his head, "Are you kidding me? There's got to be an alternative."

"None, except directing traffic with a white hat and gloves at First and Spring."

They sat quietly for a few seconds before the captain rose.

"In light of this fact that there are no good alternatives, you really need to come over to PDID. But don't worry, you will love it here. I've been around the Department a long time, and I will tell you, there is no more interesting place to work. Detective Harris tells me a big part of your commitment to Administrative Vice is being appointed to Detective. Your coming here will ensure that happens. We are a small but very tight-knit family in every sense of the word. We take care of each other like no other unit in the Department. Only a select few are ever called to work covert operations in PDID. We have more latitude than you can imagine, and we are trusted with the most sensitive information. We operate wherever we need to go to accomplish our mandate. I'll see to it that all of the paperwork and notifications are discreetly handled. Detective Harris has been assigned to help you through your transition. He is our most experienced control officer. You will learn a great deal under his tutelage."

Rabbit rose, floating in a bit of a mental haze as he shook the captain's hand. The captain placed his left hand on Rabbit's shoulder and smiled, and said affectionately, "Welcome to the program."

Rabbit thought the captain's words, "Welcome to the program" were very strange things to say. He had never heard a captain refer to his division or command as "a program." It was always "the division." He was trying to process everything that had happened in such a short time. It was a bit like a dream, and not a pleasant one at that.

As Rabbit turned to leave the office, the captain stopped him dead in his tracks, saying, "By the way, you are not to talk about this transfer with anyone, not your partner, not the people in Administrative Vice, not even your captain! He's already aware of it, anyway."

Rabbit was mystified. "What do I tell them when I say goodbye?"

"You won't say goodbye, you'll just be gone."

Rabbit left the captain's office and walked to the elevator. As he waited for the elevator car he reflected on the meeting that had just taken place. It was merely a formality. His background check obviously had already been completed, and the transfer had been approved by the powers that be, all without his knowledge. The only step left in the process was to inform him of his new assignment and date and time to report.

This was anything but good news.

Apparently PDID needed an operator with special skills that Rabbit possessed, and he fit the profile they needed. He understood all that, but the way they had made it happen wasn't right. He didn't like any part of it, and he had told Harris that when they first met. The problem now facing Rabbit was that to refuse this assignment would call into question his devotion to the Department, which would have a negative impact on his effort to make Detective. The elevator doors opened, and as he entered, he thought that surely in a few short months he could engineer a way out of the assignment and prevent further damage to his and Charlie's already-strained personal relationship, all without making waves with his new division.

The next morning the Chief of Police held his weekly intelligence briefing, which was attended by the commanding officers of Public Disorder, Administrative Narcotics, Administrative Vice, and Organized Crime. During the briefing, the CO of PDID mentioned to the Chief in front of the CO of Administrative Vice that he was processing the paperwork for the transfer of a covert operator to work the special investigation he and the chief had been talking about. When he mentioned the name Rabbit, Captain Green just about leaped out of his chair.

"That operator is assigned to my division. He's the one who has been doing all that work in the motorcycle gangs."

The PDID Captain jumped right in, "Be reasonable, Richard. Rabbit found out he was probably going to be cut, and he figured he could be of more use to us here than in uniform."

"There have been no decisions about who was going to be cut," Captain Green argued.

"Well, you know how rumors get started."

At the conclusion of the intelligence briefing, Captain Green burst back into his office as though he were on fire. His adjutant asked how the meeting had gone. Green's only reply was a demand to see Rabbit, right now. He was livid.

Within the hierarchy of any major law enforcement agency, it is intolerable to be put down by a peer in front of the big boss himself. Captain Green had more than his fair share of ego, and he took the acquisition of Rabbit by PDID as a prodigious slap in the face.

Rabbit entered the office, and before he could utter a meager greeting, Green was on him like the proverbial chicken on a June bug.

"You are one sorry-ass, ungrateful excuse of a policeman. Where did you get the balls to pull this shit on me? I took a big gamble on bringing your pitiful ass into my division, and this is your gratitude? Your goddamn package would make it tough for you to get into Parking and Intersection Control, but I was good to you. You were on your way to Detective, and this is your show of appreciation?"

The color ran out of Rabbit's face; he was dumbstruck. He had been chewed out before, but that all paled in comparison to this. He swallowed hard as the captain continued.

"Men who come into my division stay. That is called loyalty. Of course you don't get that concept. You ran around behind my back and solicited PDID for a job."

Rabbit's knees were weak, and he fumbled to be heard.

"Captain, that just is not true. May I explain?"

His remark only served to upset the captain more.

"You can't explain anything to me, but put this into your memory bank, from now on you are finished in this building. You'd better like your spy job, because I am going to see to it that you never work a special operations assignment here or anyplace else ever again. Now get your ass out of my office. I don't ever want to see your ungrateful face again."

Rabbit thought to himself that he could arrange that very easily. He could not get out of there fast enough. As Rabbit scurried past the adjutant's desk, he could hear the old man bellow, "Get that goddamn Nelson in here."

Judging from the silence in the Captain's outer office and the attitudes of his fellow cops as they went out of their way to avoid eye contact, Rabbit felt it would be in everyone's best interest if he avoided going back into the squad room and seeing all the detectives. There was no worthwhile memorabilia in the solitary desk drawer at his place on the prostitution section table; so there was no need to retrieve anything. He could always come back to the squad room on Sunday to gather his personal belongings.

In the lobby, he placed a call to Detective Harris to find out what his status was. Harris told him to go home and wait for further instructions. Rabbit was now assigned officially to PDID. There was no going back; the die was cast.

When Rabbit questioned Harris about staying at home, he was told that for now, that was his duty assignment. "Stay by the phone and don't leave the house."

One other thing: he would have to put his Harley in mothballs. His motorcycle riding had come to an end; it would not fit into this assignment. He now would project an extremely conservative image at all times.

Chapter 9
The Control

Two days later, just as Rabbit was about to go stir crazy, Harris rang the doorbell. The two of them got into Harris's city-issued two-door, the kind of car that cops refer to as a cool ride. Harris drove up the coast to Malibu, chitchatting about life in general, but actually setting the stage for a very serious dissertation.

Along the Pacific Coast Highway, the blue Pacific rolls onto the California coast, which has beauty second to nowhere else in the world. Sandy beaches gradually give way to majestic cliffs. The beaches are dotted with surfers, who ride the waves year-round. Each little town has its own distinctive features—dazzling marinas that are home to a king's ransom in luxury yachts, or oil rigs that continuously pump the liquid gold that keeps Californians on their wheels. Skaters and cyclists fill the paths, which have been dedicated to the great West Coast deity—physical fitness. Each community exudes an aura that makes it seem like the last real vestige of relaxed civilization. All the people are beautiful. The women are all blonde and tanned, and have shapes that would qualify them to be Playboy centerfolds. The men all have long hair and appear to have just walked out of Gold's Gym.

The two men spent the first part of the trip getting to know each other. They discussed their likes and dislikes; they discussed politics, sports, camping, and a great many police experiences. This was definitely not an interview; it was Harris studying Rabbit and vice versa. Harris wanted to know as much as possible about the man for whom he was to be the "control officer." It was equally important for Rabbit to know as much as possible about the man who was to be his only link with the police world as he knew it.

They stopped at a restaurant in Malibu for coffee. Before Harris could exit the car, Rabbit stopped him. Rabbit was not interested in any more small talk; he wanted to get directly to the point. He asked Harris what this operation was about and what the expectations of him were. Harris said he wanted to insert Rabbit into the radical right in order to monitor the groups that were operating in Los Angeles. Harris had been investigating several extreme right-wing groups for the past eleven years, and his partner had been working them even longer.

The number of members who subscribed to their radical philosophy had been growing over time, and that number had now become substantial. Their rhetoric had also changed. It had become more extreme and warned members to prepare for an impending revolution.

This operation was a proactive move, personally sanctioned by the Chief to enable the police to protect the citizens of Los Angeles when those groups launched their plans to cause public disorder. But there was another, far more important objective for this operation. The ultimate goal was to locate a large machine gun cache hidden somewhere in Los Angeles. The exact amount of the weapons was unknown. Harris did not share that information with him. Maybe some day he would, but this was too soon.

Harris knew this would be a long-drawn-out investigation. He had handled other undercover operators over the years, and they always burned out quickly, mostly as a result of their perceived lack of progress and their loneliness from being totally cut off from the world they knew.

It might take Rabbit years to get to the guns. Harris knew it was going to take him six months to set up an apartment, get a job for a visible means of support, make friends, and establish all the details of his new life. Harris looked for nothing of any real significant intelligence value during this time. He knew this was going to be his best and last chance to get those guns.

Rabbit had a reputation for being able to get any covert job done. His ratings consistently said there was no better operator, and his profile was perfect for this operation. He was a white Christian, born in the Midwest, and fiercely conservative. He was a hunter and an expert in wilderness survival, and he tended to be a loner. Harris's biggest task now was to get Rabbit to sign on for the assignment. Rabbit would be his perfect "Bird Dog."

Harris had learned through extensive research that in the early sixties, before he was assigned to it, the Public Disorder Intelligence Division had been known as the "Red Squad," and its purpose was to investigate subversive groups. At that time, the Los Angeles police conducted their first investigation of the militant group known as the Minutemen, and its founder, Robert DePugh.

The investigation revealed that DePugh's Minutemen organization had formed in Missouri in June of 1960. DePugh's plan was to prepare for a Russian invasion by establishing an armed resistance movement throughout the United States made up of bands of guerrillas to fight the invaders. The plan was to recruit patriots who were willing to fight and die for the cause and to incorporate existing groups of like-minded patriots into the Minutemen organization.

Although the organization seemed like a good idea to its members, the fact remained that federal law prohibited private armies. The investigation eventually revealed that the movement had spread throughout the US. Minutemen units began procuring and stockpiling a massive arsenal of machine guns, grenades, bazookas, mortars, chemical weapons, and millions of rounds of ammunition, dynamite, silencers, and other lethal weapons of war. They conducted training seminars in which tactics, goals, objectives, and philosophies were discussed. They participated in field training exercises to improve their proficiency with firearms, explosives, knife fighting, silent killing, and other aspects of guerrilla warfare.

Eventually the group quit talking and began to take action. State, local, and federal agencies began to investigate, and subsequently warrants were issued across the US. Arrests were made and weapons were seized.

Finally, after seventeen months on the run, DePugh was captured in a desert hideout near Truth or Consequences, New Mexico. He was sent to federal prison in 1969 and began serving an eleven-year sentence for violating the 1968 Federal Gun Control Act. The two Los Angeles detectives assigned to the Red Squad closed out their investigation, presuming, as had all law enforcement had, that DePugh's incarceration signaled the end of the Minutemen.

In 1973, DePugh was released early from prison. Information began slowly to filter into Los Angeles police intelligence that

DePugh had resumed his role as leader of the Minutemen. Once again, there was renewed Minutemen activity in Los Angeles. A new investigation was started.

Harris and his partner were assigned to reopen the case. The old file was retrieved from the archives and meticulously reviewed. It was a lengthy intelligence file. It contained countless interviews of Minutemen associates, arrestees, ex-members, and informants from inside the organization.

The detectives had credible information that there were substantial numbers of Minutemen in Los Angeles who were well-armed and prepared for confrontation. Their backgrounds and occupations were diverse, and they had infiltrated numerous law enforcement units and the federal government. Sources from inside the Minutemen stated that the breakdown of membership into employment categories indicated that there were Minutemen actively employed by the Los Angeles Police Department and that somewhere in the City of Los Angeles there was a very large stockpile of light machine guns. Those guns were rumored to have been shipped from the United States to some Central American country by the CIA before some kind of deal was made with that country and the guns were shipped back to Los Angeles. Somewhere, somehow, they were in the possession of the Minutemen.

That was the last entry in the report. There was no summation, no arrest, no closeout, no suggested course of action—nothing, just an abrupt end. It was very troubling and obvious that the pages at the end of the report had gone missing. The question was: by who, why, and what information was removed?

Harris had been on the job for twenty years. He knew his age and poor physical condition might force him into retirement at any time. He knew his time was limited. He had been focused for years on this investigation, and many times he had heard rumors of a major stockpile of light machine guns that were waiting for "the day" to arm an uprising. For half of his career he had worked PDID, and he was the best investigator in the division, a master of what he did. He was their foremost expert on the radical right and all its principal players. He had a link chart on all of them. He knew who had done prison time, with whom they were arrested, and where they were incarcerated. He had made follow-up contact with the suspects' arresting jurisdictions and their parole officers. He read the crime reports, arrest reports, prison files, and any piece of information he could find.

Now, finally, this was his chance to put the crown jewel in his career, to locate and seize the guns, discover where the guns had originated, put those involved behind bars, and bring the long investigation to a close. This would cinch his promotion to lieutenant. He had dedicated his life to the world of law enforcement, the LAPD, and PDID. There was not a more loyal intelligence investigator than Harris.

Harris was squirming in his seat in the car. They had been talking for over an hour, and Harris needed to get out and go into the restaurant for a cup of coffee. Once inside, they got a window table with a stunning view of Malibu Beach and the beautiful, blue ocean across Santa Monica Bay to Palos Verdes.

Harris's job now was to prepare Rabbit for the road ahead. He laid out a must-do list to get started. He gave Rabbit a map of Glendale with an encircled area and told him to rent an apartment in that vicinity.

Rabbit looked out from the restaurant at Malibu and the blue Pacific and all the beach towns lining the coast. This was where he had lived almost his entire life. Glendale was the other side of the world from Manhattan Beach. It was the end of the world. Why would he ever choose to live in Glendale?

Harris told him that it was centrally located for the places he would be frequenting, and living there would create the appearance of someone who would be strong in any ultra-right movements. Being a beach boy wasn't going to work.

Rabbit spoke up, "Listen, Sergeant, I listened to everything you have said, but this whole deal is not going to work. I am more than apprehensive about this. The folks on the right think like I do. Actually, I am probably one of them. In fact, so far what you told me, I don't see what they are doing wrong. I think if this is all there is, the Department is not only wasting resources trying to do this, but they really don't have any justification."

Harris did not want to tell him everything that he knew about the Minutemen and DePugh. He realized that while Rabbit was getting established in the radical right, if he zeroed right in on DePugh and the Minutemen, there would be a high probability of spooking DePugh. Rabbit would need somehow to do something that would cause DePugh to seek him out, not the other way around. How to do that was something he would have to figure out on his own. Trying to work off a script created by others just doesn't work in these operations.

Harris could see by Rabbit's expression that he was not getting through to him. He tried another tack. He claimed to also be a very conservative person, and assured him that this operation was not intended to hurt any good, law-abiding citizens.

"It is the extremists that we are interested in," he said. "They are no good, whether they are extreme right or extreme left. In fact, if you follow both extreme right and left from the top center to the bottom of the circle, they meet there as anarchists who want to turn our society to dust and kill a lot of innocent people in the process, including the police."

Harris reached into his briefcase and took out a blue-covered book and pushed it across the table to Rabbit. It was *Blueprint for Victory*, Fourth Edition, by Robert DePugh. He leaned close to the table and spoke in a hoarse whisper.

"Read that book by one of these modern day, right-wing extremists and you will see what this radical bullshit is all about. In the preface he distorts a famous quote that you might remember: 'Government of the people, by the people, and for the people has forever perished from the earth.'

"He continues—this is one of the extremist leaders talking—he goes on to say that, 'Never in all of recorded history has a people saved themselves from tyranny through political means alone.'

"According to DePugh, a dictator cannot be removed by legal means, and that freedom, once lost, is never regained except by violence or the threat of violence. This is a leader who advocates the formation of an underground army to provoke the first open conflict between the 'oppression' and the resistance movement.

Espionage, terrorism, sabotage, and assassination are the most effective weapons used by the underground." He leaned back for a second and then continued.

"Somewhere in those ramblings he writes, 'It was Hitler's contention that such unity could only be achieved when some one organization became so powerful that it either absorbed or eliminated all of its competitors. This case history proved that Hitler was right.'

"Do you still think you share the same political philosophy as these whacked-out radicals? Do you believe by any stretch of the imagination that they are not dangerous to the very people you are charged to protect and serve? These are fanatical assholes who happen to be extremely dangerous."

Rabbit was obviously taken aback. He said, "If that is all true, then I understand." He leafed slowly through the first few pages of the book. Other passages leaped from the pages and smacked him between the eyes.

"War is simply a continuation of politics by other means."

"We American Patriots face a war to the death and we must not be propagandized into believing that we can afford to eliminate actual military actions from those options that will be available to us."

His shoulders slumped, and he seemed resigned to the task that lay ahead. Obviously there was a lot of reading to be done, even before he thought of infiltrating any organization.

Harris never identified a specific group such as Minutemen, Posse Comitatus, the Klan, or the Nazis. It was necessary to let Rabbit find his own way. He gave Rabbit a list of books that he should read—manuals on how to set up ID and how to work undercover without fear of detection, and other books that would provide him with background on the various organizations and their philosophies. The key to the whole operation, he said, was that the local police and federal authorities were not interested in liberals and conservatives, or who was sleeping with whom; they were interested in extremists. In this case, Rabbit would be targeting white supremacist groups—hatemongers who were blind to justice and the true American way and willing to get their way through violence against those who oppose them.

They left the restaurant and drove along the famed Sunset Boulevard from one end to the other. Most of this great artery is unknown to the rest of the world, and unknown even to other parts of California. From Pacific Coast Highway, it winds its way inland past historic Will Rogers Park and polo field, through Pacific Palisades and the West Side's ultra-wealthy mansions, past UCLA (the university known for its athletic prowess), through the ever-glamorous Beverly Hills, into trendy West Hollywood and Hollywood, and through the less fortunate neighborhood of Echo Park. Sunset ends at Olvera Street and the Mission, where Los Angeles was founded so very long ago.

During this trip, Harris spoke of Rabbit finding a job to handle the additional expenses and providing him with visible means of support. He told him to develop an entirely new background and lifestyle. He was to forget he had ever been a policeman. Although he was not allowed to change his name because of legal restrictions, he was to create a background that would indicate that he had moved to LA after running away from home, and that his parents were still living in the Midwest.

By the time they finally returned to Rabbit's home in Manhattan Beach, he was exhausted from the inundation of information. Before leaving, Harris relieved Rabbit of his badge, gun, and ID card. As far as the world was concerned, Rabbit was not now nor ever had been a member of any law enforcement agency. Harris told him that from now on he was to be known as Source 757 on all written reports and in all other written communications. His paycheck would be cashed by Harris, who would give him cash. Harris gave him a week to get as much done as possible, and then he would be in touch again.

After Harris left, Rabbit fell into a chair and tried to find some semblance of reason to everything he had just been told. He felt that it shouldn't be too hard to forget he was a cop. After all, the Department had just reduced him to a well-paid informant. How the hell was he going to pull this one off? Working undercover to Rabbit was getting dressed down and hitting on a whore on a street corner (or getting dressed up and hitting on one in a fashionable bar). He would make an arrest, book the suspect, and then go home. This was all foreign to him. He had no training in infiltrating political groups. In fact, he questioned the very reason for police involvement. With the bikers, there was a criminal element to work and bring to justice. This seemed way outside the bounds of any local police jurisdiction. As time would tell, he was never going to be called in out of the cold for retraining or counseling.

He dozed off and did not wake up until long after dark. How the hell was he going to explain this to Charlie? It didn't take him too long to find out. When he told her the next morning, she didn't take it like the proverbial trouper. Especially when he got to the part about moving into another apartment—alone.

Charlie was exasperated at the mere thought. She responded that as much as she was in love, and as important as their relationship was to her, she could no longer deal with the stress of his incredibly dangerous assignments. If all that weren't bad enough, Rabbit never even knew what hours he would work, nor what days off he would have. It was impossible to plan the simplest of things and have a normal life. She was finished with all of it.

She had lived through his motorcycle escapades, and when she saw Rabbit after his beating at the biker bar, that had been enough undercover stuff for her. Rabbit had promised they were going to live a normal life, and now he had taken a covert assignment he was not at liberty to discuss with her. It was totally crazy.

Rabbit tried everything he could think of to placate her. He too was deeply in love, and he couldn't imagine not being with Charlie. After a long discussion, he cajoled her into giving him just three months to get out of this new secret assignment, but Rabbit didn't have a clue how he could keep the promises he'd made to her without pissing off his new captain.

Rabbit was blinded by his insatiable drive to succeed, earn recognition from his superiors, and be promoted to the rank of detective. He was not cognizant that his blind commitment to the Department had eclipsed his personal life as well.

Chapter 10
Agent Provocateur

Rabbit spent the next week doing all the things he had been instructed to do. He picked up the books that were on the list and began reading during every waking moment. He read the Bible of right-wing extremists, *The Turner Diaries*. He read all the books written by the Minutemen's leader, Robert DePugh. He read both right-wing and left-wing books. He read pamphlets on revolution and tax evasion, and he studied the nuances involved in creating an entirely new identity. He became a student of revolution.

He was told that he would probably have to do some traveling. He had always had an interest in working around jet aircraft, so he applied for a job with a major airline and was hired. It didn't take him too long to realize his airline job was not perfect. The noise of jet engines, the acrid jet fuel and jet blast, and the constant danger of industrial accidents made the working conditions nearly intolerable. To add insult to injury, he was being paid minimum wage, and the work of loading aircraft was physically back-breaking.

Before starting work, he spent time in Glendale looking for an apartment that was somewhere close to reasonable in the rent department. He was still paying the mortgage on the home in Manhattan Beach, so he had to find something in keeping with his new slave-wage job. He finally found a small, depressing apartment on Riverdale Drive, one block from the heavy industrial area of San Fernando Road, a major artery that had train tracks running parallel to it. The apartment was furnished in early Salvation Army, and he soon found that being an English-speaking tenant put him in the minority.

In developing a new background for himself, he was able to keep pretty close to the guidelines the Department had provided—keep it as close to the truth as possible so as not to get trapped in a lie. His cover story was that upon finishing high school he had taken all the money he had been saving from after-school and summer jobs and set off on a world odyssey.

After landing at Heathrow Airport in London, he'd taken his backpack and set off on a grand adventure—a hiking tour of Europe, Africa, and the Middle East. He learned how to get by on the basics, and in the extremes he survived by eating such delicacies as bugs, camel, and dog. He ventured down into the Sub-Saharan Africa and was totally amazed at what he saw and experienced with the tribal people.

Returning northward, he wound up in Marseille broke, hungry, and somewhat homesick for the American way of life as he had known it. He tried to bullshit his way onboard several cargo ships by pretending to be an experienced merchant seaman. After several failed attempts, he met a ship's captain who saw through the bullshit just as the others had, but who could remember a similar experience in his own past. So, this captain gave him a meaningless job that enabled him to learn much about the sea and the life of a merchant seaman.

This was his past. For the first time in his life he had to write an outline and memorize it to pull off the scam. Because of Harris's admonitions that a slipup could cost him his life, and because this was going to be a twenty-four-hour-a-day job, he wasn't about to take chances.

At Harris's direction, Rabbit visited his parents and had a long talk. He couldn't tell them what he was doing, but he asked for their trust and confidence. He needed to warn them of a ruse the underground had previously used to vet suspect members. The terrorist would utilize the phone book and call people with the same surname of the suspected individual. When the phone was answered, they would identify themselves as detectives and inform the person who answered, that their policeman son had been killed. They knew such devastating news would elicit an immediate emotional response thereby confirming their suspicions. If anything ever did happen, they would be notified in person by Detective Billy Harris of the LAPD. His mother was beside herself, but his father reassured her that their son had meant that if anyone did call, it would be a prank. His father knew better and wasn't too thrilled about the idea, but he supported his son.

At the end of the week, Harris got in touch with Rabbit and instructed him to go to an office in the Hollywood area to meet with some people. He was cryptic and refused to give him any further information, other than that it was an interview. Rabbit complied and drove to the address on Cahuenga Boulevard, which turned out to be an employment agency. A prim and proper receptionist greeted him and had him take a seat while she announced his presence. He sat there long enough to become annoyed, but not hot enough to walk away.

The dowdy receptionist finally asked him to follow her. She opened the door to an office where a distinguished looking gentleman sat behind an ornate desk. Also in the room were three other gentlemen who were somewhat younger than the first, and a young to middle-aged blonde female. All were neat, professional-looking people. The woman wore no makeup.

The gentleman behind the desk greeted Rabbit and asked him to have a seat. The people in the room were neither friendly nor cool. They had the air of people who perform mundane tasks day in and day out. They were seated in such a way as to prevent all of them from being seen at the same time. Rabbit had to turn in his seat just to see who had asked a question.

Very politely, the gentleman behind the desk said, "Tell us about yourself."

Rabbit looked around at each of them and asked, "Who are you?"

One of the men in the corner shot back, "That is not important. We will ask the questions."

Rabbit assumed this was to test him on his new background; so he related his whole life story in as brief a manner as possible. At the conclusion, each of them fired questions at him in rapid succession, except the female.

"What is your aunt's name?"

"Address?"

"What kinds of ships did you sail on?"

"Names?"

"Weights?"

"Types of cargo?"

On and on, the barrage was incessant. This was an interrogation out of a World War II movie. It was complete and exhausting. Then there was a change in tact.

"Are you uncomfortable?"

"No."

"Are you hot?"

"No."

"Are you sick?"

"No."

"Raise your hands over your head."

He complied. He knew he was perspiring profusely by now.

"You are perspiring! Are you nervous?"

"No, but I am a little warm."

Just as quickly, they bounced back to the old approach.

"You look very familiar. What high school did you attend?"

"Hollywood High."

"What years?"

"Who was the principal?"

"What classes did you take?"

"Who were the teachers?"

He didn't know the answers to most of these questions, so he made a few up and pleaded ignorance to the others. Suddenly, out of nowhere, the female stood up.

"I know you, you're a cop."

"Not me!"

"He's a damned liar. I remember seeing him in Century City in 1968, when we were having a demonstration."

"I have never been to Century City."

By now she is screaming, "I saw him beating my best friend with one of those big sticks those pigs all carry."

Everyone looked aghast as the silence fell over the room. Then one of the men suggested that he probably was a cop and that he was probably wearing a body wire.

The gentleman behind the desk told Rabbit to prove he was not wearing a body wire by removing his shirt. He complied. Inside Rabbit was boiling. Who were these bullshit people to be giving him orders? There was a time in the not-too-distant past when he would not have tolerated this situation. He was then asked to remove the contents of his pockets. Once again, he complied. He was then told to remove his pants. He looked each person in the eye and then proceeded to replace the contents of his pockets. He then picked up his shirt and put it back on. The man behind the desk appeared angry.

"Didn't you hear me? I said to remove your pants."

Rabbit simply stated, "Get fucked! I'm out of here."

With that, he turned and left.

Back at the house, he was at peace with himself. He hadn't wanted the chickenshit PDID job in the first place. When the phone rang and he heard Harris's voice, he wasn't the slightest bit concerned about hearing how he failed the interview. It might be refreshing to get back into uniform and stop being a piece of property to be checked out by anyone who wanted a dirty undercover job done. He was more than a little surprised to hear Harris tell him that he had done great. Harris had been in the next room and had listened to everything. Rabbit had carried himself off perfectly, and he had gotten further along in the interview than anyone previously had.

Regardless, Rabbit told Harris he was through, no more undercover.

Harris responded by reminding him that it wasn't as easy as all that.

Frustrated, Rabbit snapped, "You aren't paying attention, Billy! I'm through, finished, kaput, done. I'm not going to work any more undercover."

There was a slight pause on the other end of the line.

"You're the one not paying attention, Rabbit. You are assigned to PDID, not on loan. You don't get to pick up your marbles when you don't like the working conditions. If you refuse to do your job, you will get transferred in a heartbeat. Do you know what that means? It means a step back in rank and probably a transfer into Property Division for a couple of years."

Rabbit's shoulders slumped. He felt as though he had just been kicked in the stomach by a fire-breathing bull. He understood all of that very well. He was getting his mind right, and the indoctrination was working. Harris knew he had gotten through.

"Now then, have you found the apartment yet?"

Chapter 11
Embedded

Rabbit moved into the ratty apartment and started an entirely new life. It was pathetic. Charlie would continue living at the house in Manhattan Beach, and they would be able to date occasionally.

"I don't understand any of this. This is not a policeman's job. They've got you working the CIA or some other stupid thing. Whoever heard of a policeman turning over his whole life?"

She wasn't thrilled about the motorcycle gig, but this was beyond her wildest imaginations. Rabbit assured her it was a short-term assignment. Reluctantly, Charlie went along with the program. Whenever he tried to bring up to Harris the strain of this assignment on his relationship, he was reminded that only a very, very select few policemen were ever chosen to work PDID. "And besides, this is your ticket to Detective."

Working at the airport had seemed like a good idea early on, but it lost its luster now that he had such a long distance to commute. At least he avoided the rush hour traffic by reporting to work at five in the morning. His social life got a total kick in the ass, however. When he got home to his crash pad in Glendale from work at the airline, he was usually exhausted. But he had to go right to work on his operation while still in his airline uniform, smelling of jet fuel and sweat.

His established ritual was to drop in at two of the favorite haunts of right-wing extremists. The first was the Larder Bookstore in North Hollywood, in the San Fernando Valley. This was a small, musty store that was home for survivalists and soldiers of fortune. They carried every book and pamphlet imaginable on various forms of assault, stealth, weaponless self-defense, and assassination. The book list was a complete how-to, with every title from *The Anarchist Cookbook* to *The Boy Scout Handbook*. They had a variety of government manuals from everywhere, including the LAPD. There were precise manuals on how to build any size bomb or how to create a whole new persona, complete with Social Security numbers, birth certificates, and more.

The next stop in his daily ritual was the B & B Gun Store in North Hollywood. This place carried every legal weapon available anywhere on the market, including sophisticated military weaponry from Russia, Israel, England, and everywhere else. A public bulletin board was provided for the convenience of customers, and it was used by various radicals as well as ordinary members of the community who happened to be gun enthusiasts. The glib-talking Rabbit was soon a regular at B & B, and a familiar face to its clerks and patrons.

After visiting these haunts, Rabbit's routine was to go back to his apartment and read. He often thought that if he had done this much reading while he was in school, he might have become a physician. He had always been interested in survival training, ever since his early days in the Boy Scouts, so it was natural that he would spend time reading up on this subject. After all, his interest in it had helped to get him through his earlier sojourn on the other side of the world.

After weeks of these activities, his control officer Harris pointed him toward a "Tax Protest" meeting. At last he was going to actively do something positive—or so he thought.

The meeting place was a storefront on north Vermont Avenue that was in dire need of a paint job and furnished with only one table and a few dozen folding chairs. At the meeting, he met with a group of well-meaning American citizens who were sick and tired of having so much of their hard-earned paychecks go into a system that fostered uncontrolled welfare spending and a million other needless pork-barrel expenses. These folks were right-wing conservatives, but hardly extremists.

Rabbit took copious notes and forwarded them to his superiors in the form of Intelligence Reports. Meeting after meeting, storefront after storefront, the faces seemed to blend into one. Rabbit was getting bored with this activity, and he questioned its value.

Finally, he was made aware of a major tax protest that was to take place on the Queen Mary in Long Beach. He didn't know what to expect, but it turned out to be just more of the same pathetic nonsense. A large group of protesters carried a coffin, and one by one each drove a nail into it to secure the lid shut. Each nail represented a particular facet of government—one for the IRS, one for illegal taxes, etc. The group then emulated their Boston forefathers and dumped a lot of tea into Long Beach Harbor.

Rabbit couldn't help thinking this was one big bunch of wasted police time. He turned to another young man who appeared to be close to his age and stated simply, "I can't believe this."

The man asked what the problem was, and Rabbit explained that he was tired of all the Mickey Mouse bullshit. The man introduced himself as John Dolan and agreed that this was all very frustrating. He suggested that Rabbit attend an upcoming meeting at one of the hotels near the airport. It was being conducted by the Committee of Ten Million (a.k.a. the COTM) one of the groups that Rabbit had come across in the vast amount of right-wing reading material that he had been devouring.

Dolan and Rabbit left together and went to a coffee shop to talk. That led to an invitation to Dolan's home, which Rabbit accepted.

Rabbit and Dolan began to spend more time together. In time they went out to the desert for some high-powered rifle shooting and discussed survivalist wilderness training and private armies. Dolan then produced several fully automatic rifles and asked if this was more what Rabbit had in mind. They fired five hundred rounds each of .223 ammo into an abandoned car, turning it into what looked like a block of Swiss cheese. It later occurred to Rabbit that Dolan was probably the first Minuteman recruiter he had encountered.

Rabbit and Dolan became friends and shooting buddies, making many more trips to the desert, firing thousands of rounds preparing for the revolution. Dolan was a valuable contact. He took Rabbit into the network and introduced him to important members of the COTM, who in turn became sources of vital information. They all believed Armageddon was approaching, and they practiced together with firearms and other military hardware for the pending insurrection.

The Committee of Ten Million had originally been founded by the Minutemen organization, and it was an umbrella group for right-wing organizations, including the Minutemen, the Christian Patriots Defense League (a.k.a. the CPDL), the Ku Klux Klan, and others. It was used as a fishing hole from which to recruit serious members. The stated goal was to form an organization of ten million patriots within America. The thinking was fundamental: three percent of Germany under Adolph Hitler had taken over that country and created hell on earth. Three percent of Russia had taken over that country, ultimately with the same consequence. Three percent of the United States of America is roughly ten million, hence "The Committee of Ten Million."

When Rabbit reported this information to Harris, he was told that his patience was beginning to pay off. When he asked why he had not been pointed to this group in the first place, he was told that this was a necessary progression to be followed so as to reduce any kind of suspicion that might arise if he acquired the target too quickly. There was no hiding the pleasure that Harris was taking in this progress.

Two weeks later, Rabbit found himself in the main conference room of an airport hotel, where the meeting was taking place. Several tables were covered with brochures describing the various entities in attendance. Others had samples of freeze-dried foods, weapons, and pamphlets advertising survival training.

He ran into John Dolan, who took him over to a survival table and introduced him to the table manager. The manager politely challenged Rabbit to a test to determine his survival knowledge. Rabbit impressed him with tales of his travels through Africa and the Middle East, dining on camel and dog. After that, the manager's questions came fast and furious, and they were all over the place.

"What do you do if a rattler crawls into your sleeping bag? What happens if you get a snakebite? How do you set a snare? How do you get water where there is no water?"

Rabbit handled these questions to everyone's satisfaction. Dolan told him to wander around and get comfortable. Each table was devoted to a particular organization and manned by a representative who was willing to discuss ideology.

As Rabbit circulated, he picked up copies of everything available and engaged in small talk. He made a few friends and was quick to join the COTM for a paltry initial fee of ten dollars and three dollars a month in dues. It was the least he could do to help protect the freedom we all cherish so dearly.

Meetings were held once a month in various places around Southern California, but splinter groups met more frequently at various members' homes. Rabbit accepted an invitation to attend one of these splinter-group meetings.

During his first meeting he was subjected to a plethora of rhetoric about the inadequacies of local, state, and federal government. It was clear to all present that the root of all society's problems were the Antichrist Jews and their promotion of sympathy for black people. Armageddon was just around the corner. The Communists would worm their way into American society through the Jews, and as Khrushchev had predicted, capitalism would destroy itself. These folks couldn't understand why everyone wasn't preparing for the inevitable revolution. During these meetings, they each discussed the various preparations they were making.

On one occasion the host of a particular splinter-group meeting, Pete Ferris, was discussing an exercise in which they went off into the wilderness to practice their survival techniques. The lesson of that day was that people should prepare for the worst. Ferris told them about this couple who had set up their modest camp in the wilds of Griffith Park, and how the pizza they had brought along had fallen from the boxes onto the dirt, becoming almost inedible. This elicited suggestions for how to seal a pizza box, and discussions of which utensils were necessary, and how to heat and handle the pizza when it was time to eat.

Rabbit laughed to himself and found it impossible to remain mute. He announced to the group that his field of expertise was survival. Needless to say, he went directly to the head of the class, and within weeks he became the golden boy. His name spread around the community, and he was asked to attend meetings and provide helpful hints on survival. The meetings began to grow in size. Calling upon knowledge he had gleaned from his Boy Scout training, his experiences abroad, and his voluminous reading, Rabbit painted a picture of himself as a modern-day mountain man. Most of what he shared with them was basic Boy Scout information.

He instructed them in the art of catching fish without a pole, setting snares, and catching, skinning, and cooking snakes. He always warned his listeners about using snake skins as decorative clothing accessories, telling them, "You can never tell when you might be spotted by the snake's former wife or children."

He elaborated on how to determine if certain foliage was edible, how to get water when no streams were available, and a variety of other facts that few people ever concern themselves with. The "solar still" was extremely popular. These folks liked to fantasize, and they could practice that one at home in their backyards.

The reason Rabbit concentrated on survival was to provide himself with an expertise that could be devoid of guns and explosives. It was obvious to him that anyone who avoided guns couldn't possibly be associated with law enforcement. However, it was unusual for a patriot not to be obsessed with guns, so he had to walk a fine line. Most of these extremists had love affairs with their guns. They would caress them and stroke them lovingly as though they were handling the delicate skin of a beautiful woman. Every chance they got they would take them apart, clean and oil them, and then put them back together. A distant second love was their four-wheel drive trucks.

It wasn't long before Rabbit's name got around. He was able to pick and choose the groups he wanted to associate with. Pete, the "Pizza Man," soon introduced him to a local county firefighter, Mike Shuster, who was very active in the right-wing groups. Shuster was a survivalist, in addition to being a firearms expert and a martial arts black belt. His particular concern was over school bussing, which was a hot topic in Los Angeles at that time. Being the father of two very young daughters, Shuster was an outspoken opponent of bussing and professed a willingness to engage in violence.

Since school bussing was a major concern of the city, Rabbit's bosses applauded him for this contact and encouraged him to become more involved with the firefighter. This became somewhat difficult, however. Because of his paranoia, Shuster kept his distance from open meetings. Eventually he warmed up and began talking freely to Rabbit, who soon realized that he was a lightweight, and not worth pursuing.

Shuster had aligned himself with a young medical doctor and with a gun expert. The acquisition of Rabbit by this group would be considered a coup, since he had many survival skills. Shuster's goal was to develop a hardcore cadre of patriots into a special forces group. He envisioned this as a separate cell.

It was obvious to Rabbit that Shuster lacked the charisma and organizational skills to pose any kind of threat. The Department saw it differently, however, and wanted a full court press on him due to the bussing issue.

Shuster talked about a friend of his who worked for the Los Angeles Police Department, and told Rabbit that it would be good for them to meet. That was the last thing Rabbit wanted. Not knowing who the friend was, he was afraid of being burned. Then one night, Shuster invited Rabbit over to his house for some casual chitchat. During the conversation Shuster told Rabbit there was something he wanted him to see. He led him down a dimly lit hallway and stopped by a closet. Just before opening it, he turned abruptly and asked Rabbit if he was a cop. He seemed to be staring knowingly.

"Are you a cop?"

"Am I what?"

Rabbit's mouth dried up and his heart tried to leap out of his chest. All he could think of was that he must have made some kind of slip and Shuster's friend from the police department had identified him.

"You heard me. Are you a cop?"

"No, I am not a cop!"

"Are you sure?"

From a thousand replays of this scene in the past, Rabbit's instincts leaped to the foreground. He jumped on the offensive.

"What kind of shit is this? I mean, you invite me over to your house and then insult me? Are you so goddamn paranoid that you see cops around every corner?"

As Rabbit was talking, Shuster opened the closet and removed two martial arts knives with razor-honed edges, sharp enough to shave with. He went through a series of movements with the speed and precision of a master. The blades sliced the air in front of Rabbit's eyes, close enough to block the light. They circled his head, making a hissing sound as they passed his ears. Had he not remained frozen, he would have lost his nose or an ear. His heart was pounding so fiercely that he could hear it. It was like something out of *The Twilight Zone*. One slight sway of his body could have resulted in catastrophe.

As Shuster stepped slowly back and brought the knives to his side, he smiled sadistically. "If you were a cop, you would be in pieces right now. And no gun would have been able to protect you."

Rabbit remained frozen for a second. Perspiration slowly broke out under his arms and his fingers began to tremble. He fought hard to keep his voice under control.

"You know what, Shuster? You are a fuckin' psycho. You can take those knives and stick them up your ass."

With that he turned and left. As he walked out the front door, he could hear Shuster.

"Hey, man, can't you take a joke?"

The fear that had gripped Rabbit's heart turned to rage. As he drove away, he thought that if some asshole had ever done that to him while he was in uniform, he would have blown his head off. Now he couldn't even arrest the fool. Written intelligence reports could never capture the true flavor of everything that had transpired. The sterile format of those reports, reminiscent of the old TV series *Dragnet*, left no room for emotion. The reader of the report could not possibly understand the frustration, fear, and rage this incident had evoked.

The lesson Rabbit took away from his encounter with this madman with the knives was that there was no way to operate in this environment of unbalanced, irrational lunatics who fantasized about killing without being armed and able to take action to defend himself.

Rabbit knew he could not carry a gun on his person. It needed to be hidden somewhere, but available to provide him some sense of security. In short order, he rigged a hidden holster for his gun by making a cut that looked like a tear in the back of the seat in his truck. He then hung his gun by Velcro straps to the inside springs of the seat. It was a simple rig, but effective for concealment and a quick draw.

A few days later Harris met with the lieutenant and captain to submit Rabbit's latest intelligence report. As they perused the document, the captain broke into an amused chuckle when he reached the part of the report that called for the writer's professional opinion.

He turned to Harris and said, "It appears that 757 sees himself as a very quick study. In just a short time he has become the 'expert' on right-wing extremists who should be investigated."

The lieutenant gave a polite chuckle of his own and chimed in, "I love the part where he opines that we now know all there is to know about Shuster and that we should drop the investigation of him."

"Tell me, Bill, is this 757 a little faint of heart? Has he been frightened away by a little razzle-dazzle with some kitchen knives?"

Harris was at a disadvantage, but he made an attempt.

"I don't think so, sir. He's calmed down and will do anything we say—"

The lieutenant interrupted. "That's real nice of him."

Harris continued, "He just feels that this guy is a lightweight in any kind of movement, but could be very dangerous in a one-on-one situation. This guy won't do anything violent to the buses because of the kids."

The captain threw the report on his desk.

"Suppose you and 757 let me decide who is worthy of an investigation and who isn't. School bussing is the hottest political button in town right now. So he will have to stay with it whether it makes him nervous or not. Understand?"

Once more, reason had given way to a superior self-image.

Like a good soldier, Rabbit accepted the mandate of his superiors willingly, if not happily. As the weeks passed, he continued to make the rounds of the gun store and the bookstores and faithfully attended the neighborhood meetings. He did not seek out Shuster, but he did not avoid him either. Fortunately, there were no more invitations to spend a quiet evening by the fireplace.

At the same time he was told to get close to Shuster, he was also told to find out everything he could on a subject named Harry Moran. Prior to this he had reported a meeting with some members of the Posse Comitatus. He assumed that Moran was probably a member of that radical group. But Moran, like Shuster, was a zero. Neither one posed any kind of threat to the public order of the community.

Unlike Shuster, Moran was totally without color. Mr. Vanilla could walk into an empty room and immediately blend in. He was a faceless follower who wanted to be accepted as a revolutionary, much like many of these armchair warriors. He had no original ideas of his own, and could only parrot words of action that someone else had said. It was apparent that he did not quite fit in.

Moran was always nervous. He carried a short-barrel .38 pistol in an ankle holster and prided himself on how quickly he could draw the gun. He bragged that he had used that very gun to kill some gooks when he was in Vietnam. He prayed for the day the revolution would start so he could kill again.

Rabbit would refer to Moran as "the Squirrel." Shuster, Moran, and all of them were maladjusted individuals living in fantasyland, but they were hardly capable of overthrowing the United States government. Rabbit couldn't help wonder what this was all about.

Then came a big break. Dolan called and invited him to an important meeting in Orange County. This meeting would be much smaller than the one at the LA Airport because it would be only for serious patriots and would not involve mere tax protesters. Robert DePugh, founder of the Minutemen, and Reverend John Harrell, head of the Christian Patriots Defense League, would be the guest speakers. Although both of these men had served time in federal penitentiaries, no local law enforcement people had ever gotten close to them. DePugh and Harrell had founded the COTM together and were believed to be very close friends.

In preparing for his undercover assignment, Rabbit read DePugh's book on the founding of the Minutemen and learned that DePugh's closest friend was an ex-Marine named Walter Ritlin, with whom

DePugh had spent prison time. While he was in prison, officials had tried to coerce Ritlin into rolling over and informing on his associates. To accomplish this, they put him in a cellblock inhabited solely by blacks and then let the word out that he was an avid white racist. Ritlin suffered many beatings for that, but he never gave in, and this earned him DePugh's unwavering admiration. After reading the book, Rabbit decided to emulate Ritlin in every way. When he had the opportunity to meet DePugh, hopefully that demeanor would attract the attention of DePugh and enhance his chances to develop a relationship with him and gain acceptance into the movement.

Rabbit brought Charlie along as cover. Not only did it look good that he had a wife who was interested in the cause, but she was originally from Arkansas and had a lot in common with the leadership. Once inside, they listened to a variety of speakers who were really just paving the way for DePugh and Harrell.

DePugh was extremely soft-spoken and quiet in all his mannerisms. He showed no emotion, which belied his reputation as a tough ex-con. The Reverend Harrell, on the other hand, was lively and animated. He breathed fire and brimstone as he pounded the podium and vociferously sermonized for his cause of freedom and justice. He was a very emotional speaker, and like all good preachers, he knew exactly the right things to say. He could work a crowd with the best of them.

After the speeches, Rabbit stayed around to meet the honored guests. As he introduced Charlie, they were instantly taken with her feminine southern drawl and striking beauty. It wasn't difficult for Charlie to drive any man to distraction.

DePugh was not easy to get close to, so Rabbit concentrated on Reverend Harrell. He knew that if he could get close to Harrell, he would eventually get close to DePugh. The Reverend really enjoyed his chat with Rabbit and Charlie, so much so that he gave Rabbit his address and asked him to keep in touch.

Over the next two months, Rabbit kept his word and stayed in touch with the Reverend Harrell. He clipped every article he could find in the local newspapers that would be of any interest to the right wing and sent them along with a letter railing against the government to Harrell's home in Illinois. He sent clippings about crime in black communities and questionable activities by anyone with a Jewish-sounding name, and he always included a story about wilderness survival. He also kept very busy at the local meetings, continuing to make a name for himself as a survival expert.

He kept in touch with Ferris and even with Shuster, just to keep the brass happy. He still couldn't figure why he had been asked to keep track of Moran, the Squirrel, who was simply a goof who loved to show off his little two-inch .38 caliber pistol and constantly talk about killing informants.

After two months, his efforts with Reverend Harrell paid off. Harrell invited Rabbit to attend a national White Power meeting in Kansas City. The heads of all the organizations that made up the COTM would be there. Shelton from the Ku Klux Klan, DePugh of the Minutemen, Harrell of the Christian Patriots Defense League, and other organization heads from groups like the Nazis and Posse Comitatus. Harrell felt it would be good for Rabbit to meet these people and become even more actively involved.

The next morning, Harris and his boss, the Lieutenant OIC, were waiting outside the captain's office for him to arrive. When the captain arrived, the lieutenant couldn't wait to tell him about the brilliant job he had done in guiding the investigation in which Rabbit was involved. The captain agreed that Rabbit was doing great. Harris threw a little cold water on the celebration when he announced that Rabbit was concerned about traveling to another state where he had no jurisdiction and without any kind of cover.

"Is he some kind of nitwit?" the captain inquired.

Harris was quick, "Not at all, Captain. He is concerned about legality more than anything."

The captain and lieutenant smiled. They had all been down this road before in other investigations. "Calm his fears down. Have him sign a travel authority and assure him that everything is proper. I will take care of the notifications."

Chapter 12
Masters of Deception

The people at PDID had already received a flyer about the major event in Kansas City. They were beside themselves with glee over the prospect of finally infiltrating something like this. Rabbit was now about to go where no LA police undercover operator had gone before. Brass and control supervisors were aware that polygraphs were routinely administered at meetings like this. They felt in all probability that the poly would take the form of a voice stress analysis, because that is the cheapest and easiest to administer. Fortunately, it would also be easier to pass.

Someone directed Harris to order Rabbit to undergo hypnosis to purge his mind of any affiliation with police work. It was up to Harris to convince Rabbit what a wonderful plan this was.

Harris explained to Rabbit there would be time enough before his trip to Kansas City to prepare adequately for any eventuality. Arrangements had been made for him to go through several sessions with a PDID hypnotist who would hypnotize him and suppress as much memory as possible relating to the police world. This was the most help that could be provided to Rabbit to assist him with the polygraph exam that he would be required to take in Kansas City.

Rabbit was astounded.

"Wait a minute. I don't want to do that. The written Detective exam is coming up, and I want to study for it. How nuts is this? First you deny me access to the Department Manual, the Special Orders, and any other material to help me study for the exam, and now some asshole is going to work on my memory to try to erase what I do know? Is that what you are telling me? I don't think this shit is right, do you?"

Harris said to quit worrying about taking the exam, that would be taken care of.

Rabbit said, "How is it going to be taken care of?"

Harris said, "Don't worry, you are going to be made Detective. Right now you need to get ready for Kansas City. This is what is important."

Reluctantly, Rabbit went along with the program one more time. He took the address of the hypnotist. It was a single-family residence in an ordinary residential section of Downey. The houses were modest and neat. It was a nice, middle class neighborhood with neatly trimmed lawns and hedges.

Rabbit went to the door and rang the bell. He was greeted by a middle-aged, balding male who had an unkempt appearance. This man had the look of someone with more important things on his mind than the latest fad featured in *GQ*. The man introduced himself and led the way into a small den. He had Rabbit recline on a couch. After a few preliminary questions (which were more mundane than Rabbit had expected), the man began to drone on and on in a dull, flat monotone. He spoke of disassociating oneself with police work. After approximately sixty minutes of this, he informed Rabbit that the session was finished. The only thought that entered Rabbit's mind when the session was over was, *this cat is weird.*

Rabbit got into his truck and drove off. He noticed Harris's car parked surreptitiously in a driveway about half a block away and thought that the hypnosis couldn't have worked too well if he could still relate to Harris's car. *Well,* he thought, *maybe it takes several sessions.*

Harris subsequently informed him that he had been given the only session he was going to get. He wondered if the CIA or FBI worked like this. If they did, it was no wonder they were all screwed up.

Two days later, at a meeting with Harris, Rabbit reiterated his concerns about the trip. Harris, as always, gave him the party line that everything would be fine, but this time he added a new twist. In the event something were to go sideways, Rabbit was told to get the hell out of there and keep moving until he got back to Los Angeles or in touch with a federal agency.

"Do whatever it takes; just get out and don't get caught."

He wasn't supposed to take chances with local law enforcement in case they happened to be sympathizers, or even members. Harris again assured Rabbit that he was certain he could handle any eventuality.

Rabbit thanked Harris for the vote of confidence but continued to press him for help with the polygraph that was to be administered in Kansas City. In the literature published by various right-wing groups, discussions about security and rooting out informants indicated the polygraph was unquestionably the most effective tool.

Rabbit requested a meeting with the Department's chief polygraph operator for advice on how best to defeat the machine. Harris said that request had been denied by the chief on several other occasions; therefore there was no reason to even ask. Rabbit said that was nice of him—and that being the case, he wanted some dope or something, as he was not about to get on a plane to Kansas City and walk knowingly into an ambush that had been set by Ku Klux Klan security. Harris said he would work on it. To fail the test was not an option.

As Harris was leaving, he gave Rabbit a tattered business card that appeared to have been in someone's wallet for a very long time. Harris told him to take the card, go to the address, and meet Peter Keller, whose name was on the card. An appointment had been set for the following day at ten o'clock. There was the usual admonishment not to be late and to have the business card in hand when he showed up for the appointment.

Rabbit asked, "What is this all about?" Harris said it would help him in Kansas City. As Harris drove off, Rabbit looked at the card. It was an insurance agency on Wilshire Boulevard, just west of La Brea.

The following morning, a few minutes before the appointment, Rabbit arrived at the location. It was a nondescript office building, mid-block. The insurance agency was on the third floor. Rabbit opened the office door, which bore the insurance company's name in large brass letters. Inside was a generic waiting room, maybe twenty feet square. There was a middle-aged couple sitting in two of the chairs that lined the room. On the far side was a desk, behind which sat a receptionist.

Rabbit showed the business card to her and said he had an appointment. She checked the appointment book, noted his name, and told him to have a seat. It would be a few minutes, she said, as they were running a little behind. Rabbit had a seat and waited about ten minutes. He passed the time reading some out-of-date magazines on the coffee table. The receptionist finally escorted the two people ahead of Rabbit to an inner office.

Rabbit waited another twenty minutes. He was about to blow his appointment off and leave when the people who had been ahead of him came out of the inner office and left. The receptionist motioned to Rabbit to follow her. She opened the inner door and introduced Rabbit to Peter Keller, who was standing behind the desk holding several files. Keller's appearance was not what Rabbit expected of a boring insurance salesman. Keller was wearing a khaki bush shirt with the cuffs rolled up, and khaki pants with cargo pockets. He had an unkempt thick head of hair and a stubble beard. His frown lines were deep, his eyes were "no-nonsense," and he had a strong handshake. He looked more like Indiana Jones than the owner of an insurance agency that sold homeowner policies. *This is turning out to be another strange encounter*, Rabbit thought.

Rabbit nonchalantly looked around the room, the place was a mess. The desk was in complete disarray with papers and files scattered all about it. Rabbit perused the clutter half expecting to see ancient treasure hunting maps but only saw insurance actuary charts. Even Keller's name plate had been knocked over. The rest of the office didn't look much better. At one end was an old, worn, red leather couch with stacks of cardboard file boxes sitting on it. At the other end was a bank of metal file cabinets. On top of the cabinets were more stacks of cardboard file boxes. Rabbit thought this must be a very busy insurance agency.

Mr. Keller offered Rabbit a seat in the chair in front of the desk. He asked if he had been given a business card. Rabbit produced the card, and Keller took it and put it in his desk drawer. Before Rabbit could speak, Keller said they had only sixty minutes for the meeting, and because time was so short, he would speak first. After that, if Rabbit had questions and there was time, he would answer them.

He told Rabbit he knew where he was going and would tell him what to expect. It was a high-speed crash course in Interrogation 101. The man spoke quickly, with hardly a pause. He covered interrogation techniques, the questions that could be anticipated, the information the underground would be looking for, how to respond to an interrogator's questions, and how best to craft evasive answers. He explained in detail the types of polygraphs, the principle of how they worked, the training required and ability of the operators to be effective, and the best tactic for Rabbit to exercise while connected to the machine. Of paramount concern to the underground organization were federal agents, informants, and agent provocateurs.

The instructor advised Rabbit before he left for Kansas City to apply at three local police departments for employment. As normal procedure dictated, he would be screened by a sergeant who would inquire as to why he was interested in a job in law enforcement. The answer would be that he liked the idea of being a vice cop, like on TV shows, driving in high-speed chases, and getting into shootouts with bad guys. Expressing those desires would result in immediate disqualification.

The purpose of this exercise was to enable Rabbit to explain to the polygraph operator, if necessary, why the test might show deception on questions concerning whether he had ever been involved in law enforcement. He could simply say that in the past he had applied for police jobs with several departments, but he'd never gotten hired. Then, when asked on reexamination if it were true that he had tried to be a policeman but had been turned away, his answer would be truthful.

Rabbit had a thorough understanding of the polygraph. He had studied it at the police academy in Detective school, and also in college during his course studies for his degree in Police Science. He had also been subjected to it twice by experts in LAPD Crime Section prior to his assignments in Administrative Vice and Public Disorder Intelligence Division. He had even used it as an investigative tool himself, and he knew full well that an attempt to deceive a polygraph operator would only have any chance of succeeding if the operator was not a highly-trained professional. There was at least some comfort to be taken in that thought for when the moment of truth arrived.

The instructor told Rabbit to keep in mind the hypnosis that he had undergone, and to remember his fictitious attempt to join various police departments.

Exactly at sixty minutes, the intercom light on the phone was activated. The instructor stated that the meeting was over and that he had clients waiting. That was it. No goodbye, no handshake, no "Good luck."

Rabbit left the office. As he walked through the lobby to leave, he saw two old ladies sitting next to a large, faded, plastic plant on an end table. He couldn't help but wonder if these two old ladies were KGB or CIA. He wanted to ask them, but he knew what their answer would be: "Son, we operate on a need-to-know basis, and you don't need to know that."

The next day Harris met with Rabbit and gave him a dossier on the polygraph. It had a plain, dark green cover, and it was untitled and without an author credit. It appeared to have come from a government intelligence source.

Harris said to study the information and under no circumstances make a copy. He was emphatic that he needed to have the dossier back before Rabbit went to Kansas City. Rabbit spent considerable time studying the dossier and found the information it contained very helpful. It alleviated some of his anxiety about his impending encounter with the polygraph.

Chapter 13
Nightmare in Kansas City

Rabbit called Charlie and asked if she would like to take off for a couple of days and take a trip to Kansas City with him. Charlie was delighted. Maybe they could get a little normalcy back into their lives. She didn't think to ask why in the world Kansas City, and he didn't tell her why they would be going or what they would be doing.

It wasn't until they were on the plane that he told her they would be meeting with the Reverend Harrell. Needless to say, Charlie was more than a little upset to find out this was a working assignment for Rabbit. He reasoned that at least they would be together for a couple of days. They could see a place they had never been before, and she could do some shopping. She wasn't totally sold on the idea, but she was hungry for some quality time with the man she loved. *God*, she thought, *I must love this guy to put up with all this.*

They arrived in Kansas City a day early and went out on the town. Kansas City is known for its fabulous steaks, so they went out and found the best steak restaurant in town. After dinner they strolled the streets like two young lovers on a honeymoon, window shopping and giggling a lot.

Suddenly they stopped and looked into each other's eyes. They knew each other's thoughts as they entwined their arms and kissed. Without speaking, they jumped into a cab and headed back to the hotel. In the elevator they really gave the impression of being newlyweds on a honeymoon. By the time they got into the room, they were wild with desire for each other. This was to be a night to make up for all the loneliness they had both felt during the last few months.

The next morning Rabbit awoke at sunrise and looked over at Charlie as she lay sleeping. The bed sheet covered her from the waist down. She was in a semi-fetal position, and the curves of her breasts were so inviting that he had to fight off the overwhelming urge that was surging up in his loins. He realized he would need a quick cold shower to calm him enough to get started with the business at hand.

When Rabbit reached the lobby, he had a half hour to kill. He sought out the coffee shop, hoping to find the Reverend Harrell. The Reverend was just leaving as Rabbit entered, and he did a double take when he saw him. He looked as though he had just found a long-lost son, and his greeting was warm and effusive. He wrapped his arms around Rabbit and led him over to a booth where they both sat down.

He had a hundred questions to ask. How was Rabbit doing? Had his beautiful wife come with him? He hoped so. He always thought it was a good tactic to have husbands and wives together as much as possible in the movement. Females always afforded excellent cover from the prying eyes of federal agents, who were always more suspicious of lone male members than couples.

Rabbit was aware of that philosophy from his reading and from letters he had personally received from both Harrell and DePugh. That was why he had decided to bring Charlie—she was a great diversion anywhere. She was young and beautiful, with a warm, charming personality, and she was a staunch Christian conservative from Arkansas with a very heavy Southern drawl. Charlie was a perfect cover. He saw no downside to using her in this operation.

Harrell continued on with many more questions. He asked if he could take them to dinner later that evening. Rabbit found it difficult to squeeze in more than a one- or two-word answer for each question; the Reverend was a whirling dervish.

Abruptly, the Reverend rose and told Rabbit to meet him at the fifth-floor registration area, where he would brief him on what to expect. Then he left.

Charlie came down and joined him for a continental breakfast. They had a light conversation and made plans for the evening. Then they went upstairs to the registration area and were processed. They were joined by Harrell and DePugh, who was now a little more open and friendly than he had been at the Orange County meeting. He had been hearing good things about Rabbit and his talent for teaching survival. It seemed as though Ferris, the Pizza Man, was using Rabbit as a vehicle to get closer to DePugh. According to Ferris, he had known Rabbit for a long time and was using him to teach the Southern California patriots about survival.

It was all make-believe, but Ferris had turned out to be an unexpected ace in the hole for Rabbit. Harrell gave Rabbit and Charlie a briefing about the polygraph examinations that were administered to suspect people selected by the security staff, and to others who were being considered for membership in the various organizations. The security staff knew what to look for to ferret out law enforcement operators and informants. Such people had a tendency to be very nervous when watched.

This discussion sent chills up and down Rabbit's and Charlie's spines. This was the same psychological ploy used by police when giving a poly or preparing for an interrogation. If the subject sits and stews about it long enough, he will come apart at the seams.

After registration the Reverend escorted Rabbit and Charlie up to the ballroom, which was the hub of activity for the conference. As he scanned the room, Rabbit noticed several ominous-looking men in identical gray suits that gave them the appearance of uniformed security patrolling the perimeter of the ballroom. The first speaker was a middle-aged ex-Marine who had a strong military bearing and a commanding presence. He provided a briefing on the day's activities and gave them the approximate order in which the members of the Executive Council would be addressing the assembly. The Reverend Levy, a graying, heavyset minister who looked older than his fifty-five years, led the group in the Pledge of Allegiance and offered a short prayer. It appeared that it was Levy's job to warm up the crowd.

Levy had all first-time attendees stand and tell where they had come from. One by one, approximately a hundred of them stood and identified themselves as being from Arizona, Florida, Texas, Virginia, Indiana, Illinois, Arkansas, Utah, Nebraska, Kansas, Wisconsin, Alabama, Georgia, Michigan, and Missouri.

There were even six people from California. Rabbit observed that the uniformed guards who were patrolling the area took particular note of the newcomers. He reached over and grabbed Charlie's hand. It was cold and clammy. The atmosphere of the room was charged. Being an informant, Rabbit was acutely aware of the security force. Charlie whispered that she was scared out of her wits. Rabbit put up a show of bravado for her sake, but he was equally concerned. It finally dawned on him that bringing Charlie here as his cover perhaps had been a monumental screw up on his part. Both tried to avoid squirming, but the tension was getting to Charlie.

It was difficult for Rabbit and Charlie to focus on Levy, who spoke about the moral decay of America and the attack by the Communists on Christianity. His speech was fervent and stirring. Like all the leaders, he was firmly convinced of the truth of his words.

He was followed by the Reverend Harrell, who was true to form. He spoke of the many hardships that had been endured by the various leaders of the COTM. He himself had spent four years in Leavenworth Federal Penitentiary for trying to help a young soldier expose corruption in the military. The experience had destroyed him financially and caused his family immeasurable hardship. However, he did not regret having had to do the hard time. He would be willing to sacrifice his own life and the lives of his family if it meant salvation for America and his white Christian heritage.

Reverend Harrell was followed by the man of the hour, Robert DePugh, the man who had devised the concept of the Committee of Ten Million. As the founder and leader of the Minutemen, DePugh was a very quiet and introspective man who paled next to Harrell as a public speaker, but he had a certain intensity and dedication that came through.

DePugh had a message that this group would die for. He too spoke of his many years in Leavenworth Federal Penitentiary, where he had served time for violations of the 1968 Firearm Law. He was not ashamed of having been there, but he was determined that he would never go back. He opined that time in prison could have one of two effects on an inmate: it could have the effect desired by the government, which was to grind a man to dust, or it could temper him like a sword and fill him with resolve.

That was the precise effect prison had on DePugh. He had been tempered and was more determined than ever to further the cause he'd begun so many years ago. He reminded the crowd of the statistical data—that the Nazis had taken Germany with only three percent of the population and that the Soviets had also accomplished their takeover with a small percent of the population. Ten million people can effectively sway the vote in America, he said, and if necessary, ten million guns could certainly demand a recount. He went on to allay any possible fears in the audience by noting that the Federal Bureau of Investigation had been severely hampered by the courts. This was an unforeseen result of the liberal courts' attempt to weaken Democracy. The FBI was now restricted from using frivolous wiretaps and from opening undelivered mail.

Other leaders spoke after DePugh and brought their own fields of expertise to the forefront. A spokesman for the National Justice Foundation warned of a pending threat to do away with the free enterprise system. A past president of the National Association to Keep and Bear Arms warned of continuing attacks on Second Amendment rights. Speakers spoke of workshops that they would be conducting to teach members how to avoid harassment by the

Internal Revenue Service. A renowned psychiatrist from Florida who was involved in the leadership of the American Pistol and Rifle Association addressed the evils of abortion and the dedication necessary to protect Second Amendment rights. A seemingly endless parade of dedicated and vocal patriots came forth to preach the various gospels of survival in America.

Just before lunch a man named Robert Shelton stepped up and introduced himself as the Imperial Wizard of the United Klans of America. He stated that some people called him a dictator and admitted that there was some truth to it. However, he insisted that what he did was necessary in his role as Head of Security for the COTM.

"The Klan has learned a lot over the years about how to deal with the FBI," he said, "and we fight a never-ending battle against undercover agents and informants. The uniformed security force and several undercover Klansmen have been watching the audience closely and will be picking out people they believe to be agents or informants."

Anyone suspected would be required to submit to a polygraph examination. Additionally, select newcomers would also be required to take the test. Rabbit strained to maintain his calm, but his heart raced. There had been considerable dialogue about "accidents" that would happen to agents who infiltrated this organization. He thought back to that bullshit session with the hypnotist that was going to erase all police experience from his memory bank. His mind raced as he considered his options, and he remembered the warning Harris had given him about avoiding local law enforcement. He didn't have a clue as to where to go or what to do.

The Reverend Harrell approached Rabbit and told him that he had been scheduled for a polygraph examination. Rabbit's heart sank. Murphy's Law was working overtime. Harrell explained that Rabbit had a great deal of potential in the right-wing movement, and the polygraph was routine for someone like him. Charlie turned as white as a Klansman's hood. Harrell looked at her and asked if she were sick.

Rabbit interjected quickly, "She is really quite sick. We don't know if it was something she ate last night or what."

Charlie picked up on Rabbit's lead and said that she felt like dying. Maybe she would have to see a doctor. Harrell suggested that Rabbit take her to the room and then come back and meet him.

When they got to the room, Charlie grabbed a suitcase and began to pack, saying they had better get out of there. Rabbit took her over to the bed and told her to lie down. He couldn't let Charlie see that he also was in a state of near panic. He looked out the window and realized he was thirteen stories above the street. There was no fire escape and no way to gracefully make an exit.

He kept hearing Shelton's remarks about being interrogated by members of Congress, as well as the FBI and other law enforcement entities. Shelton hated cops with a passion.

Rabbit kept trying to soothe Charlie and tell her that they were in no physical danger, but he didn't believe it himself. He felt he was starting to lose his grip on the situation. The stress was becoming overwhelming; it made him feel as though he were in a deep hole and someone was shoveling dirt onto his chest.

Rabbit begged Charlie to stay dressed, but told her to get in bed with full covers over her and give him a minute to think. A knock on the door forced him to pull himself together. The Reverend Harrell entered and went immediately over to Charlie. He was genuinely concerned about her well-being. He sat on the edge of the bed, took her hand, and said he thought it might be wise to call a doctor. They both agreed. Harrell then turned to Rabbit and told him that they had to get over to the polygraph room as soon as possible.

The moment of truth was rapidly approaching. Earlier, Harrell had given Rabbit some papers to fill out that would act as control information for the examination. Rabbit apologized that he had not had an opportunity to complete the task. They returned to the main ballroom to pick up some additional papers, when suddenly an unknown young man approached Harrell and asked for his help with an urgent problem over at the registration desk.

Harrell handed Rabbit a folder that contained specific questions he and DePugh wanted asked while Rabbit was on the polygraph, and told him he would meet him at the appointed location. Rabbit knew that some questions had been designed by the Klan and DePugh to determine if he had any affiliation with law enforcement. Harrell's questions were designed to determine his commitment to Christianity and the right wing. They would certainly include questions about his alcohol consumption, his beliefs, his fidelity, and his willingness to sacrifice all for his country.

There were more than a couple of problem areas that could be disastrous for him, but his main fear was the questions that had been formulated by the Klan. These were violent psychos who were merely tolerated by the rest of the right wing so as to not cause a tremendous split in the COTM. Neither Harrell nor DePugh had any love for the Klan or the Nazis. They were regarded as clowns, albeit extremely dangerous clowns.

Rabbit took the folder and proceeded to the room where the Klan had set up the polygraph machines. As soon as he arrived he could see that the Klansman had a serious attitude problem. The Klansman asked where Harrell was and then noticed that Rabbit had failed to fill in the control questions. He let Rabbit know that he was pissed off at him and Harrell for not being ready to go. He had gone to a lot of trouble to set this up, and this was an unforgivable waste of his valuable time. He said he was going on a lunch break and that Rabbit had better fill out the questionnaire and have Harrell back there when he returned.

As soon as he left, Rabbit made a beeline down to the main hall and found Harrell. He told the Reverend that the Klansman was extremely pissed off at him and then lied, saying that they had to get up there right away. Harrell was quite even-tempered by nature, so he merely shrugged and told Rabbit, "Let's go. We don't want to upset the Klan."

When they arrived at the room and found the Klansman gone, Harrell became more than just a little annoyed. The desired effect had been achieved. He instructed Rabbit to return to the meeting room while he got this thing straightened out.

Rabbit went back to the meeting hall and checked in. He then immediately slipped out and went back to his hotel room.

Charlie looked as though she had gone through hell. He told her that she was to stay in bed and he was going to split. If anyone came looking for him, he was out looking for some medication. Charlie freaked out. She did not want to be left alone. Rabbit explained that it wasn't her they would be interested in, it was him. He convinced her—somewhat—that everything would be all right. Uncharacteristically, she was on the verge of tears. She begged him not to leave her alone, even though she knew there was no other way. Charlie would have to be his cover once more.

Rabbit gave her an in-depth explanation of the thinking of this ultra-Christian group of patriots, assuring her that they would never abuse her modesty in any way. The key to her safety was to stay in bed and continue to feign illness. She was somewhat calmed. She asked Rabbit to get her some aspirin from her suitcase. He opened the suitcase and found the bottle; unfortunately, there were only three pills left in it. Rabbit told Charlie he would go get her another bottle and be back in just a few minutes.

He took the elevator downstairs to the sundries shop next to the lobby to get a new supply—not just for Charlie, but for his own stress-induced, pounding headache.

On his way back to his room on the thirteenth floor, the elevator abruptly halted on the fourth floor. When the doors opened, in walked Shelton and one of his Klan security men. Rabbit's heart sank. It was like seeing the devil himself. Shelton spoke and said he was glad to catch Rabbit alone, out of sight of Harrell's and DePugh's men. As the doors closed again, the elevator continued two floors up and stopped. Shelton motioned to Rabbit to get out of the elevator, as he needed to speak to him in private.

Rabbit protested, displaying the aspirin that he said he had just bought for his wife, who was suffering and about to go out of her mind with a horrible, pounding headache. Shelton said he only needed a few minutes. Rabbit glanced at the security man and could see there was no viable way out of this without a physical confrontation, the outcome of which would not be in Rabbit's favor.

A few rooms down the hall Shelton opened a door, and the three men entered the room. Rabbit and Shelton sat opposite each other at a small table. The security man stood behind Rabbit blocking the exit door. Shelton looked Rabbit straight in the eye. His stare was stone cold, with no sign of emotion.

It seemed an eternity before Shelton spoke. When he did, he pointedly asked Rabbit if he were nervous. Rabbit answered he was very nervous and concerned about his wife's worsening medical condition, and this detour was not helping matters. He asked Shelton what this was about. Again there was another long pause before Shelton would speak. Finally, he asked Rabbit what he thought about the Klan.

Before Rabbit answered, he flashed on the history of the KKK and the atrocities committed under Shelton's leadership. He envisioned Klansmen blowing up the 16th Street Church in Birmingham, killing four young black girls; and lynching black boys, who were hanged kicking and screaming by the neck from trees in the back woods; and dragging black men down country roads to their deaths, tied to truck bumpers, the road tearing their limbs off one by one. That was what he knew about the Klan. They were homicidal maniacs driven by hate.

Rabbit also knew that he was an undercover policeman, hated by these people, 1,600 miles outside his jurisdiction, and equally far from any possible backup. He had been sent there to spy and report on the Klan and others—to look for weaknesses to exploit in order to disrupt their objectives.

Rabbit was now face-to-face with the Ku Klux Klan's ex-convict leader, the Imperial Wizard. No one knew where he was, and the exit door was guarded by a six-foot, four-inch, 235-pound goon with a rock-solid body that he had obviously developed over the course of many years spent in the penitentiary.

Rabbit was very nervous, and his anxiety had little to do with his wife on the thirteenth floor. This was all about the matter at hand. There was no question that the goon possessed the physical ability to toss him from the hotel room window to a sure death if this little meeting didn't go right.

Rabbit's heart was pounding, and it seemed it was about to explode. The time for his answer was up. Rabbit told Shelton that he had grown up in Indiana in the country, and that some of his neighbors had been Klansmen. He recalled that they were all church-going, God-fearing, hard-working, good men who took care of their families. He offered up the fact that his aunt's brother had been a Klansman—he knew it was safe to give that information, as it was true. Besides, that part of the family was dead, including the Klansman.

That information went a long way toward easing the tension in the room, which up until then could have been cut with a knife. Now the two men just set there, their eyes locked.

It seemed forever before Shelton spoke. He said he had read the background report DePugh and Harrell had put together on Rabbit and felt he possessed qualities that would be beneficial to the Klan. He told Rabbit that after he got past the polygraph examination, the two of them needed to sit down and talk about Rabbit's future in the movement. Shelton said that he didn't have an issue with Rabbit;

his problem was with Harrell and DePugh.

"The two of them have a real inflated sense of self-importance. They are only interested in the Klan because of the Klan's expertise in ferreting out spies and informants. They think of the Klan as underlings who work for them. Not so. It's the other way around. The Klan is getting some of their best people crossing over, and that has created a real serious attitude with them.

"I need men that are willing to take action now, not just organize for a revolution sometime in the future. I believe you could become an important member in the Klan. It's no secret that the Jews and the Feds have hurt us recently, and they continue to relentlessly hammer away at our organization. As a result of their attacks, we have lost members, and the battle has cost us a lot of money. We need to fight back as aggressively as we ever have. The Klan needs to strike violently, in many ways, to get their attention and demonstrate that we are a force to be reckoned with, not only in the South, but throughout America.

"I am in the process of reorganizing some of our special units. California has a great potential, but it needs some new people to get involved. We have some loyal, dedicated people out there already, but we need to refocus, and that will take some new blood.

"This is not the time nor the place to have this discussion with you. Reading your file, I see you can travel free working for the airlines. So here is my contact info. After this weekend is over, you fly down to Alabama and meet with us, and we'll show you around Tuscaloosa. If time permits, maybe we'll even take you out to the country. When we're finished, I guarantee you'll see what I mean. This deal with the Minutemen and CPDL isn't going anywhere.

They are a waste of your time."

Rabbit said he would think it over, but for the time being he had to go tend to his ill wife. Rabbit stood, turned toward the door, and faced off with the goon who was still blocking the exit door. It was anything but a warm, touchy-feely moment. Rabbit turned back toward Shelton and asked, "So now what?"

Shelton didn't speak. He waved his hand at the goon, who stepped aside and let Rabbit pass. As Rabbit walked from the room, he felt like he had just been released from an interrogation in a Russian prison.

Rabbit raced back to the room to find Charlie in sheer panic. She thought something bad had happened to him. Rabbit lied and said everything was okay, he'd just run into Reverend Harrell downstairs, who went on and on about her and wanted to know how she was doing and how he might be of assistance in getting a doctor or having her taken to a hospital to be examined. Reassured once again, Charlie regained her composure enough for Rabbit to determine that she could handle her situation without him. With that, Rabbit squeezed her hand gently, kissed her on the forehead, and promised her everything would be okay. He then put his plan into motion and took off for parts unknown.

When he hit the streets, Rabbit made sure that there were no drugstores in the vicinity of the hotel, and then half-walked, half-jogged as far from the hotel as he could in order to gain a safe clearance. He felt a bit like a child hiding from his parents to avoid punishment for some act of misconduct, but he knew all too well that the punishment he faced in this case would be far more serious than a spanking. He roamed the streets, pondering all the possibilities.

He had taken polygraphs before. He knew he had been psyched out in each instance, and he had just been psyched out for this one that was pending. That is the initial goal of the person who administers the test, and it had worked. He had lost the game this time.

There was no way in hell that he could flimflam the results. It would require only a minuscule amount of expertise for an examiner to determine that the subject was trying to beat the machine by perpetual movement, self-inflicted pain, or some other distraction.

Eventually he wandered into a drugstore and bought an assortment of stomach medications that would have provided sufficient care for an outbreak of dysentery involving everyone in the city. The entire trip took about two hours, which brought him back to the hotel a half-hour after the polygraph examiners had closed shop for the day.

Rabbit returned to the meeting room carrying his case of medication and he was physically exhausted and mentally stressed out. Harrell rushed over to him; he was beside himself.

"Where on earth have you been?"

Rabbit slumped into a chair and shook his head as though he had just suffered a great loss. He explained that he had gone all over the area looking for a doctor who would prescribe something for Charlie, but he'd had no luck. Rabbit told Harrell that Charlie had a tremendous fear of hospitals since her mother died in one just a year ago. Harrell was genuinely concerned. Rabbit was appreciative of his feelings, but said they would have to return home in the morning so Charlie could see her own doctor. Harrell asked him not to make it an early flight so they could put him on the poly first thing in the morning.

When Rabbit returned to the room, he had all but convinced himself that Charlie was really sick from a virus, and offered her the medication he had purchased as a cover. She immediately told him to shove the medication where the sun did not shine. He had never seen her this angry before. He called the airline to get the first available flight, but the earliest he could get was one o'clock. Murphy's Law was kicking in.

As he climbed into bed, he discovered Charlie's body was colder and clammier than her hands. In response to his "Good night," she merely stared at the ceiling. Both spent the night wrapped in their individual fears, anticipating what the next day would bring. Rabbit was filled with additional guilt over getting Charlie involved with this mess.

Self-pity was replaced with anger at the Los Angeles Police Department for putting him into this extremely dangerous situation. He thought about that one session with the hypnotist in Downey that was supposed to prepare him for this eventuality, and he wanted to kick the shit out of someone, anyone who thought that would really work.

Charlie was filled with remorse for ever having gotten involved with Rabbit in the first place. She thought of how much she had loved him, and the crazy, wonderful times they had spent together before he became consumed with this undercover work. She admitted to herself that she still loved him, but not enough to put up with this kind of life. She was determined to give him an ultimatum if they ever got back to some semblance of reality.

When the sun came up, they both were wide awake, but they did not speak. Rabbit knew it was futile even to try. They were exhausted from a total lack of sleep. Rabbit dragged himself into the shower, shaved, and dressed. He went down to the conference room like a man going to the gallows.

When Harrell saw him, he was concerned. "Rabbit, you look terrible. Is it possible that you caught something from Charlie?"

Rabbit assured him that he didn't think so, it was probably just that he hadn't gotten any sleep because he'd spent the night caring for Charlie. It suddenly occurred to him that this might just prove to be a viable alibi when he did poorly on the poly.

Harrell said that they had better get right up to the examiner's room because they were only going to be in operation for a short time this morning. En route they ran into Shelton. Harrell told Shelton that he was quite displeased at the attitude displayed and the treatment his Klansman had given Harrell and Rabbit the day before. Harrell said Rabbit's polygraph exam was the main purpose for Rabbit being in Kansas City.

Both the Minutemen and the Christian Patriots Defense League needed Rabbit tested and cleared so that he could proceed into a secure leadership position. Shelton replied that he knew about Rabbit, as he had reviewed his file, and that he had spoken to DePugh twice about the pending exam and the questions that DePugh had requested. He said that after looking over his resume, he felt Rabbit could be a far better asset to the Klan than to either the Minutemen or the Christian Patriots Defense League.

This did not go over well with Harrell. He very pointedly told Shelton the only thing the Klan had to do with Rabbit was to complete their background investigation and administer a polygraph examination—and to be clear, nothing else.

It was apparent there were serious issues between Shelton and Harrell. Shelton, bristling with resentment, accused Harrell of wasting his expert's time. A loud argument developed over who had said what to whom and at what time. Shelton said he was going to get to the bottom of this and walked off.

After a few minutes, Harrell became impatient and told Rabbit to wait there, he had other things to take care of. Instead, Rabbit immediately left and went back to his room, where he began packing.

Charlie was already packed. They spoke for the first time. He assured her that it was all over and that they would be leaving on the one o'clock flight.

In the meantime, Shelton returned to find Harrell and Rabbit missing. Not bothering to question his examiner, he walked off. Harrell came to the room to get Rabbit and stayed long enough to make sure Charlie was not on her deathbed. He then took Rabbit back to the polygraph room, only to find out that they had already packed up the polygraph and were gone. Harrell said that it looked as though they would have to do it some other time.

Rabbit would find out later that Ferris and all the other representatives from California had successfully taken the poly. DePugh would be led to believe that Harrell had put Rabbit on the poly, and since nothing was said to the contrary, he must have passed it with flying colors.

The flight home was an emotional nightmare. Rabbit attempted to engage in small talk, but it was to no avail. The only time Charlie spoke to him during the entire flight was when she turned to him and said icily through clenched teeth, "This is the dumbest fucking thing I have ever done."

Rabbit could have echoed her sentiments exactly, but realized his best course of action was to keep his mouth shut. Upon arrival at LAX, Charlie was more at ease, but the tension between her and Rabbit was still there. He realized that he was going to have to let her cool off for a while before he tried to romance her again.

He dropped her off at the beach house after driving a circuitous route, which merely antagonized her more. When she left the car, she pursed her lips tightly, as one does when chewing on a lemon, and kissed him with all the passion of a limp handshake. Rabbit realized the futility of trying to say anything.

He then retired to his hovel in Glendale.

Chapter 14
The Bomb

The next morning at four o'clock, Rabbit got dressed and prepared his gourmet lunch of peanut butter and jelly on sourdough, which he packed into his little black lunch pail, along with a thermos filled with strong black coffee. He made the long, monotonous freeway drive over to LAX and began his workday. At lunchtime he sat on the edge of the ramp with a few coworkers. One of the men present was a former Hawthorne police officer who had been the victim of severe budget cutbacks. His airline job was merely a way of filling time and keeping the wolves away from the door while he waited to be rehired by Hawthorne.

"You know what I think, Rabbit?"

Rabbit didn't even look up. "What?"

The young man spoke with his mouth full of bologna sandwich, "You should become a cop!"

Rabbit almost choked on his sandwich when he laughed.

The young man continued, "I'm serious, Rabbit. You should at least think about it. You're too smart to be busting your ass out here, and you're young and strong. The pay is a hell of a lot better, and so are the working conditions."

Rabbit was taken back by this guy's perceptions.

"To tell the truth, that job is a little too dangerous for me."

The young man shrugged and they went back to discussing some of the more important aspects of life, like getting laid.

After work that day, he resumed his networking with the fireman, the Pizza Man, and all the other fringe groups. He made his daily visits to B & B Gun Store and the Larder Bookstore.

At B & B, he met up with a man named Easton whose acquaintance he had made a few months back. Easton was a member of the Posse Comitatus, which was one of the more violent right-wing extremist groups. On that occasion Easton had mentioned that an associate of his worked for the railroad in the area of Keene and had many times observed from the train the compound of Mexican farm labor organizer Cesar Chavez. Convinced that Chavez was a Communist pawn and that he was conducting subversive activity, the Posse members were determined to find out just exactly what was going on in that compound. Their suspicions were further elevated by its armed security, which looked more like a military force than civilian.

There was no way to reconnoiter the location undetected without crossing a long stretch of difficult and remote mountainous terrain. And to accomplish this it would be necessary to use someone who had wilderness travel skills and knew how to read a topography map. Although there were no agreements requiring it, Easton spoke to DePugh and discussed his intention to conduct a reconnaissance of the Chavez compound. When he described his plan, DePugh asked how he was going to get there undetected. Easton told him that he was planning on using Rabbit to lead his team there. DePugh was familiar with Rabbit's talents through a variety of sources, and he agreed with Easton that Rabbit was a good choice.

When Easton told him of this plan, Rabbit knew that this would be another step toward gaining acceptance in the movement, and that it would take him one step closer to DePugh.

Rabbit called Harris and told him of the plot being hatched, and asked if he should back out gracefully. Rabbit was concerned about the legality of the operation and the possibility of violence. Harris was beside himself once more. Not only did he have an undercover operative deeper into the right than ever before, but now he was going to be gathering information on the left. Harris's superiors would be showering him with praise.

Rabbit also had concerns that it might be too politically hot to attempt, since it was rumored that Chavez had ties to Governor Jerry Brown. Harris allayed his fears and assured him that they would be able to cover him if something unforeseen occurred.

Rabbit began his research for the operation. He studied the map for the route to the Chavez compound from the meeting location at the Van Nuys Airport. The main highway would take them northbound on Interstate 5. In Kern County the route would transition to Highway 99. Rabbit paused at that junction and pondered the map with much trepidation. There was a problem with the route. It crossed Highway 166.

He knew that area well. It was all open land for as far as the eye could see. Twenty miles south of Bakersfield in the middle of nowhere, it was miles and miles of nothing but flat arid land. Tragically, it was the location of the infamous "Onion Field" killing, where two Los Angeles plain clothes policemen were taken after being disarmed and kidnapped by two heinous convicts in Hollywood. After being driven to the onion field, one policeman was executed, shot in the face and then several more times in the chest as he lay on the ground dying. The other policeman managed to escape. The event had happened fifteen years ago, but the passage of time didn't matter to Rabbit. It was such a cold-blooded, ruthless crime that its brutal impact would last forever, especially among police officers.

As Rabbit contemplated the location, he knew it was a bad omen. The area was taboo. He would not tempt fate. It was there the two Los Angeles policemen experienced the greatest horror possible. The price they paid made it a sacred place. He would not pass through it with three dangerous members of the Posse Comitatus who hated police and government authority with a vengeance.

Keene was only a short distance east across the barren landscape of dirt roads. It didn't matter how close it was, he wasn't going there. As far as Rabbit was concerned, this was a harbinger of terror, and he would not disregard his powerful instinct to avoid it. He would call Harris and abort the Chavez operation.

Two days later he met Harris and told him of his intuition. Harris would not consider aborting the operation. Every step was important for the overall goal of the investigation, and there was no way they were going to pass up an opportunity like this. Both men engaged in their usual verbal tug of war. Rabbit would not relent on this one—he would not take the road to Bakersfield.

Harris pulled from his glove box a well-used road map of California and opened it to view Keene. He ran his finger across the map from Van Nuys to Highway 14 north to Mojave, then west on Highway 58 to Keene. It was a more eastern route and a little out of the way, but it would work. Rabbit insisted he didn't care about another route, he was completely opposed to the operation. He felt he had received a premonition from the spirit world and would not proceed.

Harris sat quietly and studied Rabbit for a few moments. He wasn't sure what was going on inside of him, but something strange had trigged a subtle change in his attitude. Rabbit displayed an uncharacteristically sullen mood that Harris had not seen before. Harris was very perceptive when it came to his bird dog.

Maybe Rabbit was just feeling stressed, or perhaps he actually believed in a spirit world. Whatever it was, it didn't matter now. They had a job to do and it was going to be done. Regardless of what was going on in Rabbit's head, it would have to wait and be addressed at a later time. There wasn't time to get into a philosophical discussion of the afterlife and spirits. One thing for sure—Harris was determined the Chavez operation was going forward.

Then, as usual, he began a slow, gentle, but relentless cajoling and persuading until once again, Rabbit acquiesced. Harris was a master at getting compliance.

Four days later, at two o'clock on a cold December morning, Rabbit pulled his three-quarter-ton, four-by-four truck into a deserted parking lot in Van Nuys. Within moments, two other nondescript vehicles drove in and parked in close proximity. Easton got out of one vehicle and two men identified only as Gary and Greg exited the other. Easton said they were buddies of his, and that they had military recon experience and would be good assets to have along.

Rabbit produced a topography map of the mountainous Tehachapi area. He spread it over the hood of his truck, and with the help of a flashlight, he gave Easton a brief explanation of where they would be going and what to expect. He might as well have been showing him the mathematical equations necessary to put a manned satellite into orbit. As he went through his explanation, he was oblivious to what the other two men were loading into the back of his truck. Rabbit checked his watch and advised the group that they had better be on their way.

North of Tehachapi, the Ford pickup wended its way over a seldom-used mountain road that appeared to be headed nowhere. These mountains were typical of central and southern California. Almost completely barren, they were made up of rock, scrub brush, and an occasional tree. In the early morning hours when fog rolled in, or in the evening at sunset, they presented an eerie, foreboding look. The vastness and desolation could give you the feeling of being on the moon, or on another planet somewhere in the universe.

Rabbit had familiarized himself with the map. He studied the terrain as he drove slowly along on what was little more than a bumpy path weaving through the rough landscape. Finally he turned onto a narrow access road, and after approximately two hundred yards they came to a locked gate. Easton leaped from the truck and adroitly freed the gate from its rusty lock with a pair of bolt cutters. They drove on as far as practically possible and then parked.

Rabbit assured the others that this was a good place to park, and that it was a safe bet no one would come upon their vehicle, as the gate behind them had not been opened in years. As they began to unpack the vehicle in preparation for the next leg of their journey, which would be on foot, Rabbit observed Greg and Gary unloading an ice chest and three AK-47 assault rifles from his truck.

"What the hell do you think you are doing with those?"

Easton told him not to worry about it. But Rabbit protested that he wasn't going anywhere with those guns along. Easton assured him they were solely for defensive purposes and had DePugh's approval.

Rabbit thought, *this whole deal is a very bad idea.* The three play commandos then proceeded to suit up in their camouflage overalls and paint their faces black with war paint. What a sight this was turning out to be. As entertaining as it was, Rabbit was concerned about the time this production was taking and pressed the team to get moving.

Greg then opened the ice chest and very gingerly removed a package the size of a shoe box. It was wrapped tightly in brown paper and plastic wrapping tape. Rabbit's hair stood on end.

"What is in the package?"

"A little gift from us to the Mexican Communist Chavez."

Rabbit yelled, "It's a bomb! You had a fucking bomb in my truck and you didn't tell me? I ought to tear your fucking head off!"

Easton tried to calm Rabbit down, explaining it was just a small device to leave in the compound to detonate later as a warning to the Communists to cease their activity. Rabbit ordered them all back into the truck. He knew now they were absolutely crazy. It was major jail time if they were caught with this bomb. No amount of explaining would ever get them out of this.

Gary, the quiet one, stood up, pointing his loaded AK-47 at Rabbit, and said, "What is it with you and your concern for these fucking Mexicans? Is there something we don't know about you?

You better get this boy. If you don't finish what we came here to do, you are going to have a fatal hunting accident right here and now. Any questions?"

Rabbit was sure the crazy nut would shoot him. He yelled at Easton to get his man under control. He demanded to know if DePugh knew they were bringing a bomb.

"No."

"Did he tell you to plant a bomb?"

"No."

"Then we are not doing it. I'm doing this deal for DePugh, not you or the Posse Comitatus. What insane objective do you have? Blow up a totally useless farm truck that belongs to Chavez, and in the process maybe kill some peasant Mexican and get a blip on the six o'clock news? Then have the Feds all over our ass and end up in prison for forty years? Man, this just isn't going to happen."

Rabbit told Easton there would be hell to pay if they planted a bomb without DePugh's approval. This was only to be a recon, nothing else. Easton mulled it over for a couple of minutes and then agreed they would leave the bomb at the truck and proceed with the recon. Rabbit ordered them, before they took another step, to deactivate the bomb. Easton said none of them knew how the bomb was even made; they were only instructed to place it inside the compound. There was a remote trigger device for the bomb, and someone else was charged with detonation.

Rabbit was outmanned and outgunned, and knew he had gotten the best concession he was going to get. He was between the proverbial rock and a hard place. He wasn't in a position to abort the mission, but he was petrified to think what these guys might do next. He realized he had no really good options.

They proceeded with the original mission. As they began their trek, Rabbit paused and warned the three wannabe commandos to keep in mind this was rattlesnake country and to watch their step. He already had enough on his mind with this operation and didn't need to further complicate this madness with the pandemonium that would surely follow a snakebite.

The quartet made their way through the hills following the points of least resistance because, except for Rabbit, none of them were in good enough physical condition to climb up or down any steep terrain.

Eventually they came upon the compound. It was approximately the size of three football fields, with a few poorly-built buildings, a guard shack, a guard tower, and armed guards with rifles wandering about aimlessly and looking bored.

Rabbit couldn't help but question his own intelligence as he crawled with the others through the tall grass. He expected the next part of this nightmare would be to come across a rattlesnake. No matter what they had said at the start, none of them had any kind of special forces training, nor any idea what they were doing.

By this time it was broad daylight with very little cover to avoid detection. Fortunately the guards had no reason to believe that anyone would be stupid enough to want to spy on this remote location, so they weren't paying much attention to their guard detail.

This was one more bad play. All Rabbit knew was that he was someplace where a Los Angeles policeman had no business being, and he was with three possible psychos who were armed and dangerous. As far as he knew, he was the only unarmed person in the entire compound, and that wasn't a good situation.

His skin began to crawl as beads of perspiration trickled down the sides of his body. He was unnerved by several aspects of his predicament—fear for his own physical well-being, of course, but also frustration over not having any control over the situation he was in.

Easton busily made some drawings and notes and finally signaled the others to retreat. It was music to Rabbit's ears. When they were clear of the compound and could walk upright, the three members of the Posse Comitatus seemed satisfied with their recon mission.

Rabbit remained silent. He just wanted this craziness over.

When they arrived at the truck and began to load up for the long journey home, it was late afternoon and the shadows were growing long. Everyone was tired by this time, and on edge. Rabbit insisted that the weapons be unloaded before putting them in the truck. He wasn't about to take off with these nut cases and a bunch of loaded weapons in his truck. The men complied, reluctantly. They wrapped the guns in blankets and put in the back of the vehicle.

Rabbit then told Greg to put the bomb back into the truck. Easton responded, "Forget the bomb, let's get out of here."

Rabbit shot back with authority, "Bullshit. Put the bomb back into the truck. We brought the bomb out here and we are taking it back. I'm not leaving it here for some Boy Scout troop to stumble across and get their ass blown up."

There was a moment of silence. Greg and Gary got the picture and gently repackaged the bomb into the ice chest, then loaded it back into the rear of the truck. The two of them then hopped into the back, and Rabbit closed the tailgate and camper window. Easton climbed into the cab of the truck with Rabbit and they took off.

Mentally drained and physically exhausted, Rabbit missed a turnoff he was supposed to take on the deserted road. Soon they passed a gas station in the middle of nowhere with no signs of life around. From all appearances, it had been closed for a long time. Rabbit observed a California Highway Patrol car parked at the side of the building and saw an officer standing by the rear of it. He guessed that the patrolman was merely relieving himself. They continued on, and shortly they came to a dead end. It was then that Rabbit realized he had missed the turnoff. He made a U-turn on the narrow road and began to retrace his route.

As they passed the closed service station on the return trip, the CHP officer had obviously concluded whatever business he had at that location and was pulling out. As fate would have it, he pulled behind Rabbit and followed him.

Greg and Gary began to get nervous about the officer following them and announced loudly to Rabbit and Easton that if the "Chippy" decided to stop them, they were going to off him. Rabbit went into a controlled panic. His voice remained reasonably calm, but the perspiration flowed down his back and under his arms.

"Are you fuckin' crazy?"

"We don't have an alternative, man. We can't afford to be caught with these guns and that bomb."

Rabbit knew from his training that the officer would never even consider a search of the vehicle, but he could not tell his passengers that.

"Look, if he stops us, it will be to just get his ticket quota."

"Bullshit! He stops us, he's dead."

Rabbit looked into the rearview mirror and saw a sight that would burn itself into his memory until his dying breath. The CHP officer was in his late twenties, clean-shaven and wearing sunglasses, even though there was no great need for them. It was impossible to tell if he was studying the truck in front of him or if his mind was on the girlfriend he would be seeing when he got off watch tonight—if he got off watch tonight.

Suddenly there was the sickening, unmistakable sound of a banana clip sliding into an assault rifle and the roaring clang of a round slamming into the chamber. Rabbit felt like throwing up. His mind was racing at a hundred miles an hour. He pleaded and cajoled, but to no avail. These morons were convinced that it was unavoidable—this cop was merely an arm of an unjust government. As far as they were concerned, he had abdicated his right to live in a truly free democratic society when he swore to support the Jew-Communist state against the people.

Rabbit struggled to hold on to reason. If he drove perfectly, would the cop get suspicious and pull him over just out of curiosity? If he didn't drive perfectly, would the cop seize the opportunity to write a ticket? He certainly had to be somewhat suspicious of this truck driving around in this deserted area with four men, two of them in the back under the camper shell.

For a moment Rabbit decided that if the red lights came on, he would evade arrest and force a pursuit. If he could keep it going long enough for a lot of other police cars to join in, the psychos in the back of the truck might realize the futility of a shootout and surrender meekly.

No, he thought, after a moment's consideration. That wouldn't work. He knew these guys had macho and bravado up the ass. They had a distorted view of glory, and going out in a hail of gunfire would make them the subjects of folk songs and tales for years to come.

The terror that gripped Rabbit's heart was making it difficult to see the road. His heart was pounding and he was getting dizzy. With each turn in the road, the Chippy maintained the same distance. Then he heard Greg mutter that maybe it would be better if they offed him now, before he had a chance to put out a broadcast. Rabbit could hear his voice rise a couple of octaves as he tried to convince them that there was no reason to believe they would be stopped. He prayed silently that the Chippy would become bored following them and go past.

As he stared into the mirror, it became apparent that the officer was satisfied to just maintain the status quo. Rabbit then made up his mind that as soon as they reached a point in the road where there was a significant drop off, he would gun the truck and crash. Hopefully the bomb wouldn't explode, and everyone in the truck would at least be rendered unconscious. He could not let anything happen to the Chippy.

It must be true that God watches over drunks, children, and fools. Before Rabbit could find the ideal spot, a fork appeared in the road and the Chippy simply turned off.

After an initial outburst by Rabbit about the stupidity of wanting to waste a guy who probably felt the same way they did about patriotism, silence prevailed for the entire ride back to Van Nuys. He dropped off his passengers, the guns, and the bomb and headed home. He wanted desperately to get drunk, but something strange was happening to him. He stopped at a liquor store on the way home and picked up a bottle of Jack Daniel's. When he arrived at his hovel, he stared at the Jack for a long while, but never opened it. All he could think of was the need to get his reports written while everything was still fresh in his mind. This time, in addition to his usual reports for PDID, he also had to write a brief report for DePugh.

Everything would be correctly reported to the police and to DePugh except the bomb issue. Rabbit had no intention of stirring up DePugh over the bomb. Who knew what would happen after that? And as for Harris, Lord knew what crazy investigation he might feel the need to send his bird dog on.

Rabbit did not need nor want any more tasks put on him other than the ones that were already in play. He had more than he could handle. By the time he was finished with his reports, he would be able to get just a couple hours sleep before reporting for his job at the airport. But sleep was more elusive than usual that night. The face of the young Highway Patrol officer haunted him. He kept seeing a vision of high-caliber rounds ripping through the windshield of the patrol car and into the torso of the patrolman.

There had been a time when the old Rabbit would politely tell anyone in a supervisory position to buzz off if they gave him an assignment he didn't care for. This was the carefree, likable, laughing character who was the designated instigator of his watch in 77th Street Division patrol, who was given the job of driving a pain-in-the ass sergeant or lieutenant to a rubber room. But that time was gone. He didn't laugh at all anymore. This was all serious business, and he had to get his work done. He'd gotten his share of attaboys when he was doing regular police work, but he'd also gotten more than his share of dings along the way.

For the first time in his career, he was getting nothing but praise. Rabbit had underestimated Harris as an overweight, harmless, good old boy who bumbled his way through this spy business. In reality, Harris was a cool professional who could qualify for a doctoral degree in how to be a control for an undercover operator. Rabbit had no doubt that Harris was given an abundance of praise for the information he was turning in, and that was important to him. He in turn showered Rabbit generously with similar praise. He was quick to tell Rabbit that from the captain to the chief, all were impressed with his investigation.

In truth, they were indeed thrilled, but they did not have a clue who Rabbit was. Like all undercover operators in PDID, Rabbit was just another bird dog. He had a specific number, but he was usually just referred to as "Bird Dog." All Rabbit knew was that he was being recognized for doing great work. For the first time in his career, he was determined to keep the praise coming.

He would find out eventually that the incident with the CHP officer was not of any special intelligence significance; so it was to be redacted from all reports. Rabbit could never find out at which level of review such information was removed, because it was only mildly interesting in the big picture.

Chapter 15
The Snake Box

Even though Rabbit had trouble sleeping after the Chavez compound fiasco and the near cataclysm involving the Highway Patrolman, he managed to get refocused on his routine. He was attending meetings with the Pizza Man, and he was giving his droning survival lectures to small groups of well-intentioned citizens.

During the past few months Rabbit had spent considerable time talking with Reverend Harrell on the phone and communicating with him through the US mail. The objective was to establish a bond between them, and his effort achieved the desired result. He received an invitation from Reverend Harrell to attend and teach classes on wilderness survival at the First National Freedom Festival in Louisville, Illinois, about a hundred miles east of St. Louis, Missouri. Because of the near calamity back in Kansas City, Rabbit was seriously reluctant, but Harris was once more beside himself with his progress in the infiltration of the right wing. Since he would not be taking Charlie, he wouldn't have anything like the problems he'd had before. If for some highly improbable reason he had to make a hasty retreat, he would only have to deal with getting himself out.

Besides, taking her with him wasn't even an option. Kansas City had ended Charlie's undercover career. She still had not recovered from that nightmare and didn't want Rabbit to be anywhere near her. Their relationship now was down to maybe a telephone call a week, and the calls were short. Charlie's part of these conversations consisted mostly of yes, no, and uh-huh, with no response to Rabbit's tired refrain that the investigation was nearing its end. It sounded like a broken record, even to Rabbit.

So Rabbit got an extra few days off from his job at the airport and traveled to Louisville. Since it was not much more than a wide spot in the road, he was instructed to get a motel room in nearby Flora and drive a rental car to and from the festival site.

Upon his arrival at the compound, Rabbit found security to be tight. The festival was sponsored by the Christian Patriots Defense League and the Paul Revere Club, with the cooperation of the Christian Conservative Churches of America. It was held on the fifty-five-acre estate grounds of the Christian Conservative Church of which the Reverend John Harrell was the founder and president.

The grounds had seventeen buildings, all of which were in serious disrepair. The centerpiece was a fourteen-thousand square foot, twenty-four-room replica of George Washington's Mount Vernon home. This served as the headquarters of Harrell's organizations.

Admission to the festival was by invitation only. Invitations were given only to members of the participating organizations that basically made up the Committee of Ten Million. Participants also had to join the Christian Patriots Defense League, which required no dues or admission fees, only their pledge of allegiance to the white CPDL. The guards who manned the entry gates checked each entrant carefully to make sure their invitations were legitimate, and gave each vehicle a complete search. Parking was provided inside the fence line, which was a short walk from the compound and the hub of the festival.

Rabbit noted cars bearing license plates from a variety of states, from Florida to Oregon and from Pennsylvania to California. This was truly a broad representation of white, Christian America.

Once inside, each person had to complete a registration form, and those forms were double-checked against a master list of all those invited. Each entrant was given a program book with considerable information about the organizations, the topics to be discussed, the instructors, and the rules for all attendees.

Everyone inside the grounds was paranoid about possible government spies. Attendees did not identify themselves to each other, and most of the speakers were using pseudonyms. Ironically, because of recent laws prohibiting the use of aliases by undercover law enforcement officers, Rabbit kept his own name. However, at the direction of Reverend Harrell, he changed his name to an alias. Harrell was concerned for Rabbit's well-being and security, as he knew there would be government spies and informants at the festival who had slipped through the security net.

Reverend Harrell called the gathering of patriots to order. He began the festival with a moving invocation, and then presented the syllabus of the festival. Unexpectedly, he called Rabbit to the podium. Harrell recognized Rabbit for his dedication to the cause and cited him as an example of the kind of fierce young patriot warrior needed to fight the revolution.

Reverend Harrell then had Rabbit lead everyone in the Pledge of Allegiance. This was a far greater honor than Rabbit could have ever hoped for. So far the operation was running perfectly.

A wide variety of lectures were presented to the attendees, and these lectures were repeated each day. Courses included paramilitary training for guerrilla warfare, first aid, guns and reloading, knife fighting, silent killing, search and destroy, wilderness survival, archery, crossbow, SWAT training for home and community defense, racial problems and solutions, national identity, and Christian patriotic responsibility—all in preparation for the eventual revolution against Jews, blacks, the Antichrist, and all enemies of freedom.

Some classes were set up for the youth who had accompanied their parents, and several homemaking classes were designed for the women. The two biggest draws were SWAT and Rabbit's class on wildernesses survival.

Additionally, there were many lectures given by distinguished guests, designed to address the general concerns of all patriots. The Reverend Harrell gave an interesting talk about the background of the estate and his personal conflict with the federal government.

In 1961 Harrell had given aid and comfort to a young Army deserter who decried the US government's abandonment of Christian principles. Harrell provided the young man with refuge, refused to surrender him, and indicated that he was willing to engage in armed conflict.

The US Army and the FBI overran the resistance that was put up and took the young man into custody. Harrell was also taken into custody, and he spent several years in a federal penitentiary for his misguided efforts as a Good Samaritan. As is usually the case, more than one branch of the federal government got involved.

The IRS put liens all over Harrell's assets and took away all the tax exemptions normally accorded to religious institutions; ergo, the estate was in a very sad condition.

A retired Army colonel spoke of the moral decay of the country and the dire need for a Christian upheaval. The basic theme seemed to be the impending Armageddon; all speakers devoted time to this subject. All speakers were clearly anti-Semitic and anti-black. It was their belief that the Communists were using the Jews and the blacks in an attempt to eliminate white Christianity. The government had turned its back on white Americans, and had become anti-Christian and oppressive. There were predictions that before it was over, blood would be spilled and the battle for a free America, the kind envisioned by our forefathers, would be fought and won or lost in the streets. All agreed that as patriots, they would turn this country to ashes before they would give it up. The speakers whipped the crowd into a frenzy of desire to be involved in the great battles that were coming.

Needless to say, Rabbit was quite unsettled to be a spy in this camp, a declared enemy of right and an agent of the oppressors.

In this febrile atmosphere, the SWAT classes were attended by people who were eager to learn from a young man who was eminently qualified to teach the subject. He was a former Marine and highly trained in special warfare, and he had experience as a paramedic. He operated a paramilitary training business with expertise in silent killing, assassination, all forms of weaponry and knives, explosives, and various types of booby traps. People associated with him were selling sophisticated assault rifles and handguns outside the teaching area, and some of them could make available the names of others who could render these weapons fully automatic. This was a very serious business.

The training material Rabbit presented in his survival class was focused on the basics. In one hour of instruction it was not possible to turn out experts in wilderness survival. That was not the purpose of the class. The goal was to bring to the student's attention the extreme importance of being able to survive on their own when the need arose.

The class at the festival discussed the essentials—water, food, fire, and improvised shelter, with suggested reading on field medicine. Rabbit stressed that the time for learning survival was before the revolution started, not after. He told them in earnest he hoped the class would motivate and inspire them to study the subject on their own or in groups when they returned to their homes. The class was extremely well received.

The unforeseen and most important accomplishment of all was the exposure the class provided Rabbit. It established his credibility. As a result of the festival, his stature in the movement had risen to a level he had not thought possible. It also solidified his relationship to Reverend Harrell. The covert operation was exceeding all expectations.

At the end of the day, Rabbit retired to his shabby motel room in Flora. He may have been the resident expert in wilderness survival, but he also had a taste for comfort when he was not employing his skills. Unfortunately, the motel in Flora did not fulfill even the most basic expectations of comfort. Everything about it looked like the Bates Motel. The screen door was missing its lower half, allowing the hungry mosquitoes to fly through in squadrons.

The porch light was a fruit jar lit from within by an amber light bulb—and along with the bulb in the jar were a thousand dead bugs. The spider webs were big enough to catch horses.

The small, one-room space was a decorator's delight. The walls had once been painted pink, but now they were faded and peeling, revealing a moss green that had been applied at the turn of the century. The ancient air conditioner screeched like the fan belt on a fifty-year-old, worn-out car. It had one speed—full blast, which made the room feel like the arctic.

The bed was pitiful. It had to be a hundred years old. Lumps were visible in the mattress. The sheets were long overdue to be replaced and were covered with numerous disgusting, small, round, tea-colored stains. But the bathroom was the saddest part of the room. The shower had a mold farm growing in it, and there was no handle for the hot water.

This place gave new meaning to the word spartan. Everything seemed to have been built out of reinforced cardboard. A rickety table held a phone that could be used only in conjunction with the switchboard in the lobby. The chance for privacy during a long distance call was less than the chance of winning the California lottery.

The night seemed endless. All Rabbit could think of was the hate that had filled the festival—and that he represented the target of all that hate. *God*, he thought, *why can't I have Charlie by my side? Why can't I get the hell out of here and forget that the right wing ever existed?* Eventually he drifted off to sleep, but it was shallow and filled with fears and dreams of horror.

The next day was pretty much like the first, but by the end of the day, Rabbit had attained a modicum of celebrity status. Obviously Harrell had forgotten or dismissed the polygraph issue from Kansas City, or at least put it aside for the time being, because the subject never came up. He became the object of Harrell's praise, a fair-haired boy in his organization.

Harrell confided in him that he'd had a big blow-up with DePugh on the last day of the conference in Kansas City. He felt DePugh should step down as head of the COTM in favor of Dr. Tom Clark, President of the American Pistol and Rifle Association. His reasoning was that Clark had a sterling reputation, whereas DePugh and Harrell were convicted felons.

DePugh not only refused, but also wrote a blistering letter denouncing Harrell, which in turn prompted Harrell to withdraw from the COTM. Clark was so impressed with Rabbit's standing with Harrell that he offered him the role of Los Angeles County Chairman of his organization.

By the end of the day Rabbit had become very well established. He was told that as a token of appreciation for his efforts and his dedication at the festival, a fully automatic HK-91 assault weapon was waiting for him when he returned to LA. He was aware that he was being looked upon as a role model in both organizations and was expected to take advantage of both of their offers. Not to do so would cast a cloud of suspicion over him.

While everything was winding down, darkness settled over the grounds, and people began to leave for wherever they were going to spend the night. A few volunteers were cleaning up the grounds. Rabbit, the former Marine, and three of the other instructors slipped away into the woods and made their way to the little Wabash River, which coursed along the entire east property line. They built a small campfire.

It was a serene break from the stressful, unnerving day he had spent teaching survival class amid the ever-present danger that someone would recognize him as a Los Angeles Police Officer.

The flames of the small fire had a calming effect, soothing the high anxiety of the day. Sitting by the fire at the river brought back fond memories of Rabbit's childhood. He had grown up a short 246 miles away in Indiana, and it was much the same here in every way. He remembered how, as a young boy, he had camped by another fire and another river, telling ghost stories with his little Boy Scout buddies. It had been great fun, and he'd had many happy experiences. This time around it was all about killing and overthrowing the government. This was not fun.

Rabbit was snapped back to reality when he heard the Marine talking about torturing government agents and informants to death. The terrifying ghost stories were underway. Rabbit would have been uncomfortable in the best of circumstances, and these were not the best. The soft warmth of early summer gave way to a slight chill, which had no deterrent effect on the mosquitoes that filled the air. A thousand fireflies flitted about, looking like blinking Christmas tree lights. The fire cast eerie shadows that exaggerated the serious expressions of all present.

Rabbit was glad that his nervousness could be somewhat masked by the shadows. He kept his remarks to a minimum because he was in the presence of veterans who were overwhelmingly committed to the cause. He could only pray that they would not be able to tell that he was nervous—or lying.

The Marine began to tell them about the snake box he had

built. One of the men left the area and returned in a few minutes carrying two boxes. The first box was twenty-four inches square. The sides were two inches thick by eight inches high, and were made of two-by-fours set edgewise on top of each other. On one side, the two-by-fours were connected to each other by a metal piano hinge. On the opposite side there were two holes cut where the two-by-fours joined, making a stock for a man's wrist to fit into. The bottom of the box was a piece of plywood. The top was clear, half-inch-thick plastic held in place by a piano hinge above the stock. This permitted the top to be opened after the subject's wrists were placed in the stocks and his hands were inside the box, remaining visible through the plastic. Once the box was closed and locked, it would be impossible for the subject to remove his hands. It looked like a locked butterfly display case.

The other box was similar to a large fish tank with a hinged top and carrying handle. Through the sides of the glass tank, several very agitated cottonmouths could be seen twisting and turning madly, enraged from being jostled about.

The Marine said he had created the snake box specially for government informants. After the informant's wrists were in the stocks, the sides would be latched closed. Then the agitated snakes would be dumped into the box. The informant would spend the last minute of his life looking through the glass in sheer terror, watching the enraged cottonmouths snuff out his despicable, sorry-ass life.

After being bitten, the informant would be set free. Fear would motivate him to run as fast as possible for help, causing the deadly poison to travel rapidly through his veins. When the body was discovered, it would appear that another careless outdoorsman had become the victim of an ordinary snakebite.

As the Marine described the device, he paused effectively and stared into each man's eyes. Rabbit was waiting for his hands to be thrust into the box.

Silence came over the group like a pall for what seemed like an eternity. It was eventually broken by the voice of the Marine, who spoke coldly and slowly, still staring into the eyes of each man present. He knew that there had to be at least one informant or agent present at the festival—the government couldn't pass up an opportunity like this. He knew he had probably already given someone enough evidence to cause his own arrest, but that someone would be the sorriest son of a bitch that ever lived. Before he was through, the informant would beg to have his hands placed inside a snake box.

As the firelight danced in his eyes, his face became grotesque and his voice lowered to almost a hiss, as he told them he would hunt down the family of anyone who reported on him, and would torture them to death ever so slowly.

Silence came over the group once more. After waiting for his words to sink in deeply, the Marine stood up and walked off into the woods without saying another word.

If the first night in Flora was bad, the second was a trip through hell. As he tossed and turned through the night, Rabbit saw his hands placed into the snake box a hundred times and watched in horror as the snakes bit his hands over and over and his arms swelled to the size of watermelons. He awakened time after time with difficulty breathing. Overlaying the box were the ever-present, piercing eyes of the Marine, glaring in overwhelming hatred, breathing fire and threatening death. Each time Rabbit awoke, he was reminded that the nightmare would not go away with the light of day. He had convinced himself that this harbinger of death had identified him as an agent and was merely predicting the fate that ultimately awaited him.

At the closing ceremonies, Rabbit remained uneasy with the surroundings. He tried to convince himself that he was reacting to an overactive imagination, but he remained wary. If the Marine had any suspicions, he had not shared them with any of the leadership. Rabbit continued to be the fair-haired boy of the patriotic group. Harrell was eager to consider him a friend, and he was inundated with invitations to take an increasingly active part in various organizations. Prior to leaving, he was once again reminded that a fully automatic assault rifle would be waiting for him when he returned to Los Angeles.

Lastly, Harrell warned Rabbit to look out for DePugh. He told him DePugh was dangerous, and not averse to using violence to achieve his objectives or eliminate his enemies. He asked Rabbit to relay back to him anything he heard from DePugh about the festival, Harrell, or the Christian Patriots Defense League. Harrell was afraid DePugh might go as far as to set him up.

Rabbit flew back to Los Angeles with a treasure trove of intelligence he'd gathered at the Freedom Festival. His briefcase was filled with information that included names, addresses, contact numbers, organization affiliation, and networks of people of interest to the government. This information was a mother lode that would keep analysts busy for a long time.

The highly successful three-day operation had been made possible, in no small part, by Reverend Harrell. The Reverend had expressed very personal, heartfelt public praise for Rabbit's loyalty and dedication in his opening speech, and this had provided Rabbit with all the credibility of a tried and trusted, long-time friend and patriot. Such unsolicited recognition and approval put the festival attendees at ease with Rabbit, and they accepted him as one of their own, freely engaging in dialogue about sensitive matters. A relative newcomer, untested by the organization, normally would have taken much longer to earn their trust and gain access to their secrets.

Rabbit quickly and easily made acquaintances and established contact with many of the instructors, recruiters, and weapons dealers, as well as several leaders of private armies. Rabbit opted not to report on everything he learned, as he knew Harris would want him to pursue every lead, no matter where it took him, and he was becoming more concerned with each passing day about the legality of operating outside his jurisdiction. There had to be a limit to what he was allowed to do, and serious consequences for violating those rules.

The streams of communication that had been established were beyond what Rabbit could possibly handle while continuing to work his forty-hour-a-week job at the airport. And at the same time, he still had to do all his routine PDID tasks and handle covert operations for DePugh.

It was clear to Rabbit—and should have been to his superiors—that this was not even close to the jurisdiction of the Los Angeles Police Department. This ever-expanding investigation clearly belonged to the federal authorities, who had the personnel, training, and resources to handle it.

Besides, Rabbit mused, if he was busy handling this important federal investigation, who would look after the nut-case fireman and the school bus that his captain was so obsessed with?

Chapter 16
Train Station Terror

When Rabbit arrived at LAX he thought it was just like being on a vacation, compared to what he'd just left. It was early evening, which meant he would be able to get back to the Glendale rat trap and get his reports finished with enough time to get some sleep before reporting to work at the airport on Monday morning.

Any thoughts of this being a vacation quickly flickered and died. The depressing nature of his surroundings hit him like a sack of flour when he walked through the door of his apartment. Before doing anything else, he wanted to call Charlie, which he felt might help him to shake some of the depression. Just hearing her voice would give him a boost. But that was not to be. As was the case so often, he would have to be satisfied with hearing her voice say that no one was at home at the moment, but if he would leave a message after the beep, someone would be sure to get back to him.

He plunged into his work and produced a forty-two-page handwritten document that described all the events of the past weekend, listing the names, addresses, and descriptions of everyone of importance or of note who had attended the festival. He went into great detail about the subject matter of the speeches and the paranoia displayed regarding law enforcement agents and informants. In addition to the comprehensive report he gave Harris, he also submitted an index file box filled with business cards and small pieces of paper with names, contact information, and linked organizations. This time he did open the bottle of Jack Daniel's to wash away some of the fear and depression and to enable himself to get some sleep. It worked. Thoughts of the Little Wabash, snake boxes, and the PDID melted into a gooey puddle. Visions of Charlie filled the void. With a smile of contentment and bliss, he drifted off to that elusive state of happiness.

Following work at the airport the next day, he met up with Harris at a prearranged time and location to turn over his intelligence report. During the meeting he told him he would need to have the money to purchase the HK-91—five hundred dollars—if the promised gun gift did not happen. Harris agreed that it should be done, but didn't offer any money.

When Rabbit asked him for the money at their next meeting, Harris said the lieutenant wouldn't go for it. It was the opinion of the brass in PDID that Rabbit was living high on the hog. After all, he was getting paid by an airline and collecting his police paycheck at the same time.

Rabbit laughed sardonically. "I'm busting my ass at the airline job as a cover for this operation for low-life, minimum wage. To get that fuckin' minimum wage, I work with a bunch of grab-ass boys, fill my lungs with jet fuel exhaust, get my ear drums blown out with jet blast, break my back humping luggage, and then have to do the weight and balance of the aircraft. Now I take that goddamned minimum wage and pay for a rat hole of an apartment, pay dues to a bunch of organizations that in the real world

I wouldn't be caught dead in, buy beers for people I don't like, do your silly-ass police surveillance shit twenty-four hours a day, and I'm living high on the hog?"

He continued, "You tell the lieutenant if he can't come up with the money, he can stick this investigation up his ass. I don't have a life. This assignment takes every single living second of my existence. I don't have any real friends, and I don't have any personal time. I still have to pay a mortgage and property taxes on a beautiful house that I can't enjoy. And now you want me to spend five big ones on a goddamned gun that I personally have no use for?"

It was obvious that a nerve had been struck. Harris knew he had to bring his bird dog back into line. He calmed him down and told him that he would come up with the money. Rabbit had heard that tune played before, so he asked for all of the five hundred dollars up front. It would take a while, but he was willing to wait.

In parting, Rabbit pointed out that he had just finished his shift at the airport and he was on his way out to the Pizza Man's house to work on the investigation.

"Tell that asshole lieutenant he's getting his money's worth."

With that, Rabbit left the location and went back to his snooping around the gun store and bookstores. He ran into his connection from the festival and made arrangements to pick up the gun. As instructed, Rabbit followed the source to an apartment in North Hollywood. Once inside, his source went to the bedroom and pulled a large wooden bicycle box out from under the bed. The source opened the box, which had been reconfigured into a gun case. It contained twelve assault rifles. He unwrapped the treated paper and laid out a brand-new HK-91.

Rabbit raved about the beauty of it and held it to his shoulder, simulating firing.

"Nice, very nice. Who modified it to full auto?"

The source expounded, "There is a patriot in Nevada that does the work, and he is really good. There are some guys locally who claim they could do it, but who wants to take the chance of having fine pieces like these hacked up? It has to be right, especially when the firefight goes down."

The source asked if Rabbit had the money for the gun. Rabbit wasn't certain if the gift promise had not yet been communicated from the Festival or if this was just a little shakedown for five hundred dollars from one patriot to another.

Rabbit explained he did not have the money at the moment, but he should have it in about a week or so. The man took the gun and rewrapped it. He told Rabbit it would be there waiting for him when he was ready, but not to wait too long.

About a week later Harris called Rabbit in order to set up a meeting at the abandoned freight-loading dock at the top of Union Station for a briefing. He had described this location earlier as a remote, safe place to avoid being seen by anyone. Rabbit tried to beg off from the meeting. He had not slept in almost twenty-four hours, and he was exhausted. As was usually the case, Harris insisted, and his desires prevailed.

Rabbit pulled into the parking lot of that historic location at approximately 10:00 p.m. and mused about all the celebrities who had entered that Spanish-style marvel of architecture, and how they had complimented its opulence. *What a far cry from today,* he thought, as he watched low-income families carrying suitcases tied together with rope and belts.

He drove around to the back of the train station and up a ramp that led to a desolate warehouse structure covered with a corrugated tin roof. He then drove all the way back into an area that was totally deserted. It was dimly lit. Most of the lights were broken or burned out. It felt like stepping into the end of the world. Empty train tracks were separated by concrete platforms. No sounds could be heard from the outside world. The cement platforms were full of dust and dirt and trash.

As Rabbit contemplated the loneliness and emptiness, he was overcome by an uneasy feeling, although it was nothing he could put his finger on. Probably still jittery from that night in Illinois, he thought.

He could barely make out another car that slowly drove into the area with no headlights. A figure exited the vehicle and began to walk in his direction.

After what seemed like an eternity, he finally could make out the figure approaching him. It was Moran—Harry Moran from the COTM, the fucking Squirrel. How the hell could this possibly have happened? Rabbit had spent his entire drive with one eye on the rearview mirror looking for tails. It was impossible for this guy to have followed him! What the hell was he doing here?

Rabbit was still sitting behind the wheel of his truck with the window open, his mind racing at warp speed, when Moran walked up to the door and asked, "What are you doing here?"

Rabbit's hands were sweating, his heart pounding. "The question is, what are you doing here?"

As he asked the question, he tried to think. His mind went

blank. He was exhausted, but now, with this happening, his survival instinct kicked into overdrive. The only way this son of a bitch could know he was at Union Station would be if PDID had tipped him off.

Rabbit knew that Moran always carried a .38 pistol in an ankle holster. Somehow, Rabbit thought, he had to get to the .45 automatic stashed in the back of his truck seat before Moran dropped and drew down on him.

Moran was now leaning against the door of the truck. "DePugh is real interested in you. The only problem is, you look too good, way too good to believe. He told me to follow you."

The hair on the back of Rabbit's neck stood up, and he could feel every nerve in his body respond to the fear. Had he been set up? He wondered, is this stupid little zero going to off me? Who else is involved? Rabbit started to get out of the truck, but Moran was leaning against the door, holding it closed.

The Squirrel was becoming increasingly nervous. He was wearing a heavy jacket. The outside temperature was cold, but he had sweat on his forehead. He kept his right hand in his jacket pocket as he talked. He kept turning to look back down toward the ramp. White foam began to appear at the corners of his mouth, and he nervously attempted to lick it away. His face was two feet from Rabbit's, and even at that distance Rabbit could smell Squirrel's bad breath and heavy body odor.

Rabbit said, "Okay, let's you and me take a walk into the train station and call DePugh. I want to hear what he has to say about this."

Squirrel quickly answered, "No, we're going to have a talk right here."

What was this idiot going to try to do? If this were a patrol stop and Rabbit were in uniform, the rules would be different, but that wasn't the case. This was a low-level fool trying to make a name for himself in the organization, and if he was about to try to murder Rabbit at this isolated loading dock with no witnesses and no help, that was not going to happen.

Rabbit knew he could justify the use of deadly force, based on his personal knowledge that Squirrel always carried a gun—a fact that Rabbit had discussed in several written intelligence reports on Squirrel that he had submitted to Harris, outlining his fixation on killing snitches and informants like he had killed North Vietnamese soldiers. He knew that he would be the only one left standing after a shootout and that any facts essential to validating the report could be taken care of with a little creative writing. Why give this asshole the first move and take a chance on getting killed? All Rabbit needed to do now was to get his .45 auto out from the makeshift holster behind the seat.

The Squirrel turned his head one more time to look over his shoulder and down at the ramp. As he turned his head back toward Rabbit, Rabbit punched him with the back of his left fist, splitting his nose open. Blood squirted from his nose, and Squirrel grabbed his face, causing him to release his pressure on the door. At that instant, Rabbit pushed the truck door open with such force that it sent the Squirrel reeling backwards, causing him to lose his balance and fall to the ground, screaming.

As Rabbit took cover behind the truck door, he reached through the tear in the seat and pulled his gun from the Velcro straps. He had a clear shot at Squirrel, but he hesitated before pulling the trigger. He was totally perplexed by Squirrel's reaction to being knocked to the ground by the truck's door. He fully expected the Squirrel to draw the small revolver that he always carried. Instead, he lay spread-eagled on the concrete floor, hands open, frozen in position and looking toward Rabbit, screaming, "Don't shoot! Oh God, don't shoot!"

He continued yelling something, but whatever it was, Rabbit didn't hear. This was pandemonium. Rabbit's plan evaporated. He knew he could not shoot the Squirrel while he lay helpless on the ground, because the wound canal would never match the story Rabbit would recite at a coroner's inquest. His mind raced at lightning speed, trying to think of another possible course of action. There was none. It was his worst nightmare.

Then he heard the roar of a car racing up to the loading dock. He could see the Plymouth speeding toward them, dust and debris flying up from the car, headlights flashing, the horn blowing. It was Harris, waving his arm madly in the air. A second later, Harris hit the brakes. Tires squealing, the car came to a stop. Harris jumped out of the car screaming at Rabbit, "Put the gun down! Moran is a cop!"

Rabbit's thoughts were still racing in a blur—was Harris involved in this plot? He was going to take his shot. If Harris was involved, Harris would go down. If he wasn't, he would have to go along with Rabbit's story. One thing was sure: the Squirrel was finished.

Harris had his hands outstretched as he shouted, "Rabbit, for God's sake, cool it!" Rabbit was still trying to line up a frontal shot on Moran.

"Stop Rabbit, Moran's a bird dog!"

Moran looked at Rabbit, and then at Harris. It finally registered with him that Rabbit had no clue he was also a cop working undercover. He looked at the gun in Rabbit's hand and realized how close to his end he had just come. The blood drained from his face. He felt a wave of nausea as he lay on the ground and muttered a prayer of thanks.

Rabbit was now beside himself. He had been involved in five prior shootings, but had never had this kind of reaction. His hands were shaking. Nausea overcame him as he focused on how close he had come to committing a homicide—and killing a fellow police officer.

This was insane. That son of a bitch had just gone over the line. Everybody here must be fucking crazy. All he could think of was that he almost dusted another cop. That would have been impossible to justify.

He turned and screamed, "You goddamned idiot! What is your fucking problem? Are you some kind of a madman? Why would you create this nightmare?"

"Take it easy, Rabbit. No one got hurt."

"Fuck you, Harris. You are crazy!"

He could hear Harris screaming to him as he jumped into his truck and sped off. That was it for this bullshit. His heart had never beaten so hard. If he didn't have a heart attack now, he never would! He couldn't care less what they did to him. As far as he was concerned, they could send him to a Board of Rights and stick him in Property Division for the rest of his career. No one needed this madness. He was dumbfounded; he couldn't imagine how a detective sergeant could possibly have allowed this scenario to happen.

Fear and paranoia were rising within Rabbit at an alarming rate. He went back to Glendale and locked himself inside his apartment, where he once again resorted to Jack Daniel's to try and lower his raging blood pressure. When he awoke the next day, he was filled with another kind of remorse, the kind that comes when a man can't remember the events of the night before. Everything after the train station was a blur, and there was a point after which it was a complete blank. He wasn't thinking about PDID, patriots, or anything concerning the assignment. His head felt as though it were trapped in a vise, and his mouth felt like a dry, dusty dirt road.

He spent the rest of that day trying to put together his options. He made several attempts to get in touch with Charlie, but to no avail. He had been sufficiently programmed by this time not to do anything rash that would jeopardize the assignment, though he was convinced he shouldn't continue. He stayed away from all his contacts in the Valley. The next morning, though, he went in to work at the airport.

When he made it back to his apartment, the phone was ringing incessantly. He tried to ignore it at first, but finally he gave in and answered it. As he suspected, it was Harris looking for another meeting. Rabbit was still very much unnerved, and as much as he tried, he couldn't get the nightmare of the incident at the train station out of his head.

It was obvious to Harris from Rabbit's attitude that Harris's gross blunder had caused a significant problem. This was going to be difficult to get past, if not impossible. But Harris was extremely apologetic and sounded downright pitiful, so Rabbit agreed to meet.

They met for a walk along the docks at Marina Del Rey. Rabbit loved to gaze at the big sailboats and the powerful-looking twin-engine yachts. He would fantasize about the day when he could sit on the back of one of those boats and just watch the world go by.

Marina Del Rey epitomizes the American dream—sheer opulent affluence. It is one of those few places where conservatives and liberals share a commonality. They lounge around in the lap of luxury and complain to one another about how the other side is jeopardizing their lifestyle. This is a place where the line between liberalism and conservatism is blurred. These are the right- and left-wingers who cannot conceive of revolution or bloodshed in the streets. The causes they champion are focused on the environment or the presence of vagrants in the shopping centers.

However, Rabbit wasn't concerned with the plight of the rich and famous on this day. His mind was on more mundane matters like survival and peace of mind. He had gotten over his initial rage over the incident at the train station, but he was still shocked by Harris's unbelievable error in judgment. From this point on, things would never be the same.

Harris was quick to admit the stupidity of his actions. He had simply failed to anticipate the level of danger in the situation he'd created. He had seen it as an opportunity to conduct a test to see how an undercover operator would react under extremely stressful circumstances. He felt a course was needed to train undercover operators in a variety of dangerous situations, and since Rabbit was considered one of the best operators, this would be an opportunity to tape record him under extreme real-time stress. He had Moran wear a Fargo unit to record the conversation, which would be invaluable in training future operators—and which, as things had turned out, might have been used in a trial to prosecute Rabbit for murder.

Harris had failed to anticipate Rabbit's extreme response to the perceived imminent threat to his life. Rabbit would be haunted by this incident for a long time to come, and he would awaken over and over again in the middle of the night with cold sweats. That was just what he needed—one more thing to lie awake nights thinking about. Pure insanity.

One of Rabbit's strengths was his ability to move on from bullshit, but this was beyond the pale. In a way, he felt sorry for Harris, who was deeply remorseful for his admitted stupidity and extremely bad judgment, which could have sent one policeman to the morgue and another to the gas chamber.

However, this was a turning point. This particular act on Harris's part had changed Rabbit. No longer would he blindly go along with Harris, whose leadership ability was forever damaged in Rabbit's eyes. No one in their right mind would have intentionally set up the near-fatal disaster that had almost taken place on the loading dock at the train station. In fact, Harris should have been removed from PDID, put back in uniform, and demoted in rank for that insane act.

Rabbit would continue to accommodate Harris, but no longer blindly. He now questioned the entire investigation, and he wondered how much of all this had been sanctioned by the high command. This was a major problem. The critical question at hand was how to proceed without damaging the career that he had spent years rehabilitating.

His "yes boy" days were done. Rabbit's first order of business was to inform Harris that he was dumping the rat trap in Glendale and getting an apartment at the beach. He was sick of the long daily commute to the airport job and the disgusting environment he called a residence. Besides, he didn't have to go to the Valley on right-wing business every day.

Rabbit knew he had gained a major concession when Harris acquiesced to the move out of the Glendale hovel and the move back to Manhattan Beach. The only hitch was that he still could not move back into his own home. He would have to keep that at a distance.

As soon as he and Harris had parted ways, Rabbit put a call in to his old friend Buddy Brown, who was a former Marine and a decorated Vietnam veteran. Buddy had spent a short time on the Los Angeles Police Department, but had quickly realized it wasn't what he had envisioned and quit. It was the Department's loss.

Buddy's apartment was located about four blocks from Rabbit's Manhattan Beach home, just over a huge sand hill. Rabbit needed a new place to live, and as fate would have it, Buddy was having a little trouble making his rent payments. He took Rabbit's call as a blessing and didn't question his reasons for the move; he fully understood the need-to-know basis. All Rabbit told him was that he was on special assignment and couldn't talk about it. Buddy respected his wishes and never probed.

It didn't take too long for him to gather his meager belongings and bid a not-so-fond adieu to the dreaded Glendale apartment. He settled into his new digs very quickly. What a contrast it was to hear the ocean waves breaking on the beach instead of the nightly train blasting by his rat-trap apartment.

Rabbit was as happy as a little kid. He was back where he belonged and close to Charlie once again. Close enough to feel her very presence, even though he couldn't see her. He realized that he would have to be extremely discreet about contacting her, but at least she was nearby. He closed his eyes and drew the fragrance of the salt air deep into his lungs. For a moment he pitied all the antagonists in his life who couldn't saver this glorious experience.

Sharing an apartment with Buddy was an easy fit. They were both accustomed to independence and didn't intrude on each other's living space or privacy.

The first thing Rabbit did when he got settled was to call Charlie and leave a message on her answering machine. He apologized for his absence and thoughtlessness, and vowed to make it up to her. Charlie was glad to have him close by, but she found it difficult to understand why he couldn't just move home. Realistically, now that he'd moved thirty miles closer to her, she felt that just a few blocks would make very little difference. By this time, though, Charlie had long since acknowledged the futility of trying to make sense of police operations.

Chapter 17
The Minutemen

About a month passed, and Rabbit was dutifully meeting with his connections in the Valley. He even got around to picking up the HK-91 that was being held for him. The transaction didn't go exactly as he'd expected it to, however. The gift offer had apparently never made it through channels from the Illinois festival, so he had to pay for it, although Harris did give him the money. He didn't volunteer where the money came from, and Rabbit didn't care. All that was important to Rabbit was that he got reimbursed. Buddy didn't raise an eyebrow when Rabbit brought the HK-91 home. He merely shook his head when Rabbit told him that he would explain it some day.

One evening he received a call from John Dolan, who told him that DePugh was going to be in Los Angeles and would like him to attend a meeting. Ferris, the Pizza Man, had set the meeting up in the Valley and arranged for fifty people to attend.

DePugh came to the meeting and discussed various topics of interest to the members of the COTM. He never mentioned the blowup he'd had with Harrell at the end of the conference in Kansas City, or even addressed the fact that Harrell wasn't present in LA. Rabbit didn't let on that he was aware of the rift between DePugh and the Reverend.

Following the meeting, a select group was invited to stop off in the coffee shop of the hotel for a snack. This was just an affable get-together, and the topics of conversation were all non-revolutionary things—it was just a general BS session. The paunchy armchair patriots DePugh depended on for financial and moral support hung on his every word. Little get-togethers like this made them feel like insiders. Eventually, DePugh announced that he was tired and wanted to retire.

As the group got up to leave, DePugh took Rabbit by the arm and whispered to him that he should stay in the coffee shop. He said he would return when everyone else had left. Rabbit returned to a booth and waited approximately twenty minutes for DePugh, who had gone to his room to change into more comfortable attire.

When DePugh returned, he was friendlier than he had ever been. He asked Rabbit how things had gone at the Freedom Festival. Rabbit gave him a bland, no-information-of-any-consequence reply. DePugh knew Rabbit and Harrell had spent time together at the festival and asked what that was about. Again, Rabbit gave a generic answer imparting information that he knew DePugh most probably was already aware of.

DePugh warned Rabbit to be very careful around Harrell. Something was wrong, although he did not know exactly what it was. He had received information from some of his loyal followers who had attended the festival that Harrell intended to discredit both DePugh and Shelton in an attempt to take over leadership of the various right-wing organizations comprising the COTM, and that he might even go as far as to set them up. He told Rabbit to be careful he didn't get caught up in a physical conflict between

Harrell and the Klan. Rabbit could help to prevent this impending conflict if he would pass on to DePugh anything Harrell had to say about the Klan and DePugh.

DePugh said he would teach Rabbit how to effectively infiltrate and spy on both the Klan and Reverend Harrell. Disappointingly, both organizations had shown once again that they could not be trusted.

He told Rabbit his organization had been keeping track of him, and he was impressed with Rabbit's dedication and general deportment. He asked Rabbit some personal questions about his beliefs. When he asked about Charlie, Rabbit told him that the marriage was not working out as he had hoped. He said that Charlie had become a victim of the Los Angeles mystique, and that she was getting more and more into worldly things and away from their core values. Rabbit was saddened that he was going to have to get a divorce, but he knew he wanted a good, wholesome wife with whom he could have children and live out a beautiful life together. DePugh was sorry to hear about Charlie's philosophical defection, but he applauded Rabbit's decision.

After a while, DePugh looked around furtively and suggested that they go out to Rabbit's truck to continue the conversation. There were a few patrons in the coffee shop sitting around schmoozing quietly, totally unaware of these two patriots, but DePugh didn't like being within earshot of anyone he didn't know.

When they got to the truck, DePugh was silent and pensive for a few moments, and then he finally asked Rabbit if he was familiar with the Minutemen. This was the conversation that Rabbit had patiently been waiting for. He was ecstatic that he had successfully infiltrated this deeply, that the founder of this guerrilla organization was actually about to take him into his confidence.

Rabbit lied, telling DePugh that he had read about the Minutemen, but that he didn't know much except that they had broken up a long time ago. In fact, Rabbit had dedicated considerable time to researching the Minutemen, and he knew a lot about them, from their beginning in the 1960s to the present. He had studied their history and their stated objectives. He'd read books, recruiting material, magazine articles, federal, state, and local intelligence reports, and newspaper articles. He had listened to taped radio interviews and received extensive briefings from the Los Angeles police intelligence detectives.

He also knew a lot about their history. The exact number of Minutemen was not known. The numbers varied from source to source, making it difficult, if not impossible, to estimate the number of active members. It could have been anywhere from eight thousand to eighty thousand or more.

Whatever the real number was, they had become a potent force on the ultra right. There were members all throughout the US. They were organized into secret cells, usually of five to ten members. They possessed large quantities of lethal combat material. Hundreds of arrests had been made all over the country, and huge caches of weapons had been confiscated, along with hundreds of thousands of rounds of ammunition, bombs, hand grenades, land mines, and chemical weapons. The Minutemen were a force to be reckoned with.

DePugh smiled and told him that the Minutemen had never broken up nor ceased to exist. They were very much alive and well, and they were the most formidable right-wing organization in existence. The success of the organization was dependent on the recruitment of only the very best, most qualified patriots available. That was why DePugh had put together the Committee of Ten Million. The Committee was only a ruse; its purpose was to appear as a harmless organization of has-beens and armchair patriots to keep the Feds from renewing their past investigations of DePugh.

DePugh wanted to be free from the probing eyes of the government so that he could proceed with his rigorous recruitment program. He wanted to recruit qualified people from the Klan, the Posse Comitatus, and other right-wing organizations for the Minutemen. His organization would be the vanguard of the revolution in America.

DePugh then proceeded to give Rabbit a history lesson about the Minutemen and DePugh himself. Back in 1960, ten men had formed a duck hunting club and leased a small lake in Missouri. While they were building duck blinds around the lake, a discussion began about the current international crisis involving communism and Russian aggression. One of the men commented that their group would have a decisive advantage if the Russians invaded. They could retreat to their hunting club and fight as a guerrilla band.

This innocuous remark prompted some of those present to do some serious thinking. Several of them had received Special Forces training in the military and felt it wouldn't hurt Americans to know a little bit about defending themselves in the event the country were ever overrun by an enemy force. In the following weeks, training manuals were shared and read with a great deal of interest. A short time later, DePugh made overtures to develop these ideas into a serious project.

The more the members read, the more conscious they became about world politics, and the more serious they became about their own patriotism. In the course of their studies they became aware that communism had taken over seventeen nations, but only one of these takeovers had been the result of a military conquest. It was obvious that subversion was a very successful tactic.

They sought answers, delving into the writings of the most noted conservative spokesmen and right-wing organizations. A six-month program was initiated in which each member was assigned some area of research. A couple of the members even joined left-wing organizations in order to see what the attraction was that could sway otherwise intelligent, rational Americans.

At the end of six months, the group held a four-day seminar among themselves and came to some very dramatic conclusions. They decided that the war against communism was being lost and that serious patriotism was sadly waning in the United States. The most significant conclusion they came to was that the government was controlled by minority vote blocs, labor unions, and corrupt political machines. Further, they concluded that a pro-American government could no longer be established by normal political means. At some point, it would probably be necessary to violently overthrow the government. DePugh decided that the only salvation for America would lie with an organization he would form called the Minutemen.

DePugh traveled throughout the United States, expounding his views to willing listeners. He duplicated the tactics of Adolph Hitler by identifying a common enemy—Jews and blacks. These people, he reasoned, were the pawns of subversive communism and the enemies of patriotic, white, Christian America. He was able to form pockets of Minutemen everywhere he traveled, and he absorbed other small, vigilante-type groups into his organization.

One such group was the Loyal Order of Mountain Men, which was located in the San Diego, California area, and headed by William Hawthorne. At first, there were problems between the two groups, but Hawthorne felt a need to become a part of a larger, national organization, and was able to reach an accord with DePugh.

Over the next few years, the Minutemen grew by leaps and bounds. Guerrilla warfare training was being conducted on a large scale, and it was this activity that became the gravest concern of the local and federal law enforcement entities. The gathering of munitions and illegal fully automatic weapons was taking place on a massive scale, but DePugh insisted that there be no central repository for this equipment—each member should be responsible for his own weaponry. To that end, handbooks suggested the types of weapons to be gathered and concealed. They included mortars, rocket launchers, bazookas, rifle grenades, machine guns, and adaptable foreign military rifles. In addition, instructions were given out for making home-made explosive devices.

Once law enforcement became sufficiently interested, they began to infiltrate this organization and develop informants. As a result, a series of arrests were made in which illegal guns and explosives were confiscated. Eventually a conspiracy case was made against DePugh and Walter Ritlin, who both went into hiding. They were indicted in absentia by a Federal Grand Jury, and after a prolonged manhunt, they were arrested in Truth or Consequences, New Mexico and sent to federal prison.

In prison, authorities tried to roll Ritlin over on DePugh and the Minutemen. But Ritlin was a man of steel who was totally dedicated to the cause of liberty and patriotism. Nothing federal agents could do or threaten could make him bend. He was placed in a cellblock populated almost entirely by black convicts, and the word was leaked that he was a white supremacist. But Ritlin took the subsequent beatings in stride and never broke. This made him a hero in DePugh's eyes.

By now Rabbit was filled with a broad spectrum of emotions. He was elated to have broken into the inner sanctum, but somewhat apprehensive about the vast amount of sensitive intelligence he was getting into.

DePugh then invited Rabbit to join the Minutemen. He envisioned Rabbit taking an active role in California and felt he would be an asset to the "black section." This was a part of the very close inner group that could be likened to a police department's Internal Affairs Division. DePugh described the section as a special cloak-and-dagger group that would spy on other members of the Minutemen and other right-wing organizations and handle special, super-secret assignments from time to time.

Rabbit was somewhat reluctant to accept this offer, realizing that he would be putting his life in even more jeopardy than ever. He would be watched more closely by those around him, and would become extremely dangerous to the organization if he ever decided to go sideways on them. His mind raced, but the matter was decided by his own ego and dedication to his assignment, which had already prompted him to go where no other undercover operator that he knew of had ever gone before. He accepted.

DePugh was an extremely bright man in most respects, and he had learned from his mistakes. He was determined never to go to prison again and had devised a number of safeguards to protect himself. But by making this offer to Rabbit, DePugh had violated his own strict rules of security by employing a totally untested individual. He was ignoring his own safeguards—or perhaps this was some kind of test. His basic instructions to Rabbit were to continue as he always had, except he now would receive direct instructions from DePugh. He was to answer to no one else in the organization.

The first order of business was for him to get a cold phone—a public pay phone near his residence—and give the number to DePugh. DePugh utilized a code for telephone calls regarding the designated call time. When DePugh wanted to talk to him, he would phone Rabbit at home and state that he would call him back in one week. That would mean for Rabbit to go to the cold phone and await a call in one hour. DePugh explained that even the Feds could not get a wiretap on a public pay phone. DePugh had been the subject of phone taps in the past. He would not experience that again.

When Rabbit told Harris about the meeting with DePugh, Harris acted as though it was something that he had expected all along, as a natural progression of the undercover assignment. Rabbit told Harris the time had come when a choice had to be made about which group the investigation would pursue. Rabbit was well along with Harrell and the Christian Patriots Defense League, and, of course, with the Minutemen and DePugh. He also felt he could infiltrate the Klan, as Shelton, the group's leader, had expressed his interest in making Rabbit a member of the KKK. Now, every leader of these organizations were asking Rabbit to spy on some other group leader for them as a show of allegiance.

Rabbit said he could no longer straddle the fence. The question was, which group was to be the target? Of course, Harris already had the answer. It was the Minutemen. This was all about discovering and seizing the long-sought-after machine gun cache in Los Angeles. Not wanting to reveal his agenda, Harris said he would have to go higher up in the command chain for orders. Rabbit wondered whether this was true.

Harris could hardly contain himself when he brought the news to the Division. The lieutenant ushered him into the captain's office, and he was lavished with all the praise of a conquering hero. The captain couldn't say enough about his talents or how well he had done by bringing a bird dog along as far as he had. Harris, always modest, took it all in stride. He could just see the promotion to lieutenant around the corner.

Three days later, Harris would call Rabbit and tell him, "DePugh and the Minutemen are your target." Meanwhile, Rabbit kept doing his job on a day-to-day basis. He busted his ass at the airport, then hustled out to the Valley to stay in touch with the crowd from the bookstores and the gun shop. He met regularly with the Pizza Man, Shuster, and many others, and his network continued to grow. He kept pouring out reports on everything he was doing. He was keeping the analysts very busy.

In addition, he was now getting a chance to see Charlie from time to time. He had worked out a deal whereby he would go jogging and take a circuitous route through the beach alleys to avoid any kind of a tail, and then up and over into the secluded portion of Sand Dune Park, which was in close proximity to his house, his real home. On these occasions he would call Charlie and they would meet.

This was his only connection with sanity. She was angry about recent developments, but there was a deep-seated love that transcended all the other problems. Charlie loved him as much as he loved her, but she was a lot more practical and realistic. She was filled with fear—fear for Rabbit and fear for her own safety. He used her as he would a priest in a confessional or a psychiatrist. He felt free to confide everything to her, and he knew she would never reveal anything he told her, ever.

He told her everything that was going on, and she became more fearful with each new development. Charlie was starting to drink more, and so was Rabbit. Unfortunately, they weren't drinking together. Whenever they parted, each was filled with frustration and resentment that could only be eased with several swallows of whiskey.

Chapter 18
Farmhouse Bunker

As Rabbit returned from work one afternoon, he got a call from DePugh, who told him that he would call back in two weeks. He was hot and tired, to the point of being a little punchy. The last thing he wanted was to concentrate on right-wing bullshit. The pay phone was only a couple of blocks away on the corner of Marine and Highland. He thought to himself that if he left now, he could stop on his way for a couple of cold beers at Ercole's Bar over on Manhattan Avenue and 11th Street.

As Rabbit approached Ercole's, he could smell the fresh salt air wafting up from the Pacific only a block away. The cool breeze felt good. He thought of how it always felt good to be down here. The move back from Glendale had been a very good thing for his mental health.

He entered the dark bar and was filled with memories of happier, saner times. The dark, old-fashioned wood and high-backed booths were strictly a male-oriented decor. This had been a cop hangout back in the day, and he always felt comfortable here. He nodded to a few of the old-timers, who were oblivious to his recent absence from the place. But Jerry, the bartender, remembered him. He called Rabbit "Stranger," and asked where the hell he had been hiding out. Rabbit merely said he had been transferred and had screwy hours that played havoc with his social life. He wasn't lying, and Jerry pried no further. The burly bartender, who wore the scars of too many rounds in an unsuccessful boxing career, knew better than to ask for more information than was offered.

After a couple of beers and some small talk about what was going on at the beach, Rabbit left to rendezvous with the pay phone. He stood leaning against the stucco wall next to the phone booth, feeling serene. He had just had enough to drink to feel mellow.

His tranquility was shattered by the jarring sound of the telephone ringing. DePugh was very terse, and got right to the point. He wanted Rabbit for a one-day meeting in Kansas City as soon as possible.

DePugh's tone and sense of urgency struck a chord in Rabbit's early warning system. He tried to read DePugh's voice to see if he had somehow come into some kind of information about him. Rabbit's paranoia was running rampant. He tried to put DePugh off with excuses about not being able to get any time off from the airline. DePugh was insistent, however. In essence, this was an order. He merely stated that he would be waiting for him.

Rabbit contacted Harris and told him of his uneasiness. Admittedly, he didn't know DePugh well enough to interpret his idiosyncrasies, so it was easy for Harris to placate Rabbit and allay his concerns. In an earlier time, Harris would have made a fortune selling snake oil from the back of a covered wagon.

Rabbit called DePugh and said he could meet him at the airport in Kansas City, but he was only able to stay at the airport for an hour, or maybe two, as he had to catch the next flight back to Los Angeles. DePugh agreed.

Two days later, Rabbit flew into Kansas City and looked around the airport for DePugh. Instead, a nondescript white male greeted him and announced that DePugh was waiting downstairs in a car. Rabbit reminded him that that wasn't the deal; they were supposed to meet inside the terminal. The courier looked at him as though he had two heads. Apparently, Rabbit didn't understand—DePugh was waiting downstairs, and he was a very busy man.

Rabbit read more of a threat into the man's demeanor than there actually was, but agreed to follow him. Being totally unfamiliar with the area, Rabbit was reluctant to create a scene. He had no idea of who might be an associate or sympathizer of DePugh's. When he got to the car, he reminded DePugh that he only had a short time before he had to catch the next flight back to LA or his pass would expire. DePugh handed him a fully paid ticket for a later flight that evening and told him to get into the car. All Rabbit could think was that this was the end. His imagination was working overtime. He was apprehensive, but he got into the car.

As they rode in the backseat, DePugh warmed up and talked about a wide variety of topics. Rabbit failed to appreciate the serenity of the bucolic setting through which they passed. This was the heart and soul of America. Artists struggled to capture the peace and calm of this gently rolling landscape covered with wheat fields. Eventually he began to relax, but he was oblivious to his surroundings, completely transfixed by this multifaceted man.

Thirty minutes after they had left the airport, DePugh handed Rabbit a pair of wide-framed welding glasses and told him that, for security, he would have to wear them until they arrived at their destination. Rabbit complied and put them on. The lenses were solid blackout. It was not possible to see anything through them, and the wraparound frames blocked his peripheral vision. He took comfort in the thought that they probably were not going to kill him; if that were the plan, there would be no reason to cover his eyes. At least he hoped that was correct logic.

Another thirty minutes passed. The car slowed and made a sharp left turn and proceeded up a steep, bumpy road before coming to a stop. DePugh told Rabbit he could remove the blackout glasses.

They were at a farmhouse. The house sat high on a steep hill a quarter mile up from the secondary road, with a clear view of a mile in three directions. The rear of the house was about fifty yards from a thick, wooded area. The house was neat and freshly painted the color of yellow marigolds.

Next to the farmhouse were the remains of a burned-down house. All that was left was part of the brick chimney, some concrete steps, and pieces of the old foundation. It was all overgrown with weeds and rubble from the fire, which included a burned stove, kitchen sink, and bathroom fixtures. The debris was strewn about the concrete slab floor.

DePugh, the driver, and Rabbit walked up the three wooden steps of the farmhouse and onto the porch. Rabbit half expected Auntie Em to come through the screen door and offer them some lemonade.

The driver was posted at the front door, and DePugh and Rabbit entered the house. The occupants of the house were nowhere around. DePugh and Rabbit sat down in the living room. DePugh apologized for changing Rabbit's return flight. He told Rabbit that he should know by now that he didn't like to conduct business in public, and this was a very important meeting.

DePugh emphasized, "You can never be sure who is watching or listening in."

DePugh reminded Rabbit that while in California, he had offered him membership in the Minutemen. He said the offer had been extended only after a lengthy investigation, which included an intense background check. And most important, Rabbit had passed the polygraph test in Kansas City. Rabbit thought, *Thank God for that huge piece of misinformation.*

DePugh spoke about the absolute trust and loyalty to him and the organization that he demanded. He asked Rabbit if he fully grasped the seriousness of this commitment. As a trusted member, he would in time be privy to much information that, if discovered by the Feds, would result in him spending the rest of his life in the penitentiary and a lot of other patriots serving very lengthy prison sentences.

He paused for a long moment, all the while looking straight into Rabbit's eyes, and then said, "Anyone who betrays this trust, I promise, will be executed." He then asked Rabbit if he unconditionally accepted his demands.

Rabbit simply responded, "Of course."

DePugh continued, "As part of our internal security, everyone is continually tested in covert ways. It is required for the safety of all members. We cannot and will not miss a government spy. The cost of a mistake would be the end of the Minutemen. Everyone close to me fully understands the necessity of this security and willingly accepts it.

"The fully automatic HK-91 rifle made available to you in Los Angeles was one of those tests. If you had been a Fed, by now you would have put together a conspiracy case behind the automatic weapons violation. And when an arrest was made, you would have been ferreted out as the spy. Our fall guy who sold you the rifle would have gotten off with a light slap on the wrist from the court.

"I'm taking you into my confidence because you possess those attributes that the Minutemen want. I believe you are going to go a long way with the organization."

DePugh then outlined a plan: Rabbit was to be a courier for him. He was to fly Minutemen plans and strategies about the country, avoiding interception by the Feds. Rabbit had the perfect cover because he worked for an airline. Extensive travel by an airline employee on free passes would attract little or no notice.

DePugh then explained the type of information that Rabbit would be taking to different cells and other entities. He had learned to be very cryptic and careful in his speech. Even when he spoke with a trusted ally in a location that was totally safe, he acted out of habit and self-training.

It had been a long time since they had first met in Los Angeles. Rabbit and DePugh had since spent a lot of time talking on the phone and communicating by mail and together at the meetings. Rabbit had presented himself to DePugh and his organization as a dedicated, loyal member in order to gain DePugh's full confidence.

Rabbit traveled around the country with him at his own expense, doing whatever was asked. At DePugh's conferences, Rabbit's lectures on survival were always a good draw, which helped recruitment for the organization. The lectures also proved to be an excellent source of information on individual patriots and other right-wing groups, which he passed on to DePugh. Rabbit had become a loyal, faithful soldier. In return, he was becoming more and more trusted, and was now being made privy to the secrets of the Minutemen—who was who in the organization, their objectives, the network of private armies, and locations of weapon bunkers.

The most tantalizing tidbit of information periodically alluded to was that many of the automatic weapons had been provided by patriots employed by an agency of the United States government. The trust that Rabbit had worked so hard to develop had paid off.

DePugh spoke briefly of his contacts within the CIA and how he had come to be associated with them. It all started through the Minutemen's involvement with the ALPHA 66 in the Miami, Florida area. This was a group of Cuban patriots who opposed the communist rule of Fidel Castro. The Minutemen were sympathetic to their cause because of their common enemy. DePugh was never clear about his exact involvement; he said only that he had been associated with some CIA contacts. According to DePugh, these contacts provided the Minutemen with weapons and information which were funneled back into the United States from Central America.

DePugh and the Minutemen were being supported as a counterbalance to the dangerous left-wing groups that had been growing at an alarming rate in the United States. For their part of the bargain, the Minutemen would do whatever was necessary to disrupt certain targeted left-wing organizations.

This information confirmed Rabbit's belief that he and the Los Angeles Police Department were into something way over their heads, and in a place they had no business. This was FBI or CIA territory, definitely not LAPD. It was bad enough to be conducting questionable activities far from his geographic base of authority and to be dealing with ex-cons who thought nothing of murder or assassination, but now Rabbit was getting involved in international conspiracies in which US government employees were alleged to have participated.

##

It was getting late in the day. The sun was going down when DePugh ended the meeting. DePugh stood and motioned for Rabbit to follow. They walked into the kitchen, and DePugh opened a door that led to the basement. The two of them went down the steps into a well-supplied storm cellar.

It had been designed as a safe shelter from the region's fierce tornadoes. The shelter had two sets of bunk beds mounted to one wall. On the opposite wall was a small kitchen that included plumbing and a refrigerator connected to a portable generator. Next to the kitchen there was a very small bathroom. The rest of the room was dedicated to shelves that held all the necessities of survival. There were all types of canned goods, paper supplies, bottled water, a CB radio, and first-aid kit.

DePugh went to one of the shelves, reached behind some of the food supplies, and activated a concealed switch that released one of the food racks. It swung open, apparently held by a hidden hinge. The food rack concealed a thick, steel-encased door in a heavy metal frame. DePugh opened the door, and on the other side was a six-foot high walkway leading into a thirty-foot tunnel. At the far end of this tunnel was another steel door. DePugh opened it, revealing a complete military bunker. Rabbit was quite astonished at what he saw.

The setup looked as if it had been built to military specifications. It had everything—its own ventilation system, a kitchen, a bathroom, and five bunk beds on one wall. At the end of the room was a small machine shop with a lathe, drill press, grinder, acetylene torch, and hand tools. Next to it on the wall was a gun rack holding a double row of 12-gauge pump shotguns and M-16 rifles.

Without wanting to appear as though he were taking inventory, Rabbit casually perused the room. The metal racks held body armor, chemical protective gear, hand-held radios, gas masks, food, and bottled water. There was an extensive amount of medical supplies. There were cases of boxed military M-16 rifles and stacked cases of ammunition. A camo tarp covered a stack of other military hardware.

The room also had an escape tunnel made of thirty-six-inch diameter concrete drain pipe that ran underground and exited behind the barn, somewhere in the adjoining woods. DePugh said the concrete ceiling was reinforced with steel and was actually the slab of the burned down house. This was an extremely well designed, fortified bunker.

DePugh said there were many bunkers like this located throughout the US. The biggest bunker with the most military weaponry was in the mountains just outside Evergreen, Colorado. As they turned to leave the bunker, DePugh looked at Rabbit and said, "We mean business. The revolution is coming."

It was now after dark—and time to return to the airport for the flight back to Los Angeles. Before the car left the farmhouse,

DePugh handed the blackout glasses to Rabbit and told him to put them on. Rabbit complied. En route to the airport, DePugh gave Rabbit an extensive list of names that he said was of the utmost confidentiality. Next to each name there was a code number. The names were those of members of the COTM and Minutemen, and the list indicated the depth of their involvement, and therefore the degree to which they could be depended on during the imminent fall of the United States as we know it. Rabbit was told to keep it in a very safe place, and that he would receive instructions in the future for what to do with it.

DePugh had given him a prepaid ticket on United Airlines, and when Rabbit identified himself at the ticket counter as an employee of another airline who would normally fly for free, he was upgraded to first class. This turned out to be a boon for him because the drinks were free and he needed a few to help relieve his mental tension.

He reviewed the list, which was many pages long, and immediately recognized a few well-known individuals on the list. There were several from the movie industry, politics, and, of course, law enforcement. The rest probably came from all walks of life. Concern crept into his mind as he thought of the possible consequences to the people whose names appeared on this list. If his department or some arm of the federal government decided to investigate some of these people, it could be disastrous for them.

By this time, Rabbit had begun to swing philosophically more to the right than he had ever imagined he could, and as a result, he had more compassion for those who considered themselves patriots. He was sure that many of these names belonged to patriots of the armchair variety who would never take up arms against this country.

He also contemplated the possibility that the list was a setup by DePugh to test his loyalty. DePugh was sure to figure that if some of the names were prominent, most probably there would be leaks in the department that would cause them to be released to the media. If that happened, DePugh would immediately know where the information had come from. In that event, Rabbit's life would again be in grave danger.

Upon arriving back at Los Angeles, all he wanted to do was stay drunk and hide. This was beginning to be a regular outlet for him, and it was being noticed by others. Several of his coworkers at the airport had noticed a marked change in Rabbit's personality and an increase in his drinking. He called Charlie, but she was reluctant to see him. Paranoia was beginning to overtake her, too.

He put off his meeting with Harris as long as he could. When they finally got together, Harris was pissed. It had been Rabbit's responsibility to report in immediately upon arrival back in Los Angeles. Rabbit merely told Harris he had a lot of things to think about. This should have been another red flag for Harris, who should have considered the many variables that could have affected Rabbit's mental health, as well as the possibility that he was developing some kind of allegiance to the organization he was supposed to be investigating.

Rabbit gave Harris the required detailed written report on the Kansas City meeting with DePugh. Harris frowned as he went through the pages. The report began with the surprise, unscheduled car pick up at the airport and the drive with DePugh to the country farmhouse. Not included was the personal chitchat that always took place with DePugh before anything of substance was discussed.

Rabbit noted his observations when he arrived at the farmhouse. The area and the farmhouse itself were described in detail. His conversation with DePugh inside the farmhouse was also succinctly recounted. The report on the underground bunker was the most disturbing. In Rabbit's opinion, based on what he had observed, this was critical information of the highest order.

When Harris read about the bunker, Rabbit was taken aback that Harris did not display the same deep concern he felt—it seemed odd. It was almost as though Harris already knew about the bunker; maybe he was planning to give the information to the FBI or Kansas authorities at some later date, when the PDID investigation was finished.

Harris continued to study the report. When he read about the list of names DePugh had given Rabbit, his attitude immediately changed. He was no longer interested in why Rabbit was late in coming to him; all he was interested in was the list. But Rabbit refused to give it to him. He just knew this list was bad medicine, and that he couldn't take a chance on anything happening to it.

Harris pressed Rabbit until he was blue in the face, but to no avail. The tension between supervisor and Bird Dog became extremely tense, as Harris tried every persuasive tactic he could muster. Finally Harris gave up his façade in sheer desperation.

"Okay, Rabbit. I'm through fooling around with you. Give me the goddamn list."

"I haven't got it," Rabbit said, simply.

"What do you mean you haven't got it?"

"I hid it."

Harris acted like a wild man. "This is no joking matter. You have no choice here. Give me the goddamn list or I swear, you'll be transferred out of here as soon as I lay this on the captain, and you know what that means? It means your chances of ever making detective rank or working another undercover assignment again will be zip—fucking zero!"

Rabbit had never seen Harris lose his cool like this before, and he was taken aback. It took a few seconds for him to regain his own composure.

"Okay, Harris, as long as you're going to be chickenshit about this, I'll give you the list. But I'm warning you, don't let anything happen to it. 'Cause if you do, my ass is going to be in Forest Lawn cemetery."

Harris calmed down a bit.

"Rabbit, don't worry about it. We're professionals. We know how to take care of confidential materials. It will be more secure with me than wherever you have hidden it. Trust me."

Rabbit realized his mistake too late. He should never have mentioned the list in his intelligence report. He had failed to realize that once the list was given to Harris, the control of that material would be forever out of his hands. Now that Harris knew about the list and demanded a copy, Rabbit had no option but to give the list to him.

The next day, Rabbit made a copy of the list and gave it to Harris, and told him that he was out of the business for good. He was going to move back into his own home the next day. Harris told him that he was destroying his career by even thinking of such a stupid move. But Rabbit was adamant; his whole world was coming down around him and he was losing touch with reality.

Harris convinced him that he had been working too long and too hard. He suggested that Rabbit take advantage of his airline perks and go off to some far-flung place with Charlie and get back in touch with reality. Once again, Harris had successfully coaxed Rabbit back into line. Rabbit relented. He left the meeting with Harris and immediately called Charlie to request a rendezvous. She agreed.

Chapter 19
Tahiti Rendezvous

Charlie was still a little skeptical, but she was willing to take one more chance to save their relationship. To be honest, ten days in Tahiti sounded like she had died and gone to heaven.

Two days later, Charlie met Rabbit at the airport, and they sat for cocktails. At first, it was almost like a blind date. There was much to discuss, but each was reluctant to bring up anything that might spoil the moment or the near future. Mostly they stared into each other's eyes and conveyed the deep feelings that only the eyes can transmit. The drinks provided a warm glow, and they held hands as they entered the aircraft. Each hungered for the other, but it would be a long flight.

When the loving couple reached Tahiti, they checked into their hotel, which was a group of thatched huts along the beach, with one larger hut being the main building and registration area. It was early evening when they settled into their new temporary home. They wandered out to the bar, which was another thatched hut, and sat looking out over the blue Pacific at a sunset the likes of which could be seen nowhere else in the world. Soft billowy clouds tinged with gold nestled comfortably into the reddish orange background that was rapidly overtaking the deep blue beyond. Even the majestic palm trees that lined the landscape were different from the trees in Southern California. They swayed in a gentle tropical breeze with the grace of a line of ballerinas.

As they stared at the wonder before them, each caressed the other's skin and thought of the warmth and excitement that had been missing from their lives.

Slowly, Rabbit rose and took Charlie's hand, helping her to her feet. Without speaking, they turned and found their way back to their hut. Charlie removed her clothes with a series of erotic gestures, touching her fingers to her moist lips. Rabbit clumsily tore his clothes off, almost falling as his legs got caught up in his trousers. He was like a young boy struggling to get through his first sexual experience, but Charlie had far too much class to giggle at him.

When they hit the bed, Rabbit was no longer a struggling little boy. As he deftly explored her entire body with his hands and lips, Charlie responded with a passion that even she hadn't known she possessed.

The next morning proved to be all that Tahiti promised. Charlie and Rabbit had never been happier. They rented a couple of motor scooters and explored the island. They took pictures and shopped, as is expected of all tourists. The warm and friendly Tahitians made them feel as though they belonged there. Little children with bronzed bodies frolicked and included them in their games as though they had lived there all their lives. Between the tiny villages along the little winding coast road, they would stop at romantic turnouts, jump into the warm, beautiful, clear-blue ocean, and make passionate love on the beach with the sound of softly crashing waves in the background.

Charlie was able to wash away almost all the fear and recrimination of the past two years. Once more she was experiencing a happy love. Rabbit also felt a greater peace of mind, an elusive happiness that had previously been denied him.

After a few days, Rabbit was more determined than ever not to let this slip away again. He decided that as soon as they got back to Los Angeles, he was going to fulfill the promise of a church wedding he had made to Charlie in Mexico. The charade that his world had turned into was over for him. He desperately needed to get his life in order, and he knew the grip of both the PDID and Harris had to be ended. The PDID had slowly and totally consumed him, and he had to get out from under his overwhelming fear of failure, and his fear of the possible damage he might do to his career if he defied Harris. He would figure that out, no matter the consequences.

He fully realized that he had made a terrible mistake by not marrying Charlie early on in their relationship, when she had wanted to get married. But at the time, he had felt totally inadequate and unable to take care of her in the way she was used to living. As a result, he had put her off. Now he realized how wrong he had been.

As they sat on the beach under the star-filled Tahitian sky, he knew he had never seen a woman as beautiful as Charlie in his entire life. She had the face of an angel, and everything about her was perfect. She meant everything to him, and he had to be with her the rest of his life.

He took her hands and looked deeply into her eyes and told her of his deep adoration, and his desire to give her the wedding in a church that she had always dreamed of having. Charlie had prayed for this day almost from the moment she had first taken his hand, after their initial introduction in the strip club so long ago.

However, she had become hardened by the endless nights of loneliness and longing. His words brought back the memories of the fear she would experience for as long as he worked in his current assignment. It almost drove a stake through her heart, but she asked him to wait until this undercover job was finished. She wasn't prepared to further complicate their already-complicated situation.

Rabbit had shared every one of his experiences with her, and she was concerned about everything that was happening to him. She pointed out that he was no longer able to laugh at the little things in life as he used to, and mentioned his perpetual concern with his assignment.

"I love you, Rabbit. I love you with all my heart, but I'm having trouble liking you. I liked the carefree, happy-go-lucky guy who never took himself seriously. I'm afraid for the guy who broods all the time and is afraid of all the things he is doing. I'm not a cop, and I don't know a lot about police work, but I get the feeling you're wrong in what you are doing. You're going to wind up in prison one of these days, or you are going to get yourself killed. I don't want to sit at home every night and wait to hear that news."

Rabbit wanted to guarantee her that the assignment would be over in a very short time, but he had told her that many times before, and he knew she would not believe him. Even he was sick of hearing it. She was right, of course, but it was a bitter pill to swallow. At least they could go on being lovers in the interim. Their difficult conversation had dampened the spirits slightly, but it didn't extinguish the fire they had started.

Rabbit was exhausted and depressed by the struggle. He knew that to leave the assignment prematurely would not be a simple task, but for the sake of their relationship, he was determined more than ever to do that. He would first have to plan an exit strategy from the underground world he was involved in, a strategy that would ensure his safety. After that was planned, he would have to go around Harris, violating the chain of command, and meet with the captain of the division. That in itself would have serious consequences for his relationship with Harris. He would inform the captain that he could no longer work the assignment due to the extreme hardship it caused in his life. For too long the assignment had prevented him and Charlie from experiencing a normal life. They had both reached the point at which they wanted to have children, which simply was not possible working a deep undercover operation.

He knew this would not please the captain, but that was his plan. Besides, philosophically he had moved farther to the right than he had been before, and he now found himself sympathetic to some of the people he was investigating. Many of them were not the terrorists Harris had painted them as; they were just overzealous patriots. Now the only thing left for Rabbit to do was figure out the timing of his exit plan after his return to Los Angeles.

A few days later, near the end of their sojourn, Charlie and Rabbit brought their towels onto the beach and sat near an English couple with whom they'd had drinks on several occasions. All four had romped in the surf and were returning to lie in the sun and deepen their tans. Ian and Nancy were not much into tans, and had coated their reddish ivory bodies thickly in sunscreen.

As they lie there, a young American couple emerged from another hut approximately thirty yards down the beach. The young man had the scraggly beard and long matted hair of a true sixties hippie. Rabbit had battled many like him during the anti-Vietnam War demonstrations, but since his involvement with the right wing, this sight had become even more repugnant.

Without saying a word, Charlie squeezed his hand to remind him where he was and whom he was with. Rabbit relaxed and made a conscious effort to ignore the couple. He couldn't help but wonder where the hippie's money came from to afford this kind of vacation. Not everyone worked for an airline.

The young man finally opened a beach bag and removed a large American flag, which he spread on the sand to be used as a beach towel. This was not a flag-decorated towel, but a genuine stars and stripes that looked as though it had hung in a state capitol. It was intolerable to see the flag lying on the ground with sand kicked all over it, and this dirty-looking creep sprawled on top of it.

Ian spoke loudly enough for the young man to hear as he asked Rabbit what he thought of that. Rabbit told him that he didn't think too highly of the disrespect he was witnessing. If it were the Union Jack being treated like that, Ian would go down and tear the bloody bloke's lips off. Rabbit stared, seething with hatred for this long-haired freak, and decided that he was going to do just that. Charlie leaped to her feet and told Rabbit that he would do no such thing. They were in a foreign country, and he was not the appointed guardian of the American way of life throughout the free world. Further, if he did anything to this asshole, she would never speak to him again. Rabbit was hot, but smart enough to back off. He stood and picked up his gear and retreated to the hut.

Once inside, Charlie blistered him. This was just further proof of the changes in him. The fires had definitely been extinguished. Inside the hut, a deep philosophical discussion ensued. Rabbit tried to put his arms around her, but she would have none of it. She told him simply that this relationship had gone into the dumpster. Unless he could get out of this assignment and get back to normal, there was no chance whatsoever for them to continue.

Fortunately, it was the end of their stay, so the cool silence that had replaced the passion would be reasonably short in duration, even though it would seem like an eternity. They spent the remainder of that night getting drunk and talking about their problems. The next day, which was their last on the island, was cool but cordial.

They sipped exotic drinks and played the role of a happy couple in front of Ian and his wife, but never even so much as held hands.

The plane ride home was a chilling, unpleasant experience. Charlie was civil, at best, and Rabbit knew enough not to push her. When they arrived home, Charlie exited the cab and simply stated that she had had it; it was all over. Rabbit didn't really believe her, but he did not argue. He could not face the possibility of a future without her. However, he felt, as always, that this was a passing thing. With time, she'd get over it.

As he returned to his pathetic crash pad, he reflected over and over again on what Charlie had said about going to prison. He had learned to live with the fear of dying, but the thought of going to prison was overwhelming. On reflection, he thought it was certainly a possibility. He was starting to lose his way. He had been undercover too long. Whatever this assignment was about, it was not worth the price.

Chapter 20
Federal Encounter

As Rabbit sat at a picnic table inside the Travel Town Museum in Griffith Park, youngsters scurried up and down the old restored locomotives. Each one was pretending to be Casey Jones as he or she took a turn at the controls. In one of the railroad cars a small group of boys and girls were attending a birthday party. The girls were giggling and the boys were running wild, driving the few mothers crazy. Rabbit smiled, but he was glad he was not responsible for them.

Harris arrived and sat next to him. Rabbit offered him a cookie from a package he had in front of him, but Harris refused, patting his belly, indicating that he had consumed more than enough cookies over the years.

"I figured you would prefer this place to the train station."

Rabbit glanced around, "I don't think that's funny. Do you have a fixation on trains?"

Harris smiled and shook his head. "I have a fixation on privacy. How was your vacation?"

The vacation was not something Rabbit cared to discuss. Avoiding it like the plague, he launched into the concerns Charlie had expressed regarding the legality of his actions. Harris assured him that everything he was doing had been reviewed by the legal section in PDID. Rabbit was unimpressed.

"I was inside PDID for about fifteen minutes one day, and I was introduced to about four people. I don't know anything about the people who work there or their expertise with the law. I assume they don't know as much as the people from the District Attorney's office who will be prosecuting me if I get caught in one of these compromising situations."

He took a deep breath of the country-like air that seemed free of the usual LA pollutants. Of course it wasn't, but the park surroundings gave that illusion.

He told Harris they both knew full well that as part of the assignment, felonies and conspiracies were not just possibilities—they had occurred, and there are serious penalties attached to those activities. Then there was that little nagging problem of the jurisdiction of a Los Angeles Police Officer—he was running all over the US like a federal agent, spying on people, and that was probably another heavyweight set of violations involving Federal civil rights codes.

"It just doesn't sound right, and every time these subjects come up, you, a police sergeant, advise me, a policeman, not to worry about it. It's no problem, you and PDID will take care of it. That's no longer good enough, because frankly, I don't believe it. I want the chief to write me a letter that I can carry around, that I can show in case someone wants to arrest me. I want a letter that states I can do anything I want, anytime, anywhere."

Harris shot back, "Don't be funny."

Rabbit said he wanted to see case law pertaining to this kind of activity, and if there was none, then Harris had to put his transfer in for parking and intersection control. He was all finished with this insanity.

Harris could see that this time it was impossible to placate Rabbit with his routine answers. He decided that he would arrange a meeting with some people from the federal Attorney General's office to discuss these issues and to satisfy Rabbit.

A few days later Harris told Rabbit he had made arrangements for Rabbit to sit down with some federal attorneys to discuss his legal concerns. Rabbit didn't want to meet the federal attorneys face-to-face. He knew that would be a lose-lose deal. The Feds would not give anything up without getting something important in return. Rabbit told Harris just to get him copies of federal case law that pertained to undercover officers like him participating in criminal activity in the furtherance of their investigations. Harris said the Feds wouldn't go along with that; they insisted on a face-to-face meeting. Rabbit didn't like it, but couldn't see any way around it. He knew the Feds' first objective would be to identify him and the organization he was investigating. Rabbit would have to make sure they failed on both of those objectives.

Harris told Rabbit the meeting was set for the next Thursday at 2:00 p.m. at the Black Angus Steakhouse in Torrance. Rabbit knew the location well, as it was in the neighborhood he had been raised in. In fact, when he had been a little boy, his father would take him to the mall parking lot early on Sundays so he could drive his go-cart. Back then stores were closed on Sundays and the lot was empty.

Rabbit had no objection to the location, which was over thirty-five miles from the area of Los Angeles in which his investigation

was centered. However, the time was unacceptable. He knew the
Feds would want the meeting to take place during daylight hours,
which would afford them optimum conditions for surveillance on
Rabbit when the meeting was over and he left the restaurant.

Rabbit lied and told Harris the 2:00 p.m. meet time conflicted
with his airport work schedule, and if there had to be a meeting,
the time would have to be changed to Friday after 7:00 p.m. Reluctantly, the Feds agreed to the change. The new meeting time
went a long way toward allaying Rabbit's concerns about being
tailed by the Feds after the meeting was over.

The restaurant parking lot was actually part of the Del Amo
Mall, the largest mall in America, with over two and a half million
square feet of retail space and more than twelve thousand parking
spaces. On any given Friday night at seven o'clock, the parking lot
is like a zoo. It is so crowded with people and cars, a pink elephant
could give the Feds the slip.

Rabbit's plan was to arrive by taxi thirty minutes prior to the
meeting time. He would exit the taxi in the underground parking
structure of the mall and then walk the quarter mile through the
parking lot to the restaurant.

Friday night arrived, and Rabbit put his plan into motion. Of
course, he hadn't shared any of the details with Harris. It would
only serve to annoy him. Besides, as far as Rabbit was concerned,
this was one of those need-to-know situations, and since it was his
ass that needed to be covered, he would do what he needed to do
to take care of it.

Harris had instructed Rabbit to park his truck in front of the
restaurant and wait inside. When Harris saw the Feds, he would

signal Rabbit that it was okay to exit his truck. Rabbit didn't like the plan. He just said okay.

As he had planned, Rabbit arrived by taxi at the mall a quarter mile away and walked to the restaurant. He was twenty minutes early. He didn't see Harris or anything that looked like a Fed. He slipped in a side door, sat at a table in the corner at the back of the bar, ordered a double Jack Daniel's rocks, and waited.

A half hour passed. Finally, the front door opened and in came Harris with two obvious federal agents. The three of them were engaged in conversation. All the while Harris was looking about the restaurant and bar. Finally, he spotted Rabbit. He excused himself from the Feds, walked over to Rabbit's cocktail table, and not-so-politely said, "Why do you always have to be a pain in the ass?" Rabbit just smiled. He actually found some humor in Harris's annoyance.

Harris explained that the two attorneys from the AG's office had been thoroughly briefed on the reason for this meeting. The guidelines were clearly established. Rabbit did not have to identify himself and was not to discuss his assignment with them. His questions could be phrased in generalities.

The interior of the restaurant was dark. Harris led him to the booth where the federal attorneys were sitting, which was a reasonably secluded section. The western motif of the place, with its high-backed booths, afforded considerable privacy. It was an ideal location for romantic liaisons. Other patrons seeking anonymity would be unlikely eavesdroppers.

Using no names, Harris introduced all parties and left immediately. It was obvious he did not wish to hear any confessions of wrongdoing by Rabbit. As a matter of fact, he didn't want to hear anything that might jeopardize or even taint his gold mine.

Rabbit took a seat across the table from the two men, who were attired in the customary conservative dark suits, striped shirts, and drab ties. He was taking Harris's word that they were federal attorneys. They could have been anyone from any governmental agency. He knew they weren't Secret Service, because they weren't wearing dark glasses. And they couldn't be FBI, because they'd found the place. So who knew who they were.

One of the men started the conversation by telling him they understood that he had some questions about an undercover assignment he was on. Rabbit corrected him that it was not the assignment he wanted answers about, but some of the things he was getting involved with. They smiled patiently and asked him to proceed.

Rabbit was thinking specifically about the snake box, and what would have happened if they had put some poor bastard's hands in it on the night he was present, or if one of those morons had pulled the trigger on that CHP officer when they were doing their surveillance of the Chavez compound.

"Suppose I had infiltrated a group of bank robbers and became involved in the planning of a bank job with the understanding that no guns were to be used. Then, on the day of the heist, one of the others pulls a gun and kills someone? Where do I stand as far as culpability on a conspiracy or a murder charge?"

They smiled benignly and patiently and explained case law as it applied to agents who had been caught up in similar circumstances. One of the men pulled what appeared to be a trial transcript from a briefcase and showed it to him. It was a case in which a federal agent had been working undercover with the Mafia in Las Vegas. He had participated in a train wreck during an operation in which an individual had been killed. The resulting inquiry found no criminal culpability on the agent's part. Rabbit looked at the document, but all the pertinent information had been redacted with a black felt marker. Rabbit asked them to share some of the specifics of the case, but they insisted that it was extremely confidential.

Rabbit inquired, "Let me get this straight. If I'm arrested in a homicide case because I was present during the murder and didn't do anything to stop it, my defense is that two guys whose names I don't know showed me a blacked-out transcript of a case which I am ignorant of any of the facts of and told me that everything would be all right?"

"In these matters, you will never get to the point where you have to defend yourself in a court of law."

"But if I do, I just have to get hold of you guys and I'll be out of there, no problem; is that right?"

They maintained their professional federal stoicism and failed to see the humor in Rabbit's analogy. They told him that he had nothing to worry about.

Rabbit said he didn't doubt they were telling him the truth, but was concerned about things going sideways on him, especially if it happened while he was at a meeting out of state.

With that revelation, their eyes widened. They began to question him about his investigation. He reminded them of the guidelines, but that didn't slow them down.

"You are now talking about transcending state boundaries and involving yourself in federal matters. We want to know what and whom you are investigating."

Rabbit sighed. He wasn't about to give them any more information. He merely shook his head.

One of the agents leaned across the table, and in a low tone he said, "You really need to cooperate with us, or you could find yourself subpoenaed to a federal inquiry."

Rabbit had figured this was how it would go. That was exactly why he hadn't wanted to meet with them. He had had enough. He thought to himself, *Fuck 'em.*

He took a big swig of his Jack Daniel's, told them he was just after some answers so he wouldn't cross any legal lines in trying to do his job. He said he wasn't sure exactly how all this undercover stuff worked, and he couldn't tell them anything without his boss Harris being present—he just followed orders. He asked if he could get Harris, who was outside waiting for him. The one Fed directed his partner to go get Harris.

Rabbit had a key ring lying on the table with several throwaway keys to forgotten locks. Also on the table were a pair of his five-dollar reading glasses, a pad of paper, a pen, and a little bit of JD left in his glass. He told the Fed he was going to the bathroom. He left his things on the table, and before he left, he asked him if he would watch for the cocktail waitress while he was in the bathroom, and if she came by, order him another double Jack rocks. The Fed nodded, affirmative.

Rabbit smiled and thanked him. He then walked to the bathroom and kept right on going to the kitchen and out the back door. He vanished into the sea of cars and people in the parking lot. Harris would be pissed.

Chapter 21
Stakeout

By now Rabbit was operating in a perpetual paranoid state. He was totally dedicated to doing a job that he had come to hate with all his heart. Fear was his constant companion, and he perceived threats from both sides. He was living in a world of booby traps.

He knew DePugh had connections everywhere, including the federal system, and he felt sure that it was only a matter of time before his true identity became known. He was also concerned about his own side and their unwillingness or inability to grasp the depth of the danger.

By Harris's account, the brass was giddy over having one of their own policemen so deep in a federal investigation. In addition to his fears for his safety, Rabbit was overcome by the heavy burden of loneliness. He walked alone in a hostile world, and was afraid even to talk to Charlie. He realized that he had just about burned that bridge completely.

But somehow, he carried on, almost as though he were possessed. He was no longer sure of his mission, but whatever it was, he had to see it through, no matter where it took him. He had lost all touch with the police department that he loved. It was as though he had never been a part of it. He wasn't even referred to as a cop. He was a "bird dog," a coded number, like something that was checked out of the property room periodically to be used for a specific investigation.

The only cop he spoke to was Harris, and they never talked about the things cops talk about. They only talked about the right wing. He had become inundated with the right wing until there was no room in his life for anything else. He was hounded in his own mind with daily thoughts about the overthrow of the government; the killing of peace officers, judges, prosecuting attorneys, blacks, and Jews; and impending anarchy.

There was no room for laughter. This was serious business. A curtain was slowly being drawn across his mind, causing the light of reality to become dim.

When Rabbit returned from work one afternoon, he received a call from DePugh with coded instructions to go to the cold phone. DePugh had a high priority assignment for him.

This assignment involved a right-wing extremist named Karlin who had become a bitter enemy of DePugh's. Karlin had a considerable following, but his relentless, withering attacks on the Jews were very distracting, and this was having a negative effect on the right-wing movement. Karlin's anti-Semitism was so irrational that he made all right-wing patriots look like fools by association.

DePugh had expressed his concern and tried to persuade him to tone down the rhetoric. It didn't work. Karlin turned on DePugh and unleashed a vicious barrage of accusations of moral turpitude, which damaged DePugh and his organization.

DePugh wanted Rabbit to conduct surveillance on Karlin, at both his condominium and business office, and gather all the information he could, including dates and times of all activity. DePugh relayed all pertinent information he had on Karlin to Rabbit to help him in his investigation.

Once again, Rabbit was in a quandary about legality, but Harris quickly pacified him. The Department felt this was a golden opportunity for them to get information on Karlin without expending their own manpower. They did not see a problem with Rabbit handing over all his information to DePugh, because it opened the possibility that DePugh might do something they could not do that would screw up Karlin's organization, or at least disrupt his activities.

So Rabbit set out on a three-week investigation, in the course of which he actually did some real police work—ironically, for the underground organization that he himself was already investigating. It became comical—after working at the aiport, he would meet Harris, who would instruct him to hustle up to Karlin's house to do his job for DePugh. On more than one occasion he was tempted to ask Harris if DePugh could fill out his semiannual proficiency rating report.

In the course of the investigation, Rabbit scouted out suitable locations and set up vantage points from which he could monitor Karlin's comings and goings with binoculars and photograph them with a telephoto lens. In accordance with the directions he had been given, he photographed everyone entering and exiting Karlin's residence and business, especially women. DePugh knew only too well that most men share a common weakness—their inability to keep their pants on.

Rabbit also photographed the license plates of all vehicles that came to Karlin's house. DePugh said he had his own sources to run license plates, and Rabbit never questioned him. He did feel some concern though, because this was one more resource DePugh had that could lead to Rabbit's own downfall. Of course, he always had triplicate sets of photos made—one for PDID, one for DePugh, and most important, one for his own secret file, unbeknownst to Harris and PDID.

He never found out what Harris or the Department did with the information or photographs. He often thought they might have been leaked to Irv Rubin and the Jewish Defense League. Maybe the Department had decided to let them deal with the right-wing extremists.

At one point during his investigation of Karlin, DePugh called Rabbit and left him a very cryptic message, telling him to send a passport photo and his shirt size, and DePugh would get back to him with further instructions.

A week later, DePugh called Rabbit and said the situation with Karlin had become untenable, and he needed to be silenced sooner than later. Rabbit was taken aback by the word silenced. Before he could ask DePugh what he had meant by that, DePugh explained he had a man in LA who handled special projects like this, but he would need some help, and DePugh had assigned Rabbit to assist him.

"Expect a call from this man—his name is Walt. He can be trusted one hundred percent. He was in Leavenworth with me, and he's worked for the organization for over fifteen years." And with that, the call terminated.

Three days later Rabbit received a call from a person who identified himself as Walt. He said, "Our mutual acquaintance in St. Louis told me we should get together on Thursday at 6:00 a.m. for a couple of hours and talk." Rabbit agreed to a meeting and asked for a location. Walt instructed him to go to Fanny's Restaurant at Lincoln and Colorado in Santa Monica and park in the rear. The phone went dead. *Everything has to be cloak-and-dagger*, Rabbit thought.

Rabbit knew he could not get out of DePugh's assignment without destroying or seriously damaging his position. Besides, this would further prove his loyalty. So he would have to at least meet Walt and see what he and DePugh meant by "silencing" Karlin.

At the appointed time Rabbit pulled into the parking lot of the restaurant and parked at the rear of the building. A few minutes later a van pulled in and parked two stalls away. The van was two-tone, white on the top and light green on the bottom, with ladders on a rack attached to the roof. It was a telephone company repair truck.

The driver motioned Rabbit to come over. Rabbit walked up to the truck, and the driver asked him, "What are the initials of your buddy in St. Louis?"

Rabbit responded, "RBD."

The driver had the look of a badass ex-con who didn't know how to smile.

He said, "Get in. We're going for a ride. We got work to do."

This wasn't going well. Rabbit had in mind a cup of coffee, a blueberry muffin, and a little chitchat, not a clandestine operation right out of the chute.

Rabbit got in the truck and said, "DePugh didn't want to discuss this on the phone, but he told me you and I would meet and talk about the plan for taking care of his problem."

Walt brusquely snapped back, "We're not here on a date. We have a job to do. And as soon as it's over, we'll go our separate ways."

Rabbit's job had been to recon Karlin's condo and business office and then to assist Walt. Walt's job, based on the info Rabbit had provided DePugh, was to design a black-op plan for DePugh's enemy and then execute it, and that was exactly what was going to happen.

Walt explained Rabbit's participation on the drive to Karlin's condo. He handed Rabbit a telephone company uniform shirt with a plastic telephone company ID card attached. The uniform matched what Walt was wearing. The ID card had on it the passport photo that Rabbit had sent to DePugh. The name on the ID was Michael Watkins.

Walt said, "We are setting Karlin up for a fall. We have run this same op before with excellent results. We know the work habits of our target based on your stakeouts. He leaves at 7:00 a.m. The housekeeper arrives at 8:00 a.m., and between 8:30 and 9:00 a.m., the wife leaves. As soon as the wife leaves, we are going to the complex's main telephone terminal cabinet located in the parking garage, and we will disconnect the telephone line to Karlin's unit. We'll go to his door and tell the housekeeper we are there to troubleshoot a problem on the telephone line. We'll have her check the phone, whereupon she will discover it's not working. We'll talk her into letting us come in to check the telephone jacks while looking for the trouble. Okay? Got it so far?"

He continued, "Once in, we'll do our telephone service routine. We'll get the maid to show us around the condo to check the different rooms for the telephone jacks. I'll need to be in the bedroom for a couple of minutes by myself, so you got to get the maid to help you look behind the sofa and chairs in the front room for our other telephone jacks, or have her show you the bathroom or the kitchen to get a glass of water, or something. I don't care how you do it—but keep her out of the bedroom for two minutes. Got it?"

"Yeah, I got it," Rabbit replied, "but what's going to happen?"

"Don't worry about it, just do what I told you."

Rabbit pressed Walt again for an answer, but got none.

The two men pulled up to Karlin's sprawling condominium complex in the telephone company truck. Each had all the proper paraphernalia of the trade—utility belts with lineman's handsets, flashlights, and leather pouches holding all the necessary tools for telephone repair. Attached to their uniform shirts were their plastic ID tags, which boldly proclaimed that they were telephone company employees.

The two men got out of their truck and entered the subterranean parking facility in a manner that would not arouse even the hint of suspicion. Walt moved quickly to the telephone source box and opened it up. He knew exactly what he was looking for, and within a matter of minutes he had selected specific wires, which he promptly disconnected.

He looked up at Rabbit and said, "Piece of cake. Let's go."

They went directly to Karlin's apartment and knocked on the door. A middle-aged woman, presumably the housekeeper, came to the door. Walt took the lead.

"Yes, ma'am, telephone company. We've been having trouble in the complex and would like you to check your phones."

The housekeeper walked away, leaving the door open. She picked up the phone in the living room and reached down and pushed a few buttons.

"It's dead," she said.

"May we come in and check it out for you?"

"Of course."

The two men entered and walked directly over to the phone. Walt took the phone from the housekeeper and asked where the extensions were. She informed him that there were extensions in the front room, the kitchen, and the bedroom—as is the case in almost every home.

Walt directed Rabbit to go to the front room and pick up the receiver and then directed the housekeeper to go to the kitchen and pick up that receiver. As soon as the housekeeper complied, he went to the bedroom and started making scratching noises on the bedroom phone. Walt stayed in the bedroom, and Rabbit distracted the housekeeper as planned and kept her in the front room.

Rabbit was not enjoying this business at all. Whatever the reason and no matter how many kudos it earned him from Harris, it was distasteful for a cop.

Shortly, Walt exited the bedroom and flashed a sign of his success. He and Rabbit hung up the phones, and Walt called out to the housekeeper that he thought he had found the problem. She could hang up the phone in the kitchen now, and they would be right back.

The two men went back down to the subterranean garage to reconnect the wires. Rabbit went to the truck, and Walt returned to the apartment. He asked the housekeeper to try the phone again. This time she smiled broadly and proclaimed, "It's working." She couldn't thank the nice man enough for restoring the telephone service.

Once back at the truck, the men removed their utility belts and stowed them in their proper place. Walt had Rabbit pick up the orange rubber safety cones that they had placed at the front and rear of the truck and put them back inside with the rest of the equipment. They drove away.

After a few miles, Rabbit tried another approach to his inquiry about what they had just done. He told Walt that DePugh said he would learn a lot from this op, as Walt was the best. The only problem was that all Rabbit had learned was that Walt did something in the bedroom. Whatever he had done, how could it help DePugh silence his enemy?

Ego overcame Walt. He said he had planted some hardcore kiddie porn tapes with cocaine rubbed on the tape cartridges under the bottom dresser drawer. He then put the drawer back in the dresser, concealing the porn. Then he dusted the area from the dresser to the front door with some cocaine. Sometime later, he would have a woman call the cops crying in a rage and tell the cops the target had taken her little boy to his place and used dope, watched porn, and molested her kid.

The cops would take it from there. They'd go to the condo with the dope dog, which would smell the dope at the door. The dog would go on alert, and the cops would get into the condo. Once inside, the dog would make a beeline for the dresser. The cops would find the kiddie porn and the dope and make a big arrest. As soon as that happened, news of the arrest would get out to the right-wing groups and other interested parties, and with that, the target's reputation would be destroyed. He would no longer be a problem to DePugh—or anyone else, for that matter.

"Doesn't matter what happens in court, or if it even gets to court. Our job is character assassination."

Back at the restaurant, before Rabbit exited the telephone truck, Walt took back the telephone company uniform shirt and telephone ID badge. Rabbit thanked Walt for taking him along and showing him the ropes, and then asked Walt for his telephone number so he could call him sometime for a beer. Walt said he didn't drink and told Rabbit maybe he would get back to him sometime. Rabbit had wanted to ID him, but Walt—which was probably not his real name—wasn't going to help him do that.

As Walt drove off in his late-model Ford telephone van, Rabbit noted the plate number. Later, a DMV check of the plate would come back registered to a 1965 Chevrolet sedan in San Diego. Rabbit decided not to mention all the details of this little outing to Harris. It was no big deal. These little activities had started to take on a feeling of normalcy.

Besides, if the Feds said it's okay to wreck a train and kill someone, why would a little operation like this be a problem? After his meeting with the Feds—and after some of the questionable advice given by Harris—Rabbit knew without any doubt that he'd better keep a detailed journal. This was absolutely against the rules of PDID, but it was vital for his own personal survival in the event this investigation went off the rails, in which case he had no doubt he would be thrown under the bus as a rogue operator.

DePugh called Rabbit the following day and had him go to the cold phone. DePugh told Rabbit he had heard all about the great job Rabbit had done backing up Walt on the mission. The operation had gone off without a flaw. Walt had even gone as far to say he would work with Rabbit again, which was most unusual, as he almost always worked alone (Walt didn't like witnesses).

Rabbit took that as a high compliment, and it was the first time he had ever been commended for his work habits by an ex-con. He wondered if Harris could somehow include that in his semiannual department rating report.

Chapter 22
Aerial Recon

A week after the Karlin condo op, DePugh called Rabbit with instructions to go to the cold phone. As usual, DePugh called the cold phone an hour later. After some small talk, the subject shifted to the Chavez compound recon several months before.

Although DePugh considered that mission a success, and it had proved useful, it had not produced as much information as they had been hoping to get. Easton of the Posse Comitatus, who had planned the mission, was still very much fixated on the compound and its activities. He and his friend, the train engineer in the Tehachapi region, continued to gather every little scrap of evidence that they could about Chavez and forwarded it to DePugh.

Rabbit did not know what Easton had told DePugh to get him so deeply interested in Chavez, but whatever it was, it had worked. DePugh instructed Rabbit to get in touch with Easton to set up an air reconnaissance of the Chavez compound. DePugh wanted a complete aerial photo spread of the compound, and he wanted Rabbit to be the photographer.

Just thinking about the Chavez compound and the incident with the CHP officer sent shivers up and down Rabbit's spine. He wanted to ask whose brilliant idea the aerial recon was, but he knew that question was out of line. Everyone worked on a need-to-know basis, and Rabbit didn't need to know that.

Rabbit set about contacting Easton, which required a trip to the gun store to post a note to Easton on the store's bulletin board. The board had been set up by management as a public service, and it proved useful to the underground movements by enabling them to contact each other in a way that was difficult for the police to trace. People using the board never used their real names—always an alias, or maybe a play name or a number. Rabbit wondered, should he use his Bird Dog number, S757?

After several bulletin-board exchanges, Rabbit and Easton met at the coffee shop near the gun store where they had met on prior occasions. When Rabbit told Easton of DePugh's plan, Easton thought it was a great idea. He knew just the man to pilot the aircraft, and he agreed to set everything up. A few days later, Easton called Rabbit to confirm their plans, and instructed Rabbit to meet him at Van Nuys Airport.

Rabbit couldn't understand the need to meet before daybreak, but he found out when he arrived at Van Nuys. Easton was waiting with Charlie Bellows at the side of a twin engine King Air.

Easton said, "This plane flies at over 300 miles per hour in level flight and has the capability to do a lot of high-performance tricks." Rabbit didn't like the sound of that at all. Bellows, the pilot, was conducting a pre-flight check of the plane. He was a Vietnam veteran who had flown numerous combat missions, and he was, according to Easton, one of the best pilots around for the type of mission they would be flying today.

Rabbit had no desire to dispute Bellows' qualifications, but there was no special talent necessary for that which was planned. Rabbit had a Nikon camera with a telephoto lens, which would enable them to photograph the compound in detail from an altitude of five-hundred feet.

After the routine ground check, Bellows used black electrical tape to change some of the tail numbers. The trio took off and headed north. Daylight was just breaking, and there were just a few early morning clouds in an otherwise clear blue sky.

When they got over the Santa Monica Mountains, Bellows suggested that they see what this baby could do. He then put the aircraft through the kinds of maneuvers that are usually reserved for test pilots, air shows, or combat flying.

As the plane rolled, dove, and climbed, Rabbit was tossed around in the rear compartment like a lotto ball waiting to be blown free. His camera equipment was thrown all over the aircraft. Meanwhile, Bellows and Easton were whooping it up in the front seat and having a ball. Bellows sounded as though he were riding a wild Brahma. Rabbit protested, which merely made the other two laugh harder. Rabbit wasn't sure if he was going to throw up or pass out from fear. He put on a show of bravado by screaming about the damage being done to his camera equipment. Bellows finally settled down and flew straight.

Then Bellows began to reminisce about his combat exploits in Vietnam, and again he got charged up like a madman. If only a part of these stories were true, he was quite a warrior pilot, with an extremely interesting experience package. He was a man who lived for the moment and feared nothing. Certainly, he was no one to mess around with.

When they reached the compound, Rabbit instructed Bellows about the best flight pattern and altitude to ensure perfect pictures. Bellows complied by making a wide, lazy, counterclockwise circle above the compound.

Rabbit shot rapid-fire, like a fashion photographer. After exhausting two rolls of film, he sat back in self-satisfaction. He informed Bellows and Easton that it was a job well done, and that they could head back to Van Nuys.

But Bellows and Easton had other plans. Bellows instructed Rabbit to fasten his seatbelt and secure his camera gear, because they wanted to get a close-up view, personally. He then put the aircraft into a steep dive and made a strafing run at the compound just a few feet above the buildings. Rabbit could make out the excited looks on the faces of several people who scurried about in a panic. Bellows and Easton laughed and shouted as they repeated the maneuver several times. Performance flying was one thing, but this was sheer insanity.

Rabbit wondered through his panic how this story would be told if they were to crash. He was sure the Department would deny any knowledge of this escapade. There goes a life and a career down the toilet.

When the two children in the front seat had had enough fun, they pulled the aircraft up to a sensible altitude and sped out into the desert, flying very low through valleys and between the low mountains.

Bellows said he was covering his tracks. Upon their arrival back in Van Nuys, he was extremely pleased with himself.

"I'll bet you never had that much fun in Disneyland."

"You bet! We have to do that again sometime," Rabbit lied.

Cameras were never allowed anywhere around members of these radical organizations, and photographs were strictly forbidden, but on this occasion, the camera was a necessary tool. Rabbit decided to take advantage of it.

"Say, Bellows, do you want a good picture of you and the airplane?"

Bellows' eyes lit up. "Yeah, that would be a nice little souvenir of our outing."

Bellows posed proudly in front of his plane. Rabbit then encouraged Easton to join him for a small group photo. He complied.

Idiots, Rabbit thought.

Rabbit's knees were still shaking as he made his way over to his truck and took off for Manhattan Beach, but he had to giggle to himself at the way he had duped the two militants into a photo op with the plane as evidence for the files.

In the end, Rabbit was a hero once more. DePugh was thrilled with the photos and planned to use them in one of his right-wing periodicals.

Harris was a big man on campus when he proudly dropped the photos on the captain's desk. No other PDID detective ever had a bird dog like Rabbit.

Chapter 23
CIA Complicity

As the months passed, Rabbit became closer and closer to DePugh and his family. They had developed a friendship. It was extremely unusual for anyone to get that close to DePugh, but Rabbit had become an important tool in the organization.

DePugh set up a number of conferences in the Midwest and the West in order to spread the gospel according to DePugh. Although many people were drawn to hear what the founder of the Minutemen had to say and were eager to give their own patriotism a boost, it was difficult for DePugh to keep a crowd enthralled or entertained. He was a very dry and unemotional speaker with a very serious message: Armageddon was just around the corner. To alleviate these problems and maximize attendance at the conferences, he would bring Rabbit along to give lectures on survival.

Ninety percent of the people who attended were armchair survivalists, and many of them lived out their fantasies vicariously through Rabbit. The routine was pretty well set in concrete. DePugh would rent out a large conference room in a nice hotel and provide minimal refreshments. He would charge enough to cover expenses and make a small profit on the side. After a while, he even began to throw a few dollars to Rabbit, since he was part of the draw for these events. Rabbit often thought how much it would rankle the lieutenant at PDID if he knew Rabbit had an additional source of income. Discretion motivated him to keep this aspect of his lecture activity a secret.

Rabbit enthralled the crowds with simple tricks that the audience could do at home to practice survival without giving up the comforts of daily life. Always, the biggest attraction of the lecture was the solar still. Despite its simplicity and importance, relatively few people were aware of it.

The solar still is a simple way to obtain water under even the most extreme conditions. All that is required is to dig a small hole two or three feet in diameter and two feet deep, and then scatter some plant material around the bottom of the hole with a small catch container like an empty soup can and a tube extending from the container to above the hole. Cover the hole with plastic, and weigh down the edges of the plastic around the top of the hole and its center with a few stones, creating an inverted pyramid. When it is sealed properly, condensation forms on the bottom side of the plastic and drips into the catch container. It functions under the same principle as a greenhouse.

The best part was that Rabbit had learned of the solar still from the Boy Scout handbook, but he never revealed his source.

The job at the airline was never meant to be anything other than a job for means of support, but it turned out to be a boon for this particular assignment. It enabled him to travel with a minimum of personal expenses. Airline employees traveling frequently on passes would not be cause for suspicion, and DePugh was happy because he could count on Rabbit almost any time. PDID was thrilled because they didn't have to submit paperwork through the chain of command in order to finance these many questionable trips out of state.

One evening Rabbit was preparing one of his many general intelligence reports. He always tried to craft these reports in a way that would make his command happy so they wouldn't feel the need to send him in another direction and interfere with his Minutemen investigation.

His reverie was interrupted by a call from DePugh. As usual, it was a curt instruction to visit the cold phone. This time, DePugh wanted Rabbit to join him in Oregon to put on his usual survival training presentation.

Rabbit should have been accustomed to the travel by now, but he wasn't. There was always that nagging fear about being so far out of his jurisdiction and out on a limb in the event something went sideways. When he questioned Harris about the need for this investigation to continue, Harris waved the flag and told him that it was the only way to protect the country from the radical right. He assured Rabbit that they were slowly building a case that would bring down the whole movement, but in the meantime, the intelligence was invaluable.

Most of all, Harris wanted the cache of machine guns. So once again, Rabbit gave in to the dictates of his handler and threw common sense out the window. It was as though he was incapable of independent thought and judgment when it came to instructions from the Department. This flaw in Rabbit was a decided advantage for PDID.

The following weekend, Rabbit was greeted at the Portland airport by a light rain that provided a welcome change from the dry weather of Los Angeles. When he checked into the Sheraton Hotel, DePugh was waiting to accompany him to dinner.

As had become their custom, the two talked for hours on end, and with each meeting, DePugh revealed more about himself and his thinking. He never completely threw caution to the wind when he talked, however. He had learned the hard way to avoid loose talk. He often told Rabbit to be extremely careful about anything he put in writing—and doubly cautious about anything he said over the phone or in any location that lent itself to eavesdropping with shotgun microphones or body wires.

During this particular dinner, DePugh loosened up a little more and talked about gun caches that the Minutemen had stashed in various locations around the country. One favorite spot was in Colorado. For the second time, he described a cave near Evergreen, Colorado in which a considerable amount of military weaponry and various munitions were secretly stored. The entrance to this cave had been covered up with boulders and camouflaged so successfully that the cave could not be detected from the air or from the ground.

DePugh asked Rabbit if he had ever spent time in Colorado. Rabbit said that he and a friend had spent many deer seasons there. They hunted mostly in Clear Creek County in north central Colorado, not far from Denver. Rabbit's friend had a good buddy with whom he'd served in Vietnam, and who lived in a mountain cabin there and knew all the great hunting spots. Rabbit said he liked

Colorado so much that if it were possible, he would move there.

DePugh said the next time he did a seminar in Denver, he would have Rabbit join him, and when the seminar was over, they would take a drive to Evergreen to introduce him to some important people. Maybe they would even have a chance to get up to the cave bunker, which was bigger and better and had more equipment than the one outside Kansas City.

DePugh went on to describe similar locations in Hayden Lake, Idaho and other places throughout the west and in other states. When Rabbit questioned him about the Minutemen's philosophy that each member was required to provide his own weapons, he laughed. In the first place, it was necessary for the first line of defense to have their own weapons and to be familiar with them. These hidden weapons were not easily accessible in the event of an immediate catastrophe, but they would be necessary to provide sufficient arms for a small army or guerrilla force.

Once again, DePugh confided that much of this weaponry had been funneled through Central America by his contacts in the CIA and that the weapons could not be traced to anyone. He again recounted that his first contact with the CIA had been through his involvement with ALPHA 66 in Florida, following the Cuban revolution.

The more information DePugh gave him, the more Rabbit worried. He was now in possession of enough information to pose a serious threat to the Minutemen and send DePugh to prison for the rest of his life. He worried about how many law enforcement people DePugh was close to and just how far his network of information sources reached.

Rabbit didn't realize the mental toll the unrelenting stress of the constant fear of being discovered, along with the deadly consequences, was taking on him. He had lived with the stress so long that he thought it just a part of his normal, everyday life. The reality was that the stress was moving him steadily towards a psychological overload. Harris's job was to detect that, but maybe he didn't see it because he was caught up in all the praise that the extremely successful operation was generating. Or maybe he knew, but he didn't want to jeopardize the success for any reason. The symptoms that Rabbit was displaying were increasing, and he was becoming more difficult to handle. Harris found it necessary to constantly reinforce his bird dog to keep Rabbit on point. If praise failed, Harris would remind Rabbit that this was his police assignment and if he quit, he would be blowing his best opportunity to ever receive a promotion. Harris always prevailed.

Upon returning to Los Angeles, Rabbit avoided Harris for several days. Instead of going home after work, he found his way to Ercole's Bar and Grill for a beer or two. It was there he could ease his anxiety and think without Harris hounding him. From there, he dutifully returned to the Valley to wander about, connecting with the malcontents, which demanded his utmost and full attention. He judiciously saved his cocktailing for late at night when he was home safe. Most mornings, he awoke hoping that what happened the day before was just a bad dream…but it wasn't. It was reality, and the cycle continued. Rabbit could feel himself sliding deeper into the abyss but felt helpless to stop it.

When he did meet Harris at a coffee shop on Pacific Coast Highway, he was happy to see Harris smiling. Harris never smiled, and for a moment Rabbit thought maybe the investigation was over. Why else would Harris be smiling? His happiness was short-lived, however. Harris embraced him and told him how happy the deputy chief and the captain were with the work he had been doing. As a matter of fact, the captain had instructed Harris to commend Rabbit. Rabbit wondered what had brought this about.

"They are in seventh heaven over that list you gave us. The membership list DePugh gave you contains the names of several judges, a school administrator, members who have infiltrated the Jewish Defense League—"

Rabbit leaped to his feet and interrupted, "How many goddamn people have copies of that list now? You did just the thing I worried you would do. You promised me this wouldn't happen."

Harris was red-faced. He hadn't expected this kind of reaction from his bird dog.

"Just a minute, Rabbit, do you think we're playing some kind of fuckin' game here? Do you think all this intelligence you've been gathering is for you and me? It's about time you realized you're no longer a vice cop playing with whores. You've stepped up to the big time. Anything you uncover in your operation is shared by everyone in the intelligence chain of command. The reason you collect intelligence is for people a hell of a lot higher up than us to make decisions regarding this information."

Rabbit was still seething.

"You seem to be forgetting something, Detective Harris. We don't have a clue about who is close to DePugh. I'm talking about people inside our department. I'm not a fucking bird dog, I'm a human being who happens to be a police officer. I'm also standing

out on the end of a very narrow limb watching you cut away at
it. I don't give a shit about your silly-ass intelligence if it means
getting my ass blown away. Apparently, you and all the brass put
together don't give a shit about that—"

Harris saw that Rabbit was losing it. He grabbed him by the
shoulders.

"Rabbit, listen to me, I care about you. The brass cares about
you. Nobody wants to see anything happen to you. But you've got
to trust us. You're getting more valuable information than anyone
ever has. The flow of that information is very carefully guarded
against anyone seeing it who is not thoroughly cleared to see it.
There is only one copy of the list, and it is kept in a secure file."

Rabbit stared at him for a beat, and then he merely sighed.
He had no alternative but to accept what he was being told. He
had already convinced himself that there was no turning back on
this road.

Rabbit pulled out his written report and handed it over to
Harris, who began reading it immediately, pouring hot coffee
down his gullet as though it were ice water. Rabbit could see by
the expression on Harris's face that he had struck a nerve. After
reading the first two pages, he started over again. He grunted and
whistled softly as he read. It seemed like forever before he finally
finished. Finally, he set it down and began asking questions:

"What are the exact locations of these guns?

"What are the names of his contacts in the CIA?

"How many guns is he talking about?

"Who was his contact in ALPHA 66?

"What countries were the guns funneled through?"

At each question, Rabbit shrugged and shook his head. Finally, he replied, "If I had answers to any of your questions, don't you think I would have put it in the report?"

"How do we know he isn't just bullshitting?"

"He's not!"

Harris was leaning forward now, dead serious. He held up the report, "Do you realize the kind of shit you have in this? It's an indictment against a federal agency."

Rabbit smiled and nodded his head. "Affirmative. Do you mean to tell me that you don't think the CIA is dealing drugs with Columbia? Or in bed with Somoza and every other nickel-and-dime South and Central American dictator? Give me a fuckin' break."

Harris leaned closer, "This is different. This isn't conjecture. This is a law enforcement agency making a statement about the CIA. I wouldn't be too surprised if most of this information is redacted from your report."

Now it was Rabbit's turn to gloat, "What happened to strict confidentiality that you people keep up there in the ivory tower?"

Harris sighed, "Let's just say that this may be overly sensitive stuff."

The discussion turned away from the report as Harris asked about his trip and the hotel. Rabbit was just as glad to change the subject. As a matter of fact, he would have preferred to drop everything and just end the meeting. At any rate, he thought, he would be a lot more discreet about passing information along in the future.

When they had finally run out of small talk, the two men stood, shook hands, and parted.

David Poiry

Chapter 24
Iranian Package

Now that he was operating in the big leagues, Rabbit found it difficult to remain interested in his mundane connections in the Valley. When he talked to Pizza Man, he knew he wasn't going to get information worth reporting. When he met with Shuster, he knew he was going to be getting information that he had heard a thousand times before. The wannabes at the bookstores and the gun store would tell the same tired war stories and make the same dire predictions of things to come.

Word of his importance in the organization and his success on the lecture circuit had spread, however, making him somewhat of a celebrity among the extremists. He enjoyed the recognition, and it made his work more tolerable. But he wished that this were the main thrust of his assignment, and that he had not managed to infiltrate as far as he had. Unfortunately, there was nothing he could do about it now.

Most of his attempts to contact Charlie were in vain. When he did get to talk to her, the conversations were bland at best. She didn't want him coming around the house because she feared for her life. She felt that with her luck, a night she spent with him would be the same night some crazy would come looking to kill

him and get her in the bargain. For the same reason, she was reluctant to meet him at their rendezvous location in the park, so
most of their conversations were conducted through the services
of the telephone company fondly known as Ma Bell. It seemed to
Rabbit that whenever he did manage to get in touch with Charlie,
she seemed to have been drinking. That was very uncharacteristic
of her, to say the least. It gave him just one more reason to have
an extra few drinks himself.

Then one day he received another cold-phone communication. This time DePugh told him that he was sending a package
containing some letters that he wanted mailed from various Los
Angeles locations. He didn't explain the contents of the letters, but
promised he would when they next met.

When the package finally arrived, it contained ten envelopes,
each addressed to a TV or radio station. Rabbit was fearful of
tampering with the envelopes, not knowing if DePugh might
personally know one of the recipients. Instead, he strained to read
bits and pieces of each one through the envelopes. The gist of each
message was a threat to the government of Iran if the hostages they
were holding were not released. DePugh promised acts of terrorism
against Iranian people anywhere in the world they happened to
be found, starting with the Ayatollah Khomeini supporters who
lived in the United States.

Rabbit had notified Harris when he received the phone call,
and Harris had simply told him to let him know when the package
arrived. Accordingly, Rabbit prepared an intelligence report on
what he had learned and arranged to meet Harris. When Harris
read the report, he asked for the package. Rabbit apologized and

told him he couldn't. Harris attempted a patient approach at first.

"Rabbit, stop screwing around and give me the package."

Rabbit put on an aura of innocence. "I told you, I can't."

Harris's burn was very slow.

"Look, we've been through this before. The reason you got that package in the first place is because you are working for me. Now give me the package."

"Don't tell me, let me guess! You are going to protect the letters and make sure that no one opens them; is that right?"

"Cut out the bullshit. Give me the goddamn package."

"I told you, I can't."

Harris dropped the niceties. "You always have to push me, don't you? Okay. I'm giving you a direct order to give me the package."

"Stick the order up your ass, Detective Harris. I don't have the package. I mailed all the letters this morning. You'll just have to take my word about what they contained."

"You've got some goddamn nerve. I've got a mind to—"

Rabbit interrupted him, "To do what, Harris? Take me off this rotten assignment? Let me get a life for myself again?"

One more time, Harris shot back, "If I take you off this assignment now, you'll never work another one again. I can guarantee that."

Rabbit was confident now. "I've been away from the department manual for a long time, but I can remember a little bit about it. For example, I know I did not violate any orders by mailing those letters, and I haven't done anything that could get me days off. So why don't you get off my ass. I'm sick and tired of this shit job anyway. You'd do me a favor by taking me off."

Harris quickly regrouped.

"Don't go off half-cocked. You've got a shot at a great career when you wrap this thing up. Don't blow it now. Don't give up everything you've worked for. This is your ticket to promotion and a choice assignment."

Harris had opened the door a little bit, and Rabbit could see a little light. He was aware once again that he was a cop and had a future. But he was also aware that his future was not in this current assignment.

"I've had it, Harris. I can't handle this anymore. I'm going fuckin' dingy, seriously. I don't know who or what I am anymore. I've got to get back to the real world before it's too late."

Harris reverted back to the Harris of old and gave Rabbit the same bullshit that had always worked in the past.

"I know how you feel. You've been busting your ass on this case, and you're exhausted. Look, why don't you take off for a few weeks, I'll cover for you. Call Charlie, and you two can get back together. You just need a rest right now."

Rabbit knew he was being stroked, but there was nothing he could do about it. For some inexplicable reason, he couldn't let go of this assignment. He knew he was teetering on the edge of self-destruction, but like in a nightmare, he had no control over the situation. It would have been simple to walk away, but he couldn't convince himself of that. As he pondered, Harris continued.

"Pick some far off, remote place where there is no right or left wing. Just go off someplace for a few weeks and relax and think of nothing."

Rabbit knew of just such a place. It was deep in the Amazon

jungle of eastern Ecuador. In a very remote area of the rain forest, way off the beaten track in the area of the Napo and Curaray Rivers, lived the Indians of the Auca tribe. Rabbit had first become aware of this tribe in an anthropology class in college. He had read the account of five American missionaries who had been killed by the Auca in 1956 while trying to evangelize them.

He was fascinated that, in the twentieth century, there were still remote and primitive tribes that had not yet been influenced by Western civilization. He wanted to explore the area himself and, if possible, make contact with a group of the Indians and learn how they lived such a primitive, unspoiled existence. This would be another great adventure. It would be the perfect place to forget Harris, DePugh, and the dark world of PDID.

After he made his decision, he sought out Charlie. This time he knew it would work out. It took several tries before he finally got to talk to her. She knew better, but she agreed to meet him at the end of the Venice Pier.

The late afternoon breeze had kicked in when Rabbit arrived. It was about a half-hour prior to the meeting time, but he was eager to see her. It was peaceful watching the graceful sloops dancing on the blue Pacific as the wind filled their mains and jibs, causing them to heel from one side to the other as they tacked off toward the horizon, growing smaller with each beat of his heart.

Suddenly he felt as if he had been grabbed by the throat. He turned instinctively and saw Charlie strolling toward him. Her long, shapely legs moved lightly as the gentle wind caught her silk skirt and wrapped it tightly around her thighs. Her long hair bounced and swirled, giving her face a veiled, mystical look.

Rabbit's heart pounded. The rehearsed speech he had prepared flew from his mind as though the words were gulls. With each step she became more beautiful. It became nearly impossible for him to form syllables in his mouth. When he did, he was almost terse. He told her he had some time off coming and he wanted to go off with her to some far-away, exotic place where they could get reacquainted and wash away the grime of the recent past. Charlie was incredulous for a moment.

"You just don't get it, do you? We are through. I don't even know who you are anymore. I loved you with all my heart, but I don't like this paranoid creature that has taken your place. We used to laugh and smile all the time. Life couldn't have been better. But then you took this stupid job where you don't even know what you're doing. You're always looking around to see if you're being followed, and you never even smile. You've lost it. No job is worth the price you're paying. And you've got me afraid of being seen with you. You had better do some soul searching and make some drastic decisions."

There was an awkward silence as Rabbit sat, stupefied. He didn't want to accept the finality of her decision, but he couldn't find the words to argue.

Finally, she broke the silence. "Where are you going this time?"

The words came from him with no emotion. "The Amazon."

He had caught her by surprise. "The what?"

"The Amazon."

"You mean the jungle in South America? The place that's filled with snakes and weird people who've never heard of the twentieth century? Is that the Amazon you're talking about?"

Rabbit just stared at her for a second. "That's the one."

Charlie sighed. "There you have it. You just proved that you've lost it. You're going to a fucking jungle where there are snakes and spiders and flesh-eaters, and you call it a vacation. Let me tell you something, when you get to the Amazon, pull up a tree stump or whatever it is that they sit on down there, and do some serious thinking. I was afraid that this job would get you tossed into prison. Now I'm afraid that prison would be an attractive option. You really do need psychological counseling."

As Charlie turned to leave, time seemed to stand still. No kiss goodbye, no tender touching. She simply turned, and he watched as the wind caressed her skirt and outlined her perfect figure. Just like the sailboats moving gracefully toward the horizon, Charlie grew smaller and smaller with each pounding throb of his heart until she was submerged in the sea of humanity on Venice Beach.

Slowly the symphony of waves slapping the pier and crashing on the sand gave way to the cacophony of everyday life. He wanted desperately to be swallowed up by the earth. This was the lowest he had ever felt in his life. If Charlie only would have let him explain, he knew she would understand.

Chapter 25
Jungle in Ecuador

It was an uncharacteristically gray day in Los Angeles as the big jet lifted off the runway and headed out over the tranquil Pacific before making its turn south. Rabbit peered out the small window and looked at the tiny boats docked in Marina Del Rey below. *They look like toys*, he thought. The whole world looks like a toy from up here, where the air is clear and cool and beautiful. The world below suddenly seemed to be light years away. A fantasy. A dream. He settled back and waited for the flight attendant to bring him a stiff drink to help him drift even further from the world below.

After a long and uneventful flight, the lumbering jet landed in Quito, Ecuador. This was the first leg of his journey to nowhere. Rabbit gathered his meager belongings and cleared customs before making his way over to the small propeller-driven aircraft that would take him on the next leg of the excursion. There was room on the aircraft for six passengers, but Rabbit was the only soul on board for the flight. Apparently, there weren't that many people interested in going over the Andes into the Coca region.

The small aircraft couldn't make it above the majestic mountains of Ecuador, so it maneuvered adroitly through them. This particular leg of his journey gave Rabbit a feeling that he was, in fact, leaving the real world and disappearing into a hole in space.

Upon landing on a postage stamp of an air strip, Rabbit took a jeep to a small hotel near the river. He had elected to restrict the final stages of his journey to Ecuador, where the villages were far from the civilization he no longer liked. Upon checking into the hotel, he was advised that the lights and water were turned off daily at about 8:00 p.m. and would be turned back on sometime in the morning. With that, the clerk gave him a well-used flashlight. He left instructions with the clerk for his outfitter, who had failed to meet him as arranged, to meet him at 9:00 a.m.

This was a far cry from the Hilton. To say the room was basic would be the same as saying solitary confinement in Soledad lacked certain appointments.

A solitary light bulb hung unceremoniously from the ceiling without a shade or globe. It provided just enough illumination for Rabbit to study the paint peeling from the walls. He was only slightly concerned with the creatures that might have called the ancient bed home. Remembering an old police custom, he banged the dilapidated, straight-backed chair that sat adjacent to the rickety table in order to chase the roaches. That wasn't that much of a bother, as he was exhausted from the long journey.

When he awoke in the morning, he cleaned up as best he could with a cold shower. By 9:00 a.m., he was in the lobby waiting. At 10:00 a.m., with still no outfitter in sight, he left and made his way toward the river looking for him. He had made these arrangements over the phone from California, and it had been difficult, as the outfitter spoke only a smattering of English. He provided Rabbit with only minimal information and had lined up a guide who would accompany him on the final leg of his journey.

When Rabbit met up with his guide, Isidro, he realized that this was going to be a challenge. Isidro said he spoke Spanish and the local native language, but the Spanish Isidro was speaking was not like any Spanish Rabbit knew.

Before leaving, Rabbit needed to make a quick stop at an equipment supply store. He needed to buy a hammock, a big straw hat, and a few other necessities that he hadn't had time to buy before leaving Los Angeles.

Shortly, they were at the river. It was just before noon, and Isidro was ready to go. He had his well-used machete and an old, long-barrel Colt .22 revolver whose bluing had long ago worn off. Both the revolver and machete hung from his green military utility belt. He was wearing a bandana, a straw hat, and a khaki military shirt and pants. He was the quintessential jungle guide.

Isidro had already loaded his gear and the provisions for the two-week journey, including six plastic one-gallon milk containers filled with gasoline for the outboard motor. Rabbit made one final quick check of his gear in his backpack. He had his medicine kit, an ample supply of DEET, mosquito netting, salt for the leeches, flashlight, matches, Ka-Bar utility knife, a compass, energy bars, bottled water, a one-quart aluminum cooking pot, one new hammock, and trinkets for the tribe. He was set to go. The only challenge now was the nasty biting insects that were swarming over him nonstop.

Isidro was amused at the gyrations that Rabbit went through trying to keep the pests from eating him alive. He helped Rabbit load his meager provisions into the dugout canoe. This was not a Sears Roebuck facsimile, but an actual tree trunk that had been hollowed out and made into a canoe.

Rabbit thought this was exactly how it was supposed to be. It was just like National Geographic. It had been many years since he had wandered across Europe and through Africa with all his earthly possessions on his back. He'd gotten a little soft in the meantime. This was back to nature, with all the frills and niceties a lifetime away. The only thing that connected them to the twentieth century was the small but fast outboard motor that Isidro had affixed to the canoe.

As they made their way upriver, Rabbit was filled with myriad emotions and overwhelmed by new experiences—the wildlife and creatures that lived in the river were as foreign to him as the language spoken by the natives. He was also filled with awe at the raw beauty of this location. The lush landscape was thick with deep, green vegetation that appeared to be impenetrable to human beings. They were now in the Yasuni area, the ancestral territory of the Huaorani people. The sounds of the jungle were far more enchanting than any he had heard in stereophonic sound emanating from a movie screen.

It was hot and humid. The perspiration poured from Rabbit's forehead. It was like a sauna. They were going upriver, so they had to stay close to the bank and keep away from the fast-running downstream current. This meant they were an easy meal for the ever-hungry squadrons of flying insects that hung out at the river's edge.

It was a very long day, and the journey up the river was very difficult. They traveled a long distance, mostly powered by the outboard motor, but occasionally using their wooden paddles when the river was too shallow to operate the motor. Stopping only once at a very primitive fuel dock, Isidro topped off their plastic gasoline jugs. The gas was kept in glass bottles of various sizes, with corks in the openings to avoid spillage, and they sat on the muddy river bank to prevent accidental breakage. Before continuing on their journey, they took a much-needed short break to stretch their legs after spending the day crouched in a cramped canoe for hours, unable to move.

After refueling they left the Napo River and turned up a small tributary. They were in the thick of the rain forest, where the jungle canopy filters out nearly all the sunlight. They were very much alone. It was a very eerie feeling.

Rabbit felt a deep inner peace in the jungle, a peace that was not possible in the cold, cloak-and-dagger world in which he lived. This was nature in its purest form. The colors, smells, and sounds—it was beautiful. The trees, the plants, the water, and all the living creatures were in harmony with nature. Everything was following the Creator's plan. Rabbit could breathe deep and relax, without worrying about the Department, Detective Harris, DePugh, Harrell, or any of the many other players who posed a threat to him.

He even stopped obsessing about Charlie—where she was, what she was doing, and the biggest concern of all, whether she would wait. The small canoe continued making its way in the shallow water, going deeper and deeper into the jungle, and farther away from the fear and stress that haunted him in Los Angeles.

Each successive branch of the tributary they turned up became smaller, until the canoe was barely floating in little more than a dark, coffee-colored stream.

The rain forest was alive with exotic creatures—it was a biologist's Technicolor dream. There was no room for arachnophobia—spiders were everywhere. Their webs stretched across the streams like bungee cords, housing spiders the size of a man's hand.

The sun was setting, and it was nearly dark. About that time, the boat ran aground, and Isidro became frustrated at their inability to communicate. Rabbit thought he was misunderstanding Isidro's apparent suggestion that they get out of the boat and pull it; he thought Isidro couldn't possibly be suggesting such a foolhardy thing. He had seen many caimans—ferocious South American alligators—and in his limited knowledge (acquired mostly from the movies), he was certain that the river was teeming with man-eating piranha.

Isidro got out of the canoe and continued to wave his arms around and barked out what sounded like an order in Spanish. Rabbit realized he was serious. So with trepidation, Rabbit got out of the canoe and helped to drag it until it was in water deep enough to travel again.

Finally the canoe could go no farther. Isidro indicated that this was the end of the line as far as river canoe travel was concerned. This had to be the heart of the jungle. Together, the men pulled the boat ashore and made camp. There were no tents or fancy fixings, just mosquito netting and the hammocks. Isidro built a small fire to heat up some canned food, and they sat and relaxed. They attempted a bit of conversation as best they could and practiced their English and Spanish words for things like snake, spider, piranha, and alligator.

At the crack of dawn, Rabbit awoke to the smell of coffee boiling on a small fire. The pungent odor was a far cry from the delicious aroma of a Winchell's. Within minutes, Rabbit was wide awake and eager to be on his way.

The two men set off on foot through the jungle. Isidro led the way, and Rabbit was sure to step only where his guide had stepped before. When they came to a lake in the early afternoon, Isidro indicated that they would camp there for the night. Dugout canoes with paddles were on both sides of the lake for anyone to use while traveling in either direction. The lake was perhaps a hundred acres, but by the time they crossed, it would be too late to fish for supper.

Fishing, it turned out, proved to be as crude as life in general in the Amazon. This was not sport fishing from the stern of a fifty-foot boat off the coast of Baja, nor was it even remotely like fly fishing for trout in a mountain stream. Isidro took a stick and tied a long string to it. To the other end he affixed a series of crude, bent hooks that resembled old safety pins. From his backpack he took a piece of raw meat and cut off small pieces for each hook. He dropped the hooks into the water and then slapped the water repeatedly with the end of the stick. Within seconds he pulled the line from the water and had several piranhas clinging to the meat and the hooks. He repeated this a few times, and the two were ready for a feast.

Rabbit had eaten camel and dog in his youth, along with side orders of stir-fried bugs, so he was pretty much ready for anything that he could put into his stomach. Surprisingly, he found the piranha to be quite tasty. At least it provided a change from the diet of bananas and tortillas on which the two of them had been subsisting.

In the morning they took off across the lake and made their way deeper into the jungle, searching for a family of the Auca Indians that Rabbit had been reading about for many years. He wanted to spend some time with them, if possible, and experience their tribal existence firsthand.

As they made their way along, they utilized the bridges made by older trees that had been felled by nature during the heavy rainy season. This enabled them to avoid the jungle floor, which is home for the anacondas, poisonous reptiles, and other deadly forms of jungle life.

After another day's journey, they reached their destination. Following a brief introduction in a language that Rabbit had never heard before, Rabbit and Isidro were invited to sit and talk. The adults were all dressed in bark fiber dyed in brown patterns. The children, mostly toddlers, all ran around naked. The natives were very friendly, and obviously enjoyed the story Isidro was telling them about Rabbit. It was difficult to imagine these people as murderous savages.

Isidro knew this group from previous journeys into the area. He asked if he and Rabbit could stay for a few days with them. All faces were somber as they studied the white-faced, over-dressed foreigner. Rabbit understood the necessity of becoming friends with these people as quickly as possible. He removed his backpack and immediately took out gifts for all his new acquaintances. Prior to leaving the States he had loaded up on silver police whistles, compact mirrors, balloons, fishing line and hooks, and little rubber balls.

His plan worked. The gifts were well-received and brought smiles to the broken-toothed faces of everyone there. For the next two weeks he would pay for his generosity by having to listen to the shrill screech of those whistles. He also brought along a Polaroid camera with an abundance of film. The simple-living natives couldn't have been happier with a gift of the Taj Mahal. The only problem was that they kept scratching off the faces on the pictures in an attempt to see how it had been done.

Rabbit adapted quickly and assimilated into village life. On the second day he awoke with a start at the shrill sound of a whistle. His eyes opened and widened to see the bronzed face of a warrior staring at him, almost close enough to touch. Then the man's grim stare dissolved into a toothless grin. He prodded Rabbit and indicated it was time to rise and shine. Outside the makeshift hut, which was little more than a lean-to, other males stood patiently waiting for him.

The men took him hunting for monkeys, which they would bring down with blow guns. This was a far cry from the weaponry he was accustomed to. He tried to learn to use the blow gun, but never quite got the hang of hunting with it. The jungle was alive with the clatter of screeching monkeys and other amazing sounds emanating from a multitude of exotic birds and other creatures.

Rabbit was impressed with the stealth of the hunting party. They glided silently through the thick growth, stopping occasionally and freezing almost like statues as their eyes scanned the trees and vines for targets.

Suddenly, two of the natives raised blow guns to their lips, and with a whisper, two missiles sped through the heavy, humid air. The unmistakable sound of a dying animal filled Rabbit's ears. Other hunters raced gracefully ahead and returned with two large monkeys.

That night, as would be the case on each successive night, they feasted on the monkey and the catch of the day. Rabbit had no idea what else he was eating, but he decided not to probe. Besides, communication was extremely difficult. Rabbit used crude hand signs and his hosts did the same. All in all, this turned out to be a bonus he had not expected. His mind was taxed to the point of exhaustion every day, leaving him no room to reflect on the problems he had left behind.

This was an almost idyllic existence, and he was filled with happiness. Each day the children would show off their pet monkeys and bugs of all sort just to amuse him. The adults taught him their ways and treated him as one of their own. He couldn't remember having ever felt the peace he had found there.

Rabbit's time with the Auca was everything he had hoped for and more. After spending time with them, he found it difficult to imagine that only twenty years earlier, they had brutally murdered some peaceful missionaries. He couldn't help but wonder if the written account of that incident had omitted some critical facts, as often occurs. Whatever the case, Rabbit found these Indians to be hospitable.

Two weeks flew by, and it was time to start the journey back to civilization. For more than a brief moment, Rabbit considered sending Isidro off by himself. Slipping into a fantasy world, he imagined staying on in the village and never going back to LA and the endless problems waiting for him there. He had enjoyed the simple existence and the warm, friendly villagers. He didn't want to leave.

Part of it was the sadness in the eyes of his newfound friends when they realized that they would never see this funny white boy again. In the future, he would reflect back on this moment and question his judgment.

It was a long, quiet, and uneventful trip downriver back to where he had started out on this adventure—uneventful because he had rapidly acclimated himself to this beautiful, untamed land.

The caimans no longer commanded the fear they once had. He developed a feeling of belonging. Isidro sensed the change that had come over Rabbit, and although he couldn't fully understand it, he respected it. At the end of their journey, the two men stared at each other briefly and then hugged in silence. Rabbit then gave Isidro his backpack and jungle equipment as special thanks, and turned and made his way back to the dingy hotel room he was to spend one more desolate night in before flying back to the States.

As he sat on the broken springs of the dilapidated bed and looked at the peeling paint on the filthy walls, he thought very philosophically about what civilization was really about. As he contemplated, it occurred to him that he had been sober for over two weeks. As a matter of fact, he had never even thought about booze or escape. As he related the dirty surroundings in which he was sitting to the hovel he had lived in early in this assignment, he felt the urge to have a drink come over him. He shook his head at his thoughts and mused to himself, *Welcome back to civilization.*

Chapter 26
Charlie and the Gun

The loud clamor of a ringing phone broke the silence of Charlie's bedroom. She rolled over and picked up the receiver. Seconds passed before she recognized Rabbit's voice.

"What the hell are you calling me at this hour for? You know I don't get home until after three in the morning."

Rabbit was apologetic, but he knew his brief layover in Mexico City waiting for a flight back to LA was his only chance to reach her. He needed her to meet him at the airport with his pistol. Full-blown paranoia had set in, and he could no longer be without his gun. Charlie acquiesced and turned back to sleep.

Hours later Charlie came to with a start. She'd overslept and would have to rush to meet Rabbit's flight on time. First thing, she called and checked the flight's ETA. She then took a quick shower and dressed. Managing a blue collar bar in Gardena left her exhausted, and she'd only gotten a meager four hours of sleep, but tonight was check-cashing night for the regulars and she needed to make it to the bank and secure ten thousand in cash.

Charlie was adamant when it came to promptness. She knew Rabbit's plane hadn't landed yet and there would be customs to clear, but she didn't want to take any chances. So she parked the car and hurriedly made her way to the International Terminal. Rather than take a chance on missing him outside, she went inside to meet the flight. She wasn't thinking about the gun when the conveyor belt swallowed her purse into the x-ray machine.

A formerly complacent security agent suddenly became animated upon seeing the gun on the monitor. The slightly overweight woman nudged her slender male partner and nodded toward the screen. He immediately got on his hand-held radio and called for the Airport Police or LAPD, who had a substation at the airport.

Charlie was baffled when the security guard's supervisor took possession of her purse and led her to a small room nearby. She was told to accompany them and not to attempt to resist, although the thought never occurred to her. After a short wait, two uniformed LAPD officers arrived on the scene. Following a short conversation with the security guard supervisor, they took possession of her purse.

The cop approached her and asked, "Do you have any ID, Ma'am?"

"It's in my purse."

The officer reached into the purse and removed her wallet, which he handed to her. Charlie took the wallet, removed her driver's license, and handed it to the officer. He took a package of field interview cards from his shirt pocket and began copying information from the license.

"Do you mind telling me why you are detaining me?" Charlie asked, as the other officer began to search her purse.

"Yes, Ma'am. It's against the law to carry a loaded firearm."

"Well, it belongs to my husband. He's coming in on a flight from Mexico City, and he asked me to meet him with it."

About that time the other officer came upon the ten thousand dollars and immediately got on his hand-held radio to alert the substation. He then came over and whispered something in his partner's ear.

"And why would your husband want you to bring a gun to him?"

Charlie found herself between a rock and a hard place. She was afraid to identity Rabbit and the undercover assignment, but what choice did she have?

"He's an LAPD officer."

"And why couldn't he wait until he got home to pick up his gun? Or at least until he got to the car?"

Frustrated, Charlie admitted, "To tell you the truth, I forgot I had it in my purse. I thought I had left it in the car. When he called me last night from Mexico City, he was in a panic. He just said I needed to bring his gun and to meet his flight."

"What's his name?"

She told them his name.

"Where does he work?"

"Some secret assignment."

The officer reached down and took her by the arm.

"Okay, let's go. Of course, a secret assignment. Likely story."

Charlie felt the cuffs snap, and in an instant she was led through the terminal to a black-and-white. She had never been so embarrassed in all her life, handcuffed like a criminal. If there had to be a straw to break the camel's back, this was it. Of all the unhappiness Rabbit had caused in the past, this had to be the ultimate. She thought about all the love she had for him and what it had brought her. There had been good times, but they were vastly outweighed by everything that had taken place since he took on this undercover assignment.

When the car arrived at the substation, two plainclothes Narcotics Division detectives were waiting for her. The gun and the large amount of cash fit the profile of a drug smuggler. It was clear they were convinced Charlie was at the airport to meet her connection to buy a large quantity of drugs, most probably cocaine. They locked her in a small holding cell.

The detectives began their investigation by interviewing the arresting officers and running the serial number on the gun. Although they determined that it belonged to Rabbit, they couldn't ferret out where he was assigned. PDID had erased his name from the Department. Several substation officers knew Rabbit and assured the detectives he was still on the job, working some secret investigation. The substation, a branch of the Venice Division, had been Rabbit's assignment before he was transferred to Ad Vice.

This set up a whole new problem. They assumed that Rabbit was flying the narcotics in himself and planning to turn them over to Charlie, who was a courier. No one bothered to reason that if she were a courier, she wouldn't have been in possession of his gun, nor would there be a need to exchange the drugs for money at the airport. Instead, Internal Affairs Division was called and responded to the substation.

Meanwhile, Charlie was detained in a locked, bare holding cell. Eventually, she was escorted out of the holding cell to make her one phone call. She chose to call Rabbit's brother, but as she dialed the number, she heard the guarding officer behind her pick up another phone, dial a number, and begin carrying on a personal conversation with a woman.

While the policeman and his lover were making off-duty date plans, Charlie seized the opportunity. With sleight of hand she carefully slid her driver license from the center of the table toward her. It was critical that she destroy the license before they discovered the code numbers Rabbit had written on the back. He had instructed her that in the event of his demise, the address and combination would lead her to a secure lock box.

After she concluded her call to Rabbit's brother, she was escorted back to the holding cell with the now-concealed license. Charlie had no time to ponder her options. She quickly realized the only thing she could do to protect Rabbit's secret was to literally eat the license.

When she was done, she called out in her sweet, southern drawl, "Darlin', would y'all mind getting me a drink of water? I'm fixin' to die of thirst in here."

While this investigation was taking place, Rabbit's plane landed, but no one from LAPD or airport security was waiting. It didn't take Rabbit long to clear customs, since he had so few belongings. He entered the terminal and looked around in vain for Charlie. It wasn't like Charlie to be late, and he was a little concerned. However, he was exhausted from the flight, and the entire experience had made him somewhat short of patience. He began to imagine that either Charlie was still upset with him and had decided to take her time, or even worse, that she had decided to ignore him completely.

In the cab ride to his home—where Charlie was still living—he stewed, letting his imagination run amok. By the time he reached the house, he was fit to be tied. When he arrived, however, he discovered that Charlie's car was missing and there were no notes left for him to read.

He poured himself a few stiff jolts of whiskey and then called his brother to see if he knew anything about Charlie's whereabouts. His brother confirmed that Charlie had called him earlier with a cryptic message. "She said that when I hear from you, to tell you that she's in custody at the airport. Before I could ask her anything, the phone abruptly went dead."

Rabbit couldn't get any more information from his brother, so he called the substation at the airport. Not only had Rabbit worked the police division that covered the airport, he had worked a patrol car in the Westchester area where the airport was located, so he knew quite a few of the officers assigned there. Although he had transferred out of the division four years earlier, the airport detail was a choice assignment, and very few changes occur in that short a time. He didn't know the officer who answered the phone, however, so he identified himself by his name and serial number.

"I understand you have my wife, Charlie, in custody down there."

The officer put him on hold briefly and then returned.

"Yes, we have. You had better come down here."

Rabbit was a little more than hot at the moment. "Would you mind telling me what the fuck is going on down there?"

"You better come down."

Rabbit slammed the phone down and immediately contacted Harris. He was so angry that he had trouble talking to Harris.

"The motherfuckin' police have Charlie in custody and won't let me talk to her."

Harris tried to calm him down, but to no avail.

"The only reason I'm calling you, Billy, is so you'll know what it is all about when someone else calls you from the airport about me. I am going to tear the fuckin' place down. They better get a crew of badass cops to protect that wimpy-ass boy lieutenant."

"Don't go down there. I'll take care of everything for you."

"Fuck you!" Rabbit slammed the phone down and immediately called a cab.

As he was buzzed through the locked half door, he spotted Charlie sitting in the cramped, barred holding cell. He went berserk, demanding that she be released immediately. Rabbit ran to the holding cell and tried to pull open the door, but it needed a key to be opened. He was raging like a very large, pissed off bull elephant. He pounded his clenched fist on the glass and screamed, "Open this fucking door."

One of the officers grabbed Rabbit from behind in a loose choke hold. Another officer forced his arm behind him in a pain-compliance control hold. Rabbit didn't stop—now he was kicking the door. The lieutenant in charge yelled at Rabbit that if he didn't cease and desist immediately, he would give the order to choke him out, cuff him, and put him in his own cell. Rabbit tried to get loose, but could feel the choke hold taking effect. He realized his actions were not producing his desired objective.

"Okay, I'll be cool. Just let her out of the goddamn cell."

"Can't do that."

Finally, another officious-looking lieutenant entered the room and took charge. "Sit down, officer. We have some questions to ask you."

"Questions? Questions? I have a few questions myself."

The lieutenant cut him short.

"I said shut up and sit down. You have become a focal point of an internal criminal investigation. You tell us what this woman is doing with your pistol and ten thousand dollars, and meeting you on a late-night flight from Ecuador."

"You can investigate me all you want, just let her out of the cell. She hasn't done anything wrong. I told her to bring the gun to me."

With that, Harris entered the room. He must have come from downtown by jet. Rabbit, seeing Harris, began his tirade all over again. Harris managed to calm him down enough to get him seated and then took the lieutenant aside. After what seemed like an eternity, Harris returned and took Rabbit over to the cell. An officer appeared and unlocked the holding cell door.

Charlie looked up and remained seated. She looked so small and fragile sitting there. Her face was pale and devoid of any emotion, which made her look pitiful. Rabbit was overcome with nausea as he looked at her. He had never felt so bad in his life.

Before he could say a word, she simply said, "You and your fucking police world."

Rabbit stood paralyzed as Harris reached past him and took Charlie by the hand and led her out of the cell. Harris then led them outside and placed both of them in his unmarked police vehicle. A few feet away, Charlie's car sat with the doors open. The seats were out, the floor mats on the ground, the contents of the glove box dumped on the front floorboard. The trunk lid was open, the hood was open, and everything was out on the ground. A police dog was sniffing for any sign of dope. Harris told Charlie and Rabbit to wait while he went back inside to straighten everything out.

Rabbit was having an impossible time finding the words to

soothe Charlie. She stared straight ahead in a silent rage. The color was back in her face, and he could see the muscles ripple in her jaw just below her petite ear. Rabbit continued to offer profuse apologies and promises of better days ahead.

Without looking at him, she stated in a monotone, "I have nothing to say to you or any other cop. I just want to go home."

Harris returned to the car and told them he would be driving them home. His partner would drive Charlie's car and follow them.

The usually short drive from LAX to Manhattan Beach seemed like a cross-country journey. The silence was deafening. Even Harris could feel Charlie's silent wrath. Finally, Rabbit broke the silence.

"What took so long to get this thing wrapped up?"

"Well, I had to satisfy the dope cops and IAD, and convince them not to bring the dogs over to your house to conduct a search."

Rabbit went ballistic all over again.

"You mean they were going to have their goddamn dogs sniffing around my house looking for dope?"

"Charlie fit the profile of a drug courier with the gun and all that money, meeting a flight from South America."

"Let me get this straight. My wife, with my gun, was meeting me to buy drugs from me?"

"Well, it got a little screwed up. I was able to get it straightened out."

After a few more moments of silence, Harris reached into his shirt pocket and retrieved a slip of paper, which he handed to Rabbit.

"What's this?"

"It's an OR slip. It gives the date and time Charlie has to appear in court."

Charlie came to life. "I've been arrested? I've been arrested and charged with a crime?"

Harris was apologetic. "Carrying a concealed firearm."

She turned and stared icily at Rabbit, who dropped his head and spoke through clenched teeth. "That does it, I'm out of PDID. I've been shit on for three years, my life placed in danger, I ask my wife to bring my gun to me because I'm in fear of my life, and the fuckin' police department can't even quash a chickenshit thing like that without making a formal arrest?"

Harris said nothing.

"One more thing, where is my gun?"

Harris answered, "The arresting officer booked it into evidence. You'll have to go to court and see if the judge who hears the case will give it back to you."

Rabbit was in total disbelief. "My gun, which I need to protect my life, has been seized by the police department that I work for? Is that what you are telling me? If you think I'm going to go back on the street without a gun, then you are fucking nuts."

Harris said nothing. They drove in silence until they reached Rabbit's home in Manhattan Beach. When they pulled up front, Charlie made a beeline for the front door. Before Rabbit could follow, Harris grabbed him by the arm. Rabbit pulled away angrily.

"Weren't you paying attention? I'm through. Give me a call, and let me know which patrol division I'm assigned to."

Harris was gentle, but firm, "I know how you feel right now, but don't blow everything you worked for. Take a couple of days to think about it, and then we'll talk. Nothing can be done right now anyway."

"I'll take more than a couple days, and I'm not going to change my mind."

Rabbit turned and raced into the house. Charlie was in the bedroom packing a suitcase. Rabbit pleaded with her to sit and listen to him, but she ignored him. He pledged his love for her and promised that everything would get back to normal. After all, she must have heard him tell Harris that he was through.

As she closed the suitcase, she said, "I'll arrange for a van in a few days to pick up the rest of my stuff."

"You don't have to rush out. I'll be staying at the other pad for as long as it takes you to find another place."

Charlie turned and left the house with Rabbit close behind. He begged for one more chance. He couldn't imagine life without her. As she put the suitcase in the car, she turned to him for the last time. "I don't know who you are. You've given up your life and your identity. You're not even a cop anymore. The cops back at the station treated you like any other asshole who wandered in off the street. Take a look at yourself. You're a pitiful wretch who used to be a fun-loving guy. I've had more than enough of you and the assholes you call buddies. Don't ever call me again, and I mean that."

With that, she got into the car and drove off. Rabbit stood in the street watching the car fade into the distance with tears in his eyes. That was the final and cruelest cut of all. The last drop of blood had just drained from his body. The pain in his chest was almost unbearable. They say somewhere that a man feels more pain when he is abandoned by a woman than vice versa. All Rabbit knew was that no other human being had ever felt more pain than he was feeling at that moment.

Chapter 27
Court Hearing

As the days passed, Rabbit became more melancholy. His spirit was gone. He spent most of his time in a bottle, nursing his broken heart. Depression was his only companion. Whatever his goals and objectives had been, he could no longer see them. There was nothing left; it was all gone.

Harris kept him on a long leash and called only occasionally to see how he was doing and if there was anything else he could do for him. That nagging need surfaced from deep within his psyche once again. Not only did he know no other life, he couldn't imagine being anything other than a policeman. His need to succeed had become obsessive. This obsession, fueled in part by alcohol, had created a stone wall between him and rational thought.

The days turned into weeks, and Rabbit found himself reverting back to the life of a Minuteman. He was making contacts with the right-wingers in the Valley and keeping track of everything that was going on. Harris was aware of a very important seminar that was going to be held at the Ramada Inn near the airport, and he assured Rabbit that if he took part in it, he would make up for all the past injustices. By this time, Rabbit had become a hollow shell with little emotion. He felt like the walking dead. The only thing left was fear.

In the meantime, he hired an attorney to handle Charlie's case in court. On the appointed day, Harris warned Rabbit to stay away from the court.

Rabbit was less than gracious in his reply. He told Harris he fully intended to respond to Charlie's attorney's subpoena and would take the stand and lay the whole thing out in the courtroom. Under oath he would tell the judge that as a deep undercover officer, he had infiltrated the Minutemen, the Ku Klux Klan, and other radical extremists, and as a result, he feared deeply for his life, and with no other way to arm himself, he had given a lawful order to Charlie to bring him his police revolver so that he might be able to defend himself in the event of an attack. He went on to say he hoped his testimony would not find its way into the *LA Times*.

Harris now saw the entire four-year investigation being flushed down the toilet.

When Rabbit arrived at court, he learned that the City Attorney and Charlie's attorney had reached a plea bargain settlement. Charlie agreed to plead guilty to possession of a loaded firearm with straight probation and no jail time. Because it was a petty, low-profile case, the professionals in attendance and the smattering of others awaiting their turn on the judicial merry-go-round paid little or no attention to the proceedings.

As the agreement was read to the court, the judge sat in bored passivity. As soon as the case had been adjudicated, the judge took a searching look at Charlie, who was sitting in her best Sunday-go-to-meeting clothes, looking like Mary Poppins. He pardoned himself as he spoke to her.

"Young lady, will you please approach the bench."

She looked at her lawyer, who nodded assent. Charlie approached the judge.

"You don't have to answer me, because this matter is on the record and has been adjudicated. However, you've piqued my curiosity. What were you doing with a loaded firearm?"

Very patiently, Charlie described the entire incident that had taken place on the night of her arrest. The judge was dumbfounded. He asked if Rabbit was present. Rabbit stood. The judge then directed the City Attorney and the defense attorney and Rabbit to all approach the bench.

"This is the most incredible tale I've ever heard in all my years sitting on this bench. Can anyone explain this to me?"

All parties heard Charlie's discussion with the judge, and they all just shrugged.

"Are you all saying that this crime occurred as this young lady just explained?"

The City Attorney nodded. "Basically, yes, Your Honor, as I understand it."

The judge began writing feverishly on court documents. He then looked up at Charlie and declared, "In twelve months, this matter will be expunged from your record."

Charlie smiled. "Thanks, Your Honor."

Then, as an afterthought, the judge asked, "By the way, where is the gun now?"

The City Attorney looked at a folder and stated, "It's booked in Property at LAPD. Since there was going to be a plea on the matter, the arresting officers were not subpoenaed, and therefore, the gun stayed in Property."

"What's going to happen to it?"

"Inasmuch as it was booked as having been used in a crime, it will be destroyed."

"Officer, is this in fact your gun that we are talking about, and are you in fact still a police officer?"

"Yes, to both of your questions, Your Honor," Rabbit answered.

The judge shook his head and stifled a laugh.

"Are we on *Candid Camera* or something?"

The City Attorney's face reddened as he replied, "No, Your Honor."

The judge began writing feverishly again. "I'm issuing a court order to have the gun released to the officer. This is the most asinine set of circumstances I have ever heard of."

As they left the court, Rabbit and Charlie exchanged a few cordial words. She was still very cool, but no longer hostile. Rabbit was thinking with reasonable clarity for the first time in a long time. He exercised complete discretion and kept a respectful distance from her.

After leaving the court, Rabbit went directly to the Property section in the basement level of Parker Center. As far as he was concerned, his gig with PDID was over and there was no longer a need to maintain secrecy. He walked through the door and approached the wire mesh screen, where he was greeted by a civilian bureaucrat who wore a badge proclaiming him to be a property officer. Behind the property officer were rows of packages in seeming disarray, but in reality, all identified and logically placed. Most of the property, whether of evidential value or not, was in various-sized boxes or large manila envelopes.

Rabbit presented the court order to the bored, tired-looking clerk, who read it with care. He looked up and asked for an ID card. Rabbit said he didn't have one, but he would show him a driver's license if necessary.

"What do you mean you don't have an ID? You been fired or something?"

"No, I haven't been fired. Just call Detective Sergeant Harris on 4091."

The officer stared at him for a few beats and then turned and walked away without saying another word. Rabbit waited and studied the walls that were badly in need of repainting and the counter that was worn from so many officers leaning on it waiting patiently for evidence to be brought to court.

Finally, a sergeant returned with the property officer. He held the court order and stared suspiciously at Rabbit.

"Let me see your ID."

Rabbit stared at the overweight sergeant standing in his rumpled khaki uniform. His badge looked as though it had been shined with a Hershey bar.

"I tried to tell this other guy that I don't have an ID card. Just call Detective Sergeant Harris on 4091. He'll vouch for me."

The Sergeant leaned angrily on the counter with his face almost touching the wire screen.

"Every cop has an ID card. Where's yours?"

At another time, in another place, Rabbit would probably have seen the humor in this exchange at the epitome of bureaucracy. But he was still reeling from the unpleasant circumstances that had brought him here. His first inclination was to raise hell, but he bit his tongue and paused for a moment before speaking.

"Look, Sergeant, in my present assignment, I'm not allowed to carry any police ID. Please call Sergeant Harris and he'll explain it to you."

"I've never heard of such bullshit. You're walking around a police building and you're not allowed to carry ID?"

The sergeant walked away without saying a word, and the property officer busied himself with a mound of paperwork. In the meantime, several uniformed officers entered and booked items of property. In each case, the officers had to alter their reports to comply with the rules that were quoted to them.

"You forgot to put the DR number in the upper right hand corner …"

Rabbit thought to himself that he had better brush up on a lot of this crap before he went back into uniform. Hell, he could spend a whole day in here just booking a piece of property.

Finally, the sergeant returned. This time he was holding Rabbit's pistol with the cylinder open. It was a standard-issue four-inch barrel, Smith and Wesson, blue steel revolver. He placed it on the counter with a form attached to a clipboard, which he slid through a slot.

"Fill in where I marked the X, and show me your driver's license."

Rabbit complied and slid the completed form and his driver's license back through the slot.

The sergeant studied the license and stared at Rabbit before sliding the gun through the slot. As the sergeant turned to leave, Rabbit stopped him.

"Hey, Sergeant, what about the holster and the six rounds of ammo that were with the gun?"

The sergeant appeared even more annoyed that he had to explain something so very obvious to an apparently stupid policeman.

"Didn't you read this court order? It doesn't say anything about the holster or ammo."

"It's my goddamn gun, and it was in my goddamn holster with my goddamn ammo—"

The crusty old property sergeant, who had the people skills of a junkyard dog, leered at Rabbit and sternly warned him to watch his tongue and kindly govern himself accordingly or he would write him up on a Department 1.81 personnel complaint faster than a speeding bullet.

He finished by saying, "Now boy, don't give me any more shit. As I see it, your business is finished here. So just run your little old ass outta here before you get in big trouble."

It was apparent the old sergeant did not see himself and Rabbit as members of the same team. Rabbit had been away from the system too long. With no emotion, he thought to himself, *I no longer belong here.* So he turned without another word and left Parker Center.

Chapter 28
Keystone Cops

During the next few days, Rabbit spent most of his time reminiscing and sorting through the notes, photos, papers, and memorabilia that he had hidden away during the past four years. This job assignment had exacted a very heavy toll on his personal life, but what the hell, it had been an extraordinary experience. He had learned a lot about a great many things.

One of the few orders from Harris that he had ignored since the very beginning was to turn in every piece of paper he came into contact with and never to duplicate his written reports. Rabbit had not followed that directive. In fact, he kept copies of all his intelligence reports, handwritten letters from DePugh and members of his family, brochures and flyers announcing the various survival classes Rabbit had taught, photos of the recons, tape recordings sent to him by DePugh, and other stuff. He kept all of it, just in case the people who had so effectively schooled him to lie ever lied to him in turn. He was glad his life of deception was finally coming to an end.

A week passed before Harris got in touch with Rabbit. They arranged for a meeting, at which Harris asked Rabbit to do one more assignment, a big meeting that was to take place at the Ramada hotel out by the airport. Rabbit asked about his transfer. He told Harris that he did not want to stay on in PDID. It didn't matter to him where he would be transferred, he just wanted a regular detective assignment.

That was when Harris dropped the bombshell on him. It seemed as though his rank was "Policeman 3," which was classified only as a detective trainee position. This rank was normally only good for about two years, or until the trainee passed the detective promotional exam. Not only would Rabbit have to leave the division and go back to uniform patrol, but he would have to go back in a downgraded rank.

To say that Rabbit was upset would minimize the magnitude of his despair. Harris had very clearly and explicitly promised Rabbit a promotion to Detective. In fact, this promise had been made on many occasions. The burn was slow in coming, but it had the intensity of an erupting volcano.

Rabbit, fighting the urge to go into a rage, said to Harris, "You do remember that I never asked to come to PDID. I told you from the beginning that I didn't like the idea of investigating these right-wing groups, and that I actually questioned the idea of spying on individuals for their political affiliations. I was happy where I was in Administrative Vice. The captain sent me to detective school and was preparing me for promotion. Then somehow you all manipulated the system and accomplished my transfer into PDID. You promised me if I did the job you wanted me to do, PDID would promote me to detective. When I asked how that would happen, you told me not to worry about it. So was that all just one more bullshit lie from PDID?"

Harris replied, "I'm sorry, that can only happen if you complete the assignment. You can't just bail out and think you're going to be rewarded like that. Just stick with this investigation a little longer and I'll see what can be worked out."

Rabbit was devastated. The whole purpose of living in the underground, giving up his real life, and living in fear 24/7, in danger every minute from a bunch of crazies, ex-cons, and revolutionaries, was to be promoted to detective. And now Harris had twisted those promises around and added additional conditions that had never been discussed in the beginning. It was clear to Rabbit that his options were bleak. The only viable choice after all the effort he had expended was to continue on to the bitter end.

After they separated, Rabbit tried to sift through his muddled brain to find some semblance of reason in all this madness. He reflected on the start of his ongoing love-hate relationship with the Los Angeles Police Department. He thought back to the time when he'd made the decision to become a cop. It was like a vocation to the priesthood in those days. He felt it was a calling more than just a career. He never got to ride the big Harley in the same manner as that cop he'd seen from the car window as a boy, but he had managed to become one of the fabled dragon slayers. The love affair was still there, but it had cooled off considerably. He was a part of the greatest organization in the world, but they were willing to disregard the danger and hard work he had endured for so long and throw him callously away with a downgrade in rank.

His love affair with the LAPD had blossomed into an overwhelming desire to become a detective, and it was an insatiable desire that clouded his reason. He had paid an inordinate price for that goal already. He wasn't willing to give up at this point.

He resigned himself to staying with the investigation until it came to some kind of normal conclusion—whatever the hell "normal" was. Besides, there would surely be some kind of recognition if he waited until the Department called it a day.

So Rabbit one more time went back to his routine and continued to submit his standard reports about the activities of would-be revolutionaries in the San Fernando Valley.

It wasn't too long before DePugh called to make plans for the meeting at the Ramada Inn. As usual, the two men would get together before the event and spend some quality time together discussing the latest world events and their impact on white, Christian America. They would also decide when each of them would give their respective classes.

When Rabbit contacted Harris about the arrangements, Harris told him that this meeting was going to be handled a little differently. The lieutenant in his chain of command wanted to infiltrate the meeting himself, just to see firsthand what really went on and to demonstrate his undercover operating skills. In addition, there would be surveillance of the location in order for PDID to obtain up-to-date photos of all the players and to identify everyone in attendance.

Rabbit tried in vain to discourage this latest plan. He knew that DePugh would pick up on surveillance immediately, and it could very well jeopardize the entire investigation.

There was no need for current photos, except to provide the captain with some show-and-tell to impress the Chief of Police with the wonderful work he was doing. And as far as identifying the people of interest in attendance, Rabbit could tell them in advance who was going to be there. They would be the same people he had been reporting on for several years. The only different face in the crowd would be the lieutenant's, and that would cause a stir among the members.

After a long and difficult discussion, Rabbit was able to get Harris to agree to keep the lieutenant from attending, but he wouldn't budge on the surveillance or the photography.

As usual, DePugh came in to LA in the late afternoon. Rabbit met him at the airport and helped him to get settled in. They went to dinner and enjoyed the modified good life. DePugh was an introvert, and he didn't indulge in alcohol, so there weren't any raucous times between them. It was just friends hanging out. Rabbit had mailed a postcard to DePugh from his recent experience in Ecuador. DePugh seemed genuinely interested in Rabbit's journey into the remote area of the Amazon. He asked many survivor-related questions about traveling in the jungle, village life, and the food. He was fascinated to hear how proficient the natives were with the deadly blow gun, which he thought might be a good tool to incorporate into the Minutemen's arsenal.

They went on to discuss scheduling several Midwest seminars, and most importantly, some new information DePugh had on the KKK. DePugh had a reliable informant in the Missouri Klan who had learned that the Klan in Los Angeles was planning to bomb a synagogue. The idea was for the bombing to make a statement as powerful as the 1963 bombing of the 16th Street Baptist Church in Birmingham, Alabama. This time their target would be Jews rather than blacks.

The Klansmen expected not only that the act would kill some Jews and destroy their synagogue, but that it would also generate enormous press coverage, resulting in a huge surge of recruits for the LA Klan and making abundantly clear the Klan's ability to strike anywhere in America it chose.

DePugh saw another sinister opportunity in the anticipated bombing, and he designed a covert operation to capitalize on it. He told Rabbit it was another special project that required his participation. Hearing those words always set off alarm bells, sending chills up and down Rabbit's spine. He couldn't help but wonder when one of these rogue operations would go off the rails, with disastrous results totally beyond his control. Each time he hoped it would be the last operation he would personally be involved in, and all of this would end.

But that was not going to be the case. Even though he was always filled with trepidation about these projects, he knew that each one he successfully completed developed more trust, brought him closer to DePugh, and provided him deeper access to the organization's most closely guarded secrets.

DePugh's objective was to insert Rabbit into the Klan. This would be accomplished by leaking word that he and Rabbit had had a falling out over Rabbit's extreme anti-Semitic attitude, which DePugh felt was not in the best interest of the Minutemen. DePugh knew the KKK's leader, Shelton, had several times expressed interest in having Rabbit work for the Klan. Most recently he had personally solicited him to join at the National Convention in Kansas City. Rabbit wondered how he knew that.

DePugh expected that Shelton, upon learning of the split, would quickly solicit Rabbit to join the Los Angeles Klan. Once that move was made, Rabbit would be in a position to gather incriminating information on Shelton's participation in the bomb plot. After the bombing DePugh would cause this information to be relayed to the police, and Shelton would be sent to prison, where he would be out of the way forever.

They talked well into the night before retiring. For various reasons DePugh didn't like to come into LA, but he seemed to be pretty much at ease this time. Usually he was very uneasy in this city, perhaps afraid of retribution from ghosts of the past. He had never told Rabbit exactly what or who these ghosts were, but several times he'd alluded to the murder of the leader of the Loyal Order of Mountain Men.

The next morning, DePugh and Rabbit were having breakfast and going over the details of the day that lay ahead when they were joined by some of the other stalwarts of the COTM. DePugh was as jovial as he could be, treating them to some of his philosophical insights before they broke for classes. At the end of the day, they went through their usual routine. A small group met for dinner, after which DePugh feigned fatigue and announced he was going to retire for the evening.

When the others had left for the night, DePugh got together with Rabbit for a private meeting. This time he tried a full-court press to get Rabbit to move back to Missouri with him. Rabbit explained that he was very active out here and had too many roots to just pick up and leave. Besides, he thought DePugh wanted him to run the West Coast for the Minutemen.

DePugh said he had been having second thoughts about California. "There are too many flakes out here. Even the people we can draw upon are a little unstable."

Rabbit agreed that Southern California was different, but pointed out that there were a lot of good patriots out here. DePugh didn't argue that point, but he felt that they had a tendency to branch out on their own and ignore orders from a central command structure. DePugh gave him the Missouri Chamber of Commerce pitch about all the great things there were to do and the great solid patriots who lived there.

DePugh said he even had a place Rabbit could stay for a while until he decided where he wanted to relocate, that he wouldn't be starting out in a community where he knew no one. He already knew most of DePugh's family, and they liked him and spoke highly of him. DePugh went on to suggest that if Rabbit did move back there, he would put him on the payroll at his pharmaceutical company for a cover job, which would provide a way to pay him a salary. His real job would be working at the Minutemen's headquarters. DePugh felt Rabbit could be a real benefit to the organization if he accepted.

Rabbit thanked him profusely for the generous opportunity and his faith in Rabbit's potential to be an asset to the organization. He said he would think about it and see if he could work out a move.

Knowing PDID, Rabbit was afraid to tell them about DePugh's plans. They would probably tell him to go along with it and move to Missouri. He just couldn't justify in his mind being a Los Angeles Police Officer and living in Missouri.

There was a deeper concern stirring in Rabbit's mind. For some time, he had been gradually buying into the program of the ultra

Right Wing, not to the detriment of the Police Department, but enough that he began to believe in the possibility of an imminent, violent overthrow of the United States government. He had become convinced that Armageddon was just around the corner, and he didn't want to get caught back in Missouri when the revolution began.

The next day, DePugh was more withdrawn than usual. When the group broke for lunch, DePugh excused himself and went to his room, where he stayed by himself. When the convention ended that Sunday afternoon, DePugh didn't want to get together with anyone. He spoke only to those he absolutely needed to speak to. When the last class ended, DePugh went straight to his room and packed. He declined an offer from Rabbit to take him to the airport, saying that he would just take a cab. Rabbit knew enough not to question him. DePugh merely told him that he would call him soon.

That evening at Parker Center, PDID held a debriefing. Unlike most detective divisions, there was very little horseplay in the inner sanctum of this division. The great majority of men and women who were assigned to PDID were hand-picked, talented investigators whose loyalty and dedication knew no bounds. They were all hard-working, tenacious officers who could be depended upon to function in an outstanding manner on any assignment throughout the Department.

While assigned to PDID, though, they were similar to the men and women assigned to Internal Affairs. This was serious business, and displays of grab-ass were frowned upon.

On this particular evening, however, the mood was lighter than usual. Lighter, that is, except for the martinet who bore the rank of lieutenant. He wore his customary air of arrogance, looking like the Hollywood version of a Gestapo official preparing to interrogate a downed American flyer. His manner quickly changed when the captain entered the squad room.

The captain had been given a preliminary briefing and was well aware of what to expect. As usual, his mood was pleasant as he greeted all the personnel present by their first names. He was all smiles as the lieutenant extolled the brilliant manner in which the surveillance of the Ramada meeting had been carried out—no one knew they were there. The lieutenant and one of the detectives had managed to attend the classes, and the lieutenant's star bird dog had stolen the show with his classes on survival. They shot about a dozen rolls of film and got photos of everyone. The captain was filled with unaccustomed glee.

"Wait until I show this stuff to the boss. Nobody has ever infiltrated this far into the extreme right before."

The lieutenant added a bit more fuel, "I guess the captain over in Ad Vice will be a little unhappy when you lay out the incredibly successful deep cover operation that 757 pulled off for us, especially since we stole our operator from under his nose."

"A little unhappy? That arrogant bastard will be totally pissed off. Besides, the boss really needs something like this. He's getting so much flack from those commie assholes on the left and the ACLU, he'll be able to say that we work both sides of the fence."

That was the most important aspect of this entire investigation, looking good in the eyes of the chief. It didn't matter that the chief would have forbidden many of the methods and techniques that were utilized. Unfortunately, the chief was not always informed of these things. The overriding concern was one-upping the other captains. This would truly be one of those coups for PDID.

Rabbit didn't sleep especially well that night. He knew what was bothering DePugh. Hell, it didn't take a rocket scientist to see all the cops that were around the Ramada Inn. Everyone in the Minutemen avoided having their pictures taken. They were always on the lookout for cameras. Rabbit saw an awful lot of cameras over the weekend. He could also spot the cars carrying detectives all around the hotel perimeter. He knew DePugh had seen them. He tossed and turned all night wondering if he would become the suspect in the tipping off of the cops. That fear stayed with him for the next couple of days.

On the way home from work on Tuesday, he drove his habitual route, which took him along Vista del Mar, past Dockweiler Beach. On this day, he decided to break from his normal routine and stop to walk along the beach. As is always the case on beaches in Southern California, there were many sun worshipers seeking the perfect Coppertone tan. Thanks to a total lack of waves there were almost no surfers. If this had been Rockaway Beach in New York or Myrtle Beach in South Carolina, Rabbit would have been totally out of place strolling along the sand, fully dressed in his airline uniform and work boots.

But California is the beloved land of the free spirit. Rabbit wasn't even noticed as he plodded along the sand and talked softly to himself. Even the tourists looked at him and assumed he was a poet in the throes of creation, or perhaps just another California fruitcake.

Rabbit couldn't have cared less. He had far too much on his mind to be concerned with the thoughts of unimaginative tourists. He had to conjure up a story for DePugh to explain why the police might have been at the Ramada Inn. He couldn't believe everything that had transpired. Here were the super sleuths, the Department's answer to the CIA. Spies, masters of the secret investigation! Surveillance specialists! They looked to him like something out of a Mack Sennett Keystone Cops comedy. It might not have been as apparent to others, but as far as he was concerned, the cameras were ubiquitous. There were so many detectives that they seemed to be falling over each other.

His own safety was of course Rabbit's primary concern. It didn't occur to him that most of what was evident to him was only obvious because he knew they were going to be there—he knew who and what to watch for.

As he ambled along the beach, he drifted into a trance. The paranoia had a strange hold on his mind, which prevented him from viewing anything rationally. He was so preoccupied in his thoughts about the surveillance fiasco, he was oblivious to the tide, which had come in and was splashing water up over his boots. The cold water snapped him back to reality. He suddenly realized he had walked nearly a mile from where he'd parked his truck. As tired as he was, he turned around and jogged back to the truck, climbed in, and drove home. He had a report to prepare.

When he walked into the house, he was greeted by Buddy, his roommate.

"Man, Rabbit, you look like the wheels came off your cart. Grab a beer from the fridge and come out on the patio. Let's sit back and watch the most beautiful chicks in the world go by."

Rabbit grabbed a yellow tablet and sat down at the kitchen table to start writing his report. He knew Harris would be on his back for it.

"Can't. Got work to do."

Buddy stopped and stared at him for a beat. Buddy was a highly-decorated Marine Corps veteran of Vietnam. He had done several tours over there and could be classified as a true, proven patriot. When Buddy had finally been discharged from the Marines, he'd joined the LAPD for a short while, so he was no stranger to the machinations of the Department.

Early in their current relationship, Buddy had asked only once what the nature of Rabbit's investigation was. When Rabbit said he couldn't talk about it, Buddy had accepted that and never brought it up again—until now. The wiry, handsome man pulled up a chair and straddled it. He leaned on the back of the chair with his forearms and sipped slowly from a long-necked Budweiser. Rabbit ignored his stare and kept writing.

Finally, Buddy broke the silence, speaking barely above a whisper, "What the hell is going on, man?"

Rabbit looked up at him. "What are you talking about?"

"I'm talking about you. I don't know if you are aware of it or not, but you are all screwed up."

Rabbit shook his head and went back to his writing. "I don't know what you are talking about."

Buddy slowly rose from the chair and took a long swig from the bottle before talking again.

"Rabbit, take a look at yourself. You used to have a reputation of being a big-ass party animal, always fun to hang out with. Any time someone was down, all they had to do was come around and Rabbit would get them to laughing and feeling good again. I can't remember the last time I heard you laugh. I don't know what you're supposed to be doing for the Department, but it ain't right. I've read some of the books you've been keeping, and it's all dangerous bullshit. You're running around with a bunch of psychos, and it's rubbing off on you."

Buddy threw the empty bottle in a trash can, which caused a loud clatter. He jerked open the refrigerator door and pulled out another beer.

Rabbit threw down the pencil he was using. He said, "Listen, Buddy—"

But Buddy interrupted, "No, you listen. You're destroying your whole life. You had a dynamite woman who loved you and you threw her away. You said a million times that she was the love of your life, and now she's gone. You don't have any friends anymore, and you don't even care. You're a fuckin' robot who is consumed by this revolutionary bullshit 24/7. You bought into it lock, stock, and barrel, and it has taken you way over the edge. Brother, you got to snap out of it, this shit's not real."

Rabbit pushed away from the table. "You don't get it, do you? This whole society is about to blow up in your face, and all you can think about is beer and broads. We're about to see a revolution in this country, and its not something to laugh about. Maybe that's why I don't laugh anymore."

Buddy shook his head and put the beer on the table. He walked over to the door and opened it. Just before leaving, he turned around and made one more attempt at getting through to Rabbit.

"You poor fool, in addition to your loaded AR-15 rifle with the banana clip under the bed and your 9mm pistol under the pillow, your room is packed floor to ceiling with freeze-dried food, cases of bottled water, guns, ammo, and enough survival equipment to equip a Marine battalion. Man, you don't get it, you have some serious issues. For your information, you left reality a long time ago."

Chapter 29
Target Spooked

Rabbit had finished his report for Harris and very judiciously left out the majority of his criticisms of how the amateur surveillance had been conducted. As he sat at the table reflecting, his mind returned to what Buddy had said earlier about him drifting off from reality. That really bothered him, as he had a great deal of respect for Buddy and his opinion. On the other hand, he knew Buddy wasn't getting the big picture—he didn't have the depth of information Rabbit had. Maybe in time Buddy would get it, but right now that was too depressing to think about, so he decided to pour himself a stiff drink and relax before retiring to bed.

About the time he was starting to get a slight glow on, the phone rang. It was DePugh calling with coded instructions to get on the cold phone. The glow left him immediately. This was about to be the moment of truth. He still had no idea what to say if DePugh asked him for an opinion. The only thing he could think of was to marvel at DePugh's powers of observation and tell him he hadn't noticed anything unusual. He got dressed and jogged over to Marine and Highland to await the call.

After a few minutes, the phone rang with a shattering clang. His heart pounded as he answered it. DePugh was matter-of-fact in his tone.

"Rabbit, I hope I didn't alarm you the way I left after the seminar on Sunday. I had to get out of there as quickly as possible, and I didn't want you to drive me because that would have drawn extra attention to you."

"What are you talking about, Bob?"

"You may not have noticed it, but that place was crawling with cops. I have become very sensitive to it over the years; a few years in Leavenworth will do that to you. I spotted several cops taking pictures of us, and others sitting in cars all around the hotel."

Rabbit tried to sound concerned. "Are you sure they weren't just tourists?"

DePugh was almost in a panic. "No, they weren't tourists. The cops had an army out there. I don't know if they were feds or locals, but it doesn't make any difference. I do know one thing for sure, though: that's the last time I'll ever go to Los Angeles or any other place in Southern California. It's just too hot for me, and too easy for me to be set up. I'll never go back to prison again."

"Is there anything I can do for you?"

"No! Just try to keep a low profile for a while. I'll explain a lot of things the next time I see you. I don't want to discuss it, even over a cold phone. I'll be in touch soon."

With that, he hung up. Rabbit was more relieved than he had been in months. The end was finally in sight. He went back to the apartment and took out the report to put in a description of the phone conversation. He picked up the bottle of Jack once again, but this time in a different frame of mind. The result, of course, would be the same—a protective wall from reality.

Work dragged on interminably the next day. Rabbit had a meeting scheduled with Harris, and for a change there would be nothing but good news, at least from his perspective. He was feeling so good, he asked for the meeting to take place at Gladstone's, where Sunset Boulevard runs into Pacific Coast Highway near Malibu. This was a special kind of place where the patrons and the employees all seem to enjoy themselves.

Rabbit got there early and got a booth next to the window. As he sat and sipped his coffee, he looked out at the beautiful, peaceful Pacific and watched the throngs of seagulls swoop down on the beach to pick up morsels thrown by diners who were determined to spoil these graceful creatures. He was at peace with the world. Let there be a revolution. Maybe he could get Charlie and take off for some safe haven like Tahiti or Australia.

Rabbit's reverie was soon interrupted by reality. Harris slipped into the booth across from him, and they exchanged greetings. A pretty, young waitress approached the table and set down a menu. Harris waved her off brusquely, telling her he wanted only coffee.

Rabbit quickly added, "My dad is always in a bad mood until he finds out that I'm not going to borrow money."

The waitress giggled politely and hustled off. Rabbit slid the report over to Harris and said, "The end is in sight."

Harris scanned the report briefly and gave Rabbit a quizzical look before poring over the papers slowly. He didn't acknowledge the waitress when she placed the coffee in front of him. She looked at Rabbit and wrinkled her nose.

When he'd finished the report, he looked up and said, "What are you talking about, 'the end is in sight'?"

Rabbit couldn't believe that he didn't get it.

"It's right there! DePugh is never going to come to Southern California—and especially LA—again."

"So what?"

"So, if he's not in Los Angeles, what business do we have investigating him?"

"The Minutemen are still in this city."

Rabbit shook his head.

"The would-be patriots in this city don't pose any kind of realistic threat without DePugh. They're mostly armchair warriors and weekend survivalists who like to do a lot of talking."

"Wrong! These are still the same dangerous bunch of assholes who could go off the deep end at any time. It's even more important than ever for you to keep in close touch with DePugh now."

Rabbit turned and stared out the large window and seethed. He was totally depressed. He felt like he was in a maze with no way out. He now realized Harris no longer had control of the investigation. Whoever had seized control was using Rabbit to accomplish some agenda without any regard for him. It was clear to Rabbit that Harris had been reduced to a messenger.

The only time he felt even the least bit safe while operating was when he was close to home. He felt totally naked when he was out of state and away from any kind of protection. Now it looked as though he would be expected to work almost entirely out of the city.

"You just don't give up, do you? I mean, when do we call it a day? Am I going to stay with this until it's time to retire? Am I never going to get a chance to study for a promotion exam? This is bullshit, man. I want to be a cop again. I want to hold up my head and be proud of what I do. I'm getting sick and tired of being scared to death all the time, waiting to make a slip and have some son of a bitch off me."

Harris's usually professional manner softened. He had been warned by his superiors that this was a gold mine, and ordered to keep Rabbit at all costs.

"Listen, you're the best we got. You're too smart to make any slips. I don't know when we are going to terminate this investigation. It's not my call. But you've got too much invested already not to see it through. It shouldn't be that much longer. Just hang in there."

Rabbit got up and threw a couple of bills on the counter for the tip. He knew that Harris would be frugal.

"I'll keep in touch."

Harris sat there for a while longer and stared out the same window. He didn't see the same things Rabbit had seen earlier, but he began to relax.

He really liked Rabbit, but he was the consummate supervisor, totally dedicated to carrying out the wishes of his superiors. He knew that Rabbit should probably be pulled from his assignment, but that wasn't going to happen—at least not now. Rabbit was just a bird dog, but Harris himself wasn't much higher on the totem pole. Besides, he still wanted the long sought-after machine gun cache and a chance to make lieutenant. Rabbit and this investigation were his ticket to that end.

Chapter 30
Machine Gun Confirmation

It occurred to Rabbit that this assignment was not one of life's vicissitudes. This in fact was his life. It was just as well, though, because he would be on the ground floor when the revolution came, and there was no doubt in his mind that it was imminent. At least he would have a head start in running for the hills.

He continued to meet with the locals and to visit the appropriate locations. He continued to submit meaningless reports about plans that would never reach fruition. The bravado of a few fools was enough to keep several analysts busy, and that was probably all that really mattered. His heart was no longer in the investigation. It was just a fog that he now lived in.

By now it was December, and very little was happening. Christmas was coming, and everyone seemed too busy to be involved in radical activities. The slowdown in revolutionary activities made Rabbit even more depressed. As stressful as the job at the airport was, it didn't give him enough to think about to keep his mind off his misery.

This holiday season would be the first in a long time without Charlie, and that gnawed at his heart. Every moment with her had been special, but Christmas had been even more meaningful. His

self-pity made him even more vulnerable to the paranoia that had
seized his brain. He could no longer envision anything bright or
happy in life.

Just prior to Christmas he came home from work and found
that Buddy had decorated the Christmas tree with little rubber toy
soldiers in different fighting poses. Rabbit couldn't find the humor
in it, and he and Buddy had words. Buddy genuinely felt sorrow
for what was happening to his friend, but there was nothing he
could do for him. Over the past few months, their interactions had
been civil, but cool. Neither invited the other to partake in any
kind of camaraderie. Buddy was sure Rabbit was losing his grip on
the rope, but he was at a loss for what to do. He couldn't believe
Rabbit's control could not see it—he had to be blind.

For the next few months Rabbit roamed the San Fernando
Valley like a zombie, drained of all emotion and life. Ever the actor,
he concealed his depression well enough that it was only evident
to those who really knew the man he had been.

Winter and spring passed, and summer came around. Rabbit
received a summons from DePugh to meet him in Sacramento
for another seminar. There was nothing unusual about this, but it
gave him something to do. If not for the deception and the danger,
he would have enjoyed the experience—it got Harris off his back,
and there was only so much he could report from the bookstores
and gun stores.

When he checked into his hotel in Sacramento, DePugh contacted him almost immediately. Ever since Rabbit had told him that he
was divorcing Charlie because she was growing unsympathetic to
the cause, DePugh had tried to bring him closer to his own family.

He and DePugh's daughter Rose became close friends, but they never quite became romantically involved; Rabbit's deception made that impossible. In another time and another place, it certainly could have happened, however, and by all appearances Rabbit seemed like the ideal type of man to become Bob DePugh's son-in-law.

The two men and the young lady had been in touch with each other by telephone and letters, but this was the first time Rabbit and DePugh had been face-to-face since that day at the Ramada Inn. DePugh reiterated that he was disappointed that Rabbit couldn't come back to Missouri for the Christmas holidays, but he certainly understood.

That first night, DePugh spent a great deal of time reminiscing about the past, and how much he missed the excitement of the field work he used to do. In a bizarre move, he then took Rabbit outside to demonstrate his prowess at conducting reconnaissance under the cloak of darkness. Dressed in ordinary sportswear, slacks, and polo shirts and wearing leather street shoes, the two proceeded to crawl through a bushy area that bordered a freeway, and then over a chain-link fence. They then managed to cross four lanes to the center divider, which was another chain-link fence raised about eighteen inches above the asphalt. This one they crawled under. Then they darted across four more lanes of traffic to the far side of the freeway without being detected. Rabbit expressed concern about what would happen if they got caught by a Highway Patrol officer.

DePugh proclaimed that to be impossible. He was far too skilled to be detected. After catching their breath, the two made their way back across the freeway into the relative safety of the darkened bushes. DePugh pointed out that one of the reasons he was so opposed to smoking was that if either of them had been smokers, this would have been a time for them to light up, which would have given away their position to the enemy. He also said that he was in pretty good shape for his age, but he would have to improve very quickly. Rabbit took that as an ominous sign.

When they returned to the hotel room, DePugh slipped into a melancholy, reflective mood. He appeared to be wrestling with himself about something.

Rabbit's paranoia was rising faster than Missouri flood waters. "Something bothering you, Bob?"

DePugh studied Rabbit for a second and then sighed. "Do you remember when I left Los Angeles abruptly and said I was concerned that there had been a setup?"

Rabbit thought he was about to be uncovered. "Yeah."

DePugh leaned back in his chair and stared briefly at the ceiling. "I think I already told you the story about William Hawthorne and the Loyal Order of Mountain Men, but I didn't tell you all the details." He leaned forward and gently rubbed his forehead with one hand. Rabbit half expected him to say, "Bless me father."

DePugh continued in his soft monotone. Ordinarily, he was not given to long stories, which was good, because his speech was sleep-inducing. But he held Rabbit's attention during this soliloquy.

Soon after the Minutemen organization was formed, DePugh traveled around the United States on a recruitment mission. It became obvious that there was a dire need for a platform for ultra-conservative ideas. The Cold War had had a profound effect on the minds of mainstream America, and predictions of communist world dominance were running rampant.

It seemed, however, that the only voice being heard was the voice of liberalism, due to the liberal views of the vast majority of news media.

As a result, DePugh was greeted with open arms by a large audience of patriotic Americans. His recruitment effort was directed toward the radical right, but he realized that he needed support and sympathy from the reasonable right, which was and is the heart and soul of America.

When he came to California, DePugh became aware of a group of right-wing radicals called the Loyal Order of Mountain Men. This group, led by a man named William Hawthorne, was based in Southern California. DePugh and Hawthorne had a great deal in common and soon became fast friends. The Mountain Men were a little more radical than the low-key DePugh preferred, but it was an alliance he couldn't pass up.

Together they did quite a lot to build their respective organizations, and they carried out a number of hate missions against the radical left and various other groups. It wasn't long, however, before familiarity bred contempt. Eventually, DePugh said, he began a clandestine relationship with Hawthorne's wife. When Hawthorne eventually found out about it, their friendship was over.

DePugh didn't admit it, but Rabbit would come to find out some time later that the FBI suspected DePugh had been involved in Hawthorne's murder. At any rate, DePugh told Rabbit, Hawthorne was dead and his son and closest followers held a vendetta against him. He was afraid for his life, and he was certain that a faction of the Mountain Men had set him up with the police at the Ramada Inn.

There was no way that DePugh would ever go back to jail again. He wasn't opposed to confronting his enemies, but he couldn't cope with law enforcement surveillance. For that reason, he would never again return to Los Angeles.

DePugh then told Rabbit about a large cache of machine guns hidden away in the Los Angeles area. A woman named Joan had been holding onto them for years, but it was time for him to relieve her of that responsibility. Something had happened, and Joan was worried about being in control of the guns.

"She is getting older, and she is afraid of getting caught and doing a long prison term, and maybe taking her old mother down with her. The mother is in frail health and is a real liability. If she fell into the hands of the Feds, she would cause a lot of damage. It could bring us all down."

He wanted Rabbit to take possession of the guns and hold onto them until given further instructions. DePugh sensed that the end was rapidly approaching and that they would have to get the guns distributed quickly to the units in the area that needed them.

DePugh went on to explain that after Rabbit had control of the guns, he would receive further orders. DePugh then took out a dollar bill and tore it in half. He gave half to Rabbit and told him that he would give the other half to Joan. Rabbit would be contacted later with a phone number to call Joan, at which time he would be given further instructions.

Then as an aside, he asked Rabbit if he still had that list of names of members that he had given to him earlier. Rabbit's heart raced as he lied. He said that he had hidden it away so that no one would ever see it. DePugh gave one of his rare, soft laughs.

"That list contains many phony members. I put it out as a test of our security. It is peppered with the names of a lot of prominent people who don't even know we exist. Even intelligence agencies have lapses, and I knew that some of those prominent names might find their way to the press if the authorities got their hands on it. In its present form, the list is meaningless."

Rabbit couldn't hide the expression on his face, but fortunately DePugh misinterpreted it. "Now don't be offended. Nobody suspected you of being a spy or anything like that. This was one of the standard operating procedures I told you about in which we conduct security tests on our members."

DePugh instructed Rabbit not to throw the list away. In a short time he would receive a letter in the mail containing a code that would enable him to decipher the list. Printed on the letter would be seemingly random numbers and alphabetical characters that, when applied to the list, would separate the phony names from the true names and indicate their level of involvement. Instructions on how to employ the code would be sent in a second letter. Both letters would be delivered to Rabbit at his airline work address in order to avoid the possibility of the Feds intercepting his mail at his personal residence.

The seminar went according to plan, with no glitches like the ones that had occurred in Los Angeles. DePugh reverted back to his old self, and once again it was business as usual.

After the seminar, Rabbit returned home, but he was more somber now than ever. He had an ominous feeling about the ramifications of his next mission.

Chapter 31
The Exigent Report

When Rabbit arrived in L.A. he went straight to a phone and called Harris to request a meeting. He then went home and began writing his report on the explosive information he had just gotten from DePugh. When he was finished, he went to bed, but sleep was more elusive than usual. His mind raced, and he had cold sweats. Even nightmares would have been better than this—if he could only get to sleep.

He finally did fall asleep, but it wasn't very long before the irritating talk radio voice emanating from his alarm clock shattered the early morning silence. Why is it, he wondered, that after sleep finally kicks in, it's impossible to awaken fully for what seems like an eternity? Even a shower failed to bring him to a fully-conscious state. After gulping down a full pot of coffee, he was ready to face the make-believe world he had created.

After work he met Harris at a coffee shop on Manchester Boulevard, near the airport. As usual, he got there first and selected a seat that afforded him a view of everyone entering the shop and enabled him to protect his back, which placated his paranoia.

He studied the people sitting at various tables and at the counter and thought about the microcosm of humanity they represented.

There was the couple in their late teens who shared a look of young love. They stared at each other and giggled and played with each other's food. Rabbit wondered if he had ever been that young or that much in love.

At another table, a harried couple with two small children gulped their food as they tried to keep the children amused and quiet. The youngest, just a baby, sat in one of those terrible contraptions used to restrict the movements of infants. He was more than a handful for his mother, who was kept busy picking up everything he threw on the floor.

Not far from them, an overweight matron sat smiling at every movement the baby made and repeated over and over how cute he was. Her paunchy husband failed to see anything cute about the little one, however, and he wore a mask of disdain for the infant's squeals.

Rabbit thought about the blissful ignorance they all shared. America was about to come apart at the seams, and they were preoccupied with meaningless concerns. The saddest part of all, Rabbit thought, was that they represented the whole spectrum of age and social strata.

His thoughts were interrupted when Harris entered and took a seat, completely unaware of Rabbit's precautions and not remotely concerned with safety.

"Hi, how was the trip?"

Rabbit shoved the report over to him. "Not bad."

A waitress brought over a previously ordered cup of coffee, which Harris sipped as he began to peruse the report. He went through it quickly, with half a smile on his face.

Rabbit studied him, waiting for a response.

Harris suddenly turned somber, and then his mouth dropped open with astonishment. He went back to the previous page and read the material more carefully.

Finally, he asked, "Where are the guns?"

"I don't know yet."

"What kind of machine guns? How many?"

"You know as much as I do, Billy."

"When are you going to pick them up?"

"Billy, it's all in the report. I have to wait for instructions."

Harris shook his head and stuffed the report into the leather folder he always carried. "This is pure dynamite."

"I thought you would find it interesting."

Rabbit was displaying an uncommon bravado, but his stomach was churning. He knew it would be senseless to ask any questions about his own future at this point, so he slipped into his operating shell. Harris usually stretched out these meetings with Rabbit in order to keep their bond in place, but he had to get this information up to his boss right away. He threw a couple of bills on the table and excused himself.

"I've got to get this up to the lieutenant. He'll jump up and down when he sees this. Of course, he's not going to be overly happy when he finds out that the secret list you gave us was a phony."

Rabbit stared blankly back at Harris. "Why would that surprise you? Did you think we were dealing with a fool?"

Harris ignored the remark and turned to leave. "See ya."

"I'm sure."

As Harris left the restaurant, Rabbit stared into his coffee as he spun the cup around on the table. He felt a peace of mind about his own safety, having discreetly left out of the report DePugh's intention to forward him the code to decipher the list. Harris and PDID would now believe the original list was a complete phony of no value, and would stop investigating the names on it, eliminating the possibility of a security leak. It was now as if the list had never existed.

##

Harris scraped the bottom of his car as he mounted the driveway and sped past the small guard shack and into the underground parking area at Parker Center. He swore mildly as he drove up and down the aisles looking for a parking space. He mumbled to himself, "Why the hell aren't some of these bozos out investigating a crime or doing something like police work?"

For some reason, even the taboo spaces along the fire lanes were filled. Frustrated, he drove back out and around the block to the upper deck. The civilian guard recognized him and let him enter. The upper deck was reserved for select personnel vehicles and police cars that were not used in undercover work. Harris found a space and made his way into the building.

As he waited for an elevator, he wondered what had ever happened to old "Mr. Otis." That had been the nickname of the elderly gentleman who had monitored the elevators in Parker Center back when it was called PAB, the Police Administration Building (it was still called PAB by the old-timers). Mr. Otis was always on duty in front of the bank of four elevators, with the clicker he used to alert people to the arrival of the elevators that had been summoned for them. He constantly fidgeted with the electronic panel on the wall, giving all present the impression that he actually controlled the elevators. Whether he did or not, the elevators always seemed to work more smoothly when he was on duty.

Harris finally managed to squeeze onto an elevator that had filled up on the ground floor level. When he entered the secure offices of PDID, he went directly over to the lieutenant's desk.

"757's report. It's hot."

The stiff, somber martinet initialed a document he had been reading and threw it in his out basket. He took the report from Harris, leaned back in his chair, and began reading. His reactions were the same as Harris's had been when he'd first read it. He grimaced about the secret report.

"Damn! We've disseminated some of that list already. We're going to look like fools if we try to recant. If the list was made up, how do we know that this business about machine guns isn't all bullshit?"

"Well, we don't know that, but I don't think DePugh would have told the truth about the list and then turned around and tested him again."

The lieutenant asked the same question Harris had asked Rabbit earlier, and received the same answers. He leaped to his feet. "C'mon!" he said.

He led the way into the captain's office. The captain was finishing up a phone conversation, and with a smile waved for the two men to take a seat. As they waited, the lieutenant leaned over to Harris, "Are we sure this isn't some kind of a setup?"

Harris whispered back, "757 is as good as gold with DePugh. We can take this to the bank. Unless, of course, you want to gamble…"

The captain hung up the phone and turned to the men. "Good news, I hope?"

The lieutenant's reluctance was hardly perceptible.

"Good and bad, sir."

He handed the report over to the captain, who put on his reading glasses and began reviewing the document. Like Harris and the lieutenant before him, he reacted when he got to the part about the phony list and the machine guns. Once again, basically the same questions were asked, with the same responses.

The captain leaned back and smiled. "The chief needs something like this right now. He's still getting a lot of flack from the Left and needs to show that he doesn't favor the Right."

The lieutenant was very matter of fact. "I doubt that the liberal muckrakers will ever find anything positive to say about the chief or any of us."

"True, but at least it gives him some ammunition." He pressed the comm-line button on his phone and spoke. "Helen, call the chief's office and see if I can get a few seconds. It's very important."

The captain adopted a serious air and leaned forward, "I want both of you to stay on top of this. This is going to be our number one priority."

He turned to Harris, "Stay on that bird dog's ass until we get those guns."

A female voice on the comm-line interrupted the conversation. "Captain? The chief can see you right now."

"Thanks, Helen."

The captain stood up and started out of the office. Harris and the lieutenant also stood, as though on command. The lieutenant hurriedly asked, "Would you like me to accompany you, sir?"

"That won't be necessary," the captain replied. Suddenly he stopped in his tracks, as though he had remembered something. "You mentioned something about bad news?"

The lieutenant cleared his throat nervously. "If you read further in that report, you will see that the membership list given to 757 by DePugh was a phony."

The captain looked as though he just passed gas during a wedding ceremony. "What the fuck do you mean, 'phony'?" he shouted. He immediately began to scan through the report. Before anyone could respond, he had found the information they were talking about.

"I'll be a son of a bitch! Let's keep this confidential for the time being."

As the captain took the stairs two at a time down to the sixth floor, he thought, *Why should I share a moment like this with anyone else or dampen the boss's spirits with bad news?* He strolled down the hall, cheerfully greeting everyone he passed. He intentionally took a circuitous route so that he wouldn't have to pass the office of his boss, who was an assistant chief.

The captain entered the outer office and glanced around at the familiar array of desks and personnel there. The chief's driver and bodyguard sat at the first desk, fielding a phone call from some malcontent who felt the chief should spend more time in a specific area of the city. The young policeman was handling the call with the aplomb of a senior ambassador.

No one bursts into the chief's office, so the captain waited dutifully in front of the chief's secretary's desk. The secretary, Anne, was fondly referred to as the chief's "Type A from Taipei." No one got access to the chief until she cleared them.

After Anne had let him in, the captain entered the inner office, where the chief sat behind a long conference table. He didn't care for the table, which had been left by his predecessor, but it was the personal handiwork of an officer assigned to Supply Division, and the chief would not hurt his feelings by discarding it.

Ever pleasant, the chief greeted the captain jokingly. "What sort of emergency have you concocted for today, Bob?"

The captain remained serious as he related the contents of Rabbit's report. It was a gift that certain captains seemed to have—they could memorize a report in seconds and then relate it as though they had done the investigation themselves.

When the captain finished, the chief sat pensively for a few seconds and then asked, "Has any of this information been verified yet?"

"Well, no. But our undercover is so well placed in the organization, it is unlikely that they would have given him false information."

"I would suggest that we try to determine the accuracy of this information before we get too excited."

"Oh we will, Chief! We will!"

"What about the undercover officer? Is he in any kind of increased danger as a result of this?"

"No, not really."

The chief drummed his fingers on the desk for a second. Then he concluded by admonishing the captain, "I know security for him is difficult at best, but keep an eye on him. I don't want him taking any unnecessary risks."

The captain shrugged as though that were a given. "Believe me, Chief, that's always my first concern."

The meeting was over, and the captain left, having omitted the part of the report that indicated he had been duped by a secret list peppered with false names. He would work around that one some other time.

Back in his office, he reiterated the chief's concerns about the reliability of the report, and leaned heavily on Harris to stay with Rabbit until the existence of the machine guns could be substantiated. The captain had stuck his neck out before on information provided by Rabbit, and he had better not wind up with egg on his face this time.

Meanwhile, Rabbit was back out doing what had become so familiar to him. If nothing else, he knew that no one could get in touch with him while he was roaming.

Rabbit had been back in Los Angeles for two weeks, since he had the meeting in Sacramento. Three envelopes from DePugh arrived in the mail for him, as expected. Each one was a different size and type of envelope, and each had a different company name and return address. One was postmarked from Kansas City, one Seattle, and another from Los Angeles.

Rabbit opened them. Each letter contained a part of a code that he needed in order to decipher the original list of member names, and ascertain who the operational members were. The birth dates were the key. The dates were not the actual month and day, but had been adjusted slightly by DePugh. The birth years, however, were correct.

Any birth dates listed in even months were to be eliminated. Dates in the first half of the month had to be checked against the past calendar years and if they were a Saturday or a Sunday, they were identifying the cell leaders of ten men. These units were fully operational and were prepared for an open, armed conflict against the government.

Along with the key was an order to give a phone call to the leaders. They were already expecting a call from Rabbit, in which they would plan a meeting to discuss the coordination of the planned operations in the Los Angeles area.

The order for Rabbit ended with the message, "Time is short. Get your plans set, as the day is fast approaching." Everything in the letters had been typed out, and as normal operating procedure for secrecy dictated, it was anonymous.

In the envelope that came from Kansas City, there was an additional message:

```
Burn the three envelopes
   and their contents.
Remember, they are watching.
```

Rabbit had no way of knowing if this was true, or if it was a security test. Whatever the case, he didn't care. For his own security, he decided to keep this from Harris.

…At this point, no one could be trusted.

Chapter 32
In the Attic

It did not take long for Harris to get in touch with Rabbit and set up another meeting to discuss the machine guns. Rabbit drove over to the mall in Torrance. The mall always amazed him—it was hard to believe how many people had so few obligations in life that they could afford to fritter away their time at a shopping mall. The vast parking lot was crowded, yet no one seemed to be carrying packages. Rabbit wondered to himself if window shopping was an addiction similar to booze or drugs.

Harris arrived, and they drove around for a while with no destination. Harris let Rabbit know that this was the biggest breakthrough he had made since the investigation had started. He also told him that they would now be in closer contact than before, because of the nature of this information.

Harris was eager for a follow-up, to see who had been in possession of these guns for such a long time, and exactly what type and how many there were. At this time, however, what happened next was totally out of Rabbit's control. He had to wait to hear from DePugh about the plans that were being made for him to meet the contact. Rabbit assured Harris that he would let him know as soon as he heard from DePugh, but that wasn't good enough, for

Harris, who ordered him to call in every day, whether he heard anything or not. Rabbit was sure that Harris was losing it, but there was no sense in arguing about it.

A couple of weeks passed without word from DePugh. Rabbit faithfully called every day to relay that information to the powers above him. Rabbit was actually glad that he hadn't heard anything. He had a terrible feeling in the back of his mind.

Finally, he received a call from DePugh with instructions to go to the cold phone. When he made contact with DePugh, he was given a phone number to contact Joan. DePugh had discussed the matter with her, and she would be waiting for Rabbit to contact her. When he hung up, he was glad that Ercole's was close by so he could have a few drinks around "real" people. He decided to fortify himself with a couple of Jack Daniel's before notifying Harris of the contact.

He felt warm and relaxed as he sat at the bar inside Ercole's. A few couples sat in the oak booths, looking into each other's eyes. Bittersweet melancholy swept over Rabbit as he remembered the many times he had sat in those booths with Charlie. He had taken so much for granted.

Rabbit knew a few of the patrons were off-duty policemen, but he avoided getting into a conversation with any of them. He exchanged greetings, but turned his attention to his drink.

It's funny how booze works. Sometimes it enhances a pleasant feeling and sometimes it brings on depression. It's almost impossible to anticipate which effect it will have on any given occasion. Rabbit knew enough not to get looped in public, especially in the presence of other cops, so he left while he was just slightly numb and not yet in the throes of depression or hilarity. Also, he needed to call Harris or he would feel his wrath the next morning.

Harris could hardly wait for Rabbit to get off work from his airport job the next day. He was like a kid who knew he was getting his first bicycle for Christmas and had to wait until morning to examine the presents under the tree. If he'd had his way, he would have crawled into Rabbit's hip pocket for the rest of this investigation. On top of his own anxiety, he was getting a constant barrage of questions and suggestions from his superiors. The lieutenant and captain were taking a more active interest in this case than they had ever taken in any case before.

When he met Rabbit, he asked him why he had not yet gotten in contact with Joan. Rabbit explained that he didn't want to contact her until he could comply with any directions she might give to him. With that, he went to a pay phone with Harris and dialed the number DePugh had given him.

A female voice answered the phone, and the conversation was rather cryptic.

"Hi! This is Rabbit. I'm a friend of Bob's."

"How is Bob?"

"He's well. He suggested that you and I could get together."

"That's possible. Call me tomorrow at exactly 9:30 sharp, in the morning." There was an immediate click on the other end of the phone, so Rabbit hung up.

Harris was beside himself. "What was that all about? Why

would she act like that?"

"I have to call her back again tomorrow morning."

"Why?"

"How the hell am I supposed to know? I do know that I'm going to have to call in sick to the airport, though."

"I wouldn't worry about that if I were you. I mean, it's not your real job."

Rabbit wondered for a beat. He wasn't sure just exactly what his real job was anymore.

Harris suggested that they get together before he contacted Joan in the morning, but Rabbit balked. There was no way in hell that he was going to let this investigation get burned at this point by an overeager detective who didn't have a clue how to deal with this side of the operation. Harris reluctantly gave in, and Rabbit agreed to stay in touch with him and keep him apprised of everything that transpired.

Rabbit was hoping that this meeting would be delayed indefinitely, but he did not know why. He was very uncomfortable about meeting Joan. In the first place, he knew that he would have no control over what happened. He was used to operating by the seat of his pants while undercover, but he tried to maintain a certain amount of control whenever possible.

That night, when Buddy came home, Rabbit was sitting in an over-stuffed chair with his bottle of Jack Daniel's on the table beside him. He was fondling a glass of Jack and ice cubes, transfixed by the television set, but totally unaware of the news events being reported on it.

Buddy took one look at him and said, "Why don't you let me

set up an IV for you so you don't get tennis elbow from so much bending."

"Very funny."

Buddy went over to the fridge and took out a beer. He might as well join Rabbit, since he wasn't going to discourage him.

He made a few attempts to start a conversation, but to no avail. The only responses he could elicit were grunts. Eventually Buddy set his beer down and went out to get a bite to eat. Sometime later, Rabbit was able to pry himself from the chair that had enveloped him and make his way to bed.

By the following morning, he had made a miraculous recovery. He had no hangover. He showered, shaved, and prepared to set up the meeting with Joan.

Buddy questioned him about not going to work, and Rabbit told him that he had made other plans for the day and taken a day off. They sat at the table drinking coffee and making small talk. Buddy knew something was bothering Rabbit, but he knew enough not to broach the subject—when Rabbit was ready to talk, he would. Eventually, Buddy got up and grabbed his jacket.

"Well, one of us has to get off our dead ass and go to work." As he walked through the door, Rabbit merely said, "See ya!"

Rabbit took out his wallet and withdrew the piece of paper with Joan's phone number on it. He studied it for a while and then took a deep breath, picked up the phone, and dialed. He counted the rings. After the fourteenth ring, he placed the phone back on the cradle and sighed with relief. Maybe a good long jog would get his mind right, he thought.

So he put on some ratty old sweat gear and took off for a jog along the beach. When he reached the alley behind the apartment, he remembered the many times he'd started out on this route as a subterfuge to conceal a clandestine meeting with Charlie in the park. When he got to the corner, he was thinking about Charlie and the good times, but instead of turning left, he turned right and headed for the sand and the water.

A million thoughts darted through his mind like the strobe lights at a disco, but he couldn't seem to put them into any kind of logical order. It really didn't matter, though, because he was drifting beyond rational thought on most of the matters that filled his life. He went longer than usual, and running in the soft sand was more tiring than he expected.

Eventually, he threw himself onto the moist sand that had recently been lapped by the waves. He lay there looking out over the ocean, contemplating its vastness. Suddenly his problems weren't all that overwhelming. He picked himself up and walked back to the apartment.

After another shower, he called Joan's number again. After only three rings, a female voice softly answered, "Hello."

"Joan, this is Rabbit."

"How long would it take you to get to the Silver Lake area from where you are?"

"Where's the Silver Lake area?"

"Just east of Hollywood, toward Downtown."

"About an hour, hour and fifteen minutes."

There was a short pause, and then Joan spoke again.

"It's 10:05 now. At exactly 12:00 noon, I want you to call me again from a phone booth on the southeast corner of Sunset and

Santa Monica Boulevard. It's where Santa Monica Boulevard begins."

Rabbit quickly grabbed a pencil and began writing down her instructions. He was vaguely familiar with the area, but feigned ignorance.

"Okay, I got it!"

"Good!"

Joan simply hung up.

Rabbit decided not to say anything to Harris yet, because he did not want to take a chance on having the meeting burned by sloppy surveillance. He left immediately in order to ensure that he would be able to get there in plenty of time to reconnoiter the area and spot any of Joan's people who might be setting him up. His heart raced as he headed down the San Diego Freeway to the Harbor Freeway, which would take him through downtown Los Angeles and up into Hollywood.

He was getting the adrenaline rush that he used to get whenever he was doing an undercover vice assignment. Most of the time, the rush was from his fear that the investigation would get burned and no arrests would be made. This time, the stakes were higher. A blown cover would lead to a funeral with full honors. Whenever the piper played "Amazing Grace," he wanted to be around to hear it.

His truck snaked through the four-level interchange and veered off at Alvarado Street. He followed Alvarado up to Sunset and made a left turn. He was about two miles from his destination, but he studied the entire route, knowing that he would eventually be directed to a location somewhere in this general vicinity.

When he reached Santa Monica Boulevard, he saw that there was a long stretch of Sunset where there were no buildings. It would be easy to spot any surveillance. He located the phone, and then drove around the neighborhood, making mental notes of the best and widest streets on which to beat a hasty retreat if necessary.

It was only 11:15 a.m., so he parked and went into a nearby taco stand where he could keep an eye on the phone and the surrounding area. Rabbit's stomach was in no condition to digest the spicy fare that was offered in this place, so he settled for coffee. There wasn't too much call for coffee in this eatery, so he was given a cup from a pot that had been prepared much earlier in the day. It was nearly a solid mass, but he sat and sipped it as he concentrated on every movement he could see through the windows, which had become nearly opaque from decades of grease and steam.

After checking his watch for the thirteenth time, he eased off the stool and walked over to the public phone on the southeast corner. At exactly noon, he dialed Joan's number.

"Hello!"

"This is Rabbit."

"You're very prompt. Now, please go to the corner of Sunset and Micheltorena and wait for me to call you. It's just a few blocks east of where you are right now. The phone is on the southwest corner." With that, she hung up.

Rabbit drove to the appointed location and pulled up to the phone. As he got out of his truck, the public phone on the wall of a market was ringing. He picked up the phone and identified himself. Joan instructed him to proceed to Maltman Street, make a left turn, drive almost to the top of the hill, and park across from number 410.

He got back into the truck and followed Joan's directions. As he turned away from the fabled Sunset Boulevard, he entered a neighborhood that looked like Small Town USA. The street was filled with old, two- and three-bedroom stucco houses. From the top of the hill looking south, he could see Downtown Los Angeles. It was incongruous for this modest neighborhood to be in the center of the entertainment capital of the world. You might see a neighborhood like this in the Valley or in the suburbs, but certainly not here.

Rabbit parked across the street from 410 Maltman and stared at the modest one-story frame house. A rickety fence protected the small patch of grass from intruders. There were a few steps up to a small porch, which, like the rest of the house, was in dire need of paint.

He pushed the doorbell, but heard nothing from inside, so he opened the screen and knocked on the door. After a few seconds, the door opened a crack, stopped by a safety chain. He could barely make out the figure who was pressed against the crack on the inside. A voice Rabbit recognized from several cryptic phone conversations quietly asked, "Do you have something to show me?"

Rabbit retrieved his wallet and removed his half of the dollar bill DePugh had given to him. He slid it through the crack in the door. A hand grasped it from inside and the door closed securely. He stood there awkwardly for several minutes, until finally he heard bolts sliding and locks unlocking. The door opened and there stood Joan Becker.

She appeared to be a woman in her fifties, dowdily dressed in a faded but clean housedress that buttoned down the front, and plain in overall appearance—not plain as in unattractive, but plain as in vanilla, with no frills or pretensions. She wore no makeup, and her graying hair was neatly combed, but not styled. Rabbit guessed that in her youth, she had probably been very attractive.

She was extremely soft spoken, and she invited him to come into the parlor. The interior of the house, like the exterior, could have used a fresh coat of paint. The walls had a few Norman Rockwell prints hung on them and a crucifix above the mantle. The furniture was very old fashioned. The sofa and stuffed chairs had lace doilies neatly pinned to each arm. On a small coffee table lay a well-worn Bible. Everything in the house looked as though it had come from a neighborhood antique store.

Joan ushered Rabbit over to the couch and asked if he wanted coffee or tea. When he said he would have whichever was easiest, she informed him that she had prepared both in anticipation of his visit. He opted for coffee.

Joan retreated to the kitchen, and in moments returned with a tray carrying two cups of coffee, a small pitcher of cream, sugar, and a small dish of cookies. Rabbit felt as though he had some-how stepped through the looking glass. He was here on a very dangerous mission to obtain machine guns from a representative of a very dangerous organization, and he had been greeted by a kindly, middle-aged lady who was now serving him coffee and butter cookies that she herself had baked.

Joan sat on the edge of a high-backed chair and served her guest. The conversation began with small talk. She asked Rabbit where he came from and where he had grown up. She was interested in everything he had to say, not as an interrogator, but as though she were the mother of a girl he was dating for the first time.

She did not mention DePugh or the political right. The whole conversation reminded Rabbit of his initial interview with PDID years earlier. Many of the questions were identical, as far as he could remember. He couldn't help but wonder, was there some sort of script used by people in the spy business?

Joan said nothing about herself. The small talk lasted for over an hour, during which she periodically refilled his cup. It had been a long time since he had told the invented story of his youth, but he had been living the lie for so long that it came out naturally. He wondered if he would sound as though he were lying if he told the truth about himself.

Finally, Joan stood and asked Rabbit to follow her. They walked to the hallway, where she lowered a ceiling ladder, ascended the steps, and led him into a small attic. Once inside, she retracted the folding stairs and closed the wooden trap door over the opening.

The room was totally barren except for a small table, two straight-backed wooden chairs, and a small old-fashioned radio. The electric cord from the radio was plugged into the same socket as the low-watt light bulb that hung from the ceiling. There was no shade, just the bare bulb.

Joan sat down and told Rabbit to remove his shirt. Rabbit flashed back to that earlier meeting and feigned incomprehension. She insisted that it was absolutely necessary for him to do this, so Rabbit complied. Joan asked him to hand the shirt to her.

As she ran her fingers over every inch of his shirt, she instructed him to turn around. Satisfied that he was clean, she returned

the shirt and told him to put it back on and to have a seat. She
then turned the radio to a local talk show and spoke even more
softly than she had earlier. Rabbit had to strain to hear her. She
raised her voice very slightly to accommodate him and then
began to explain.

"We learned a long time ago not to take any chances. My
mother is very frail, and it would be disastrous for me to have to
leave her to go to prison. I have never met you before. I know only
what you have told me. If you were a policeman or a federal agent,
you would have come prepared with a story, so the best security
tactic available to me was to search you to make sure you weren't
wearing a body wire. The reason for the radio is that if anyone is
using a spike mike or any other listening or recording device, it
will pick up the voices on the radio before it will pick up the live
human voices. I have no idea why that happens, but it does. Now
we can talk without fear of being overheard."

It was stifling hot in this room, which had no windows or ventilation. Rabbit was extremely uncomfortable, but also relieved—the
heat was more than enough reason for him to perspire without
appearing to be nervous about detection. He was not in the hands
of a novice, and this room wasn't designed as a sewing room. He
was almost in awe of this woman.

From this point on, she would do most of the talking. She gave
Rabbit some background on her involvement in the Minutemen,
starting at the beginning in order to give him proper perspective
on who she was and to explain about the guns.

Bob DePugh had come to California in order to enlist young
patriots into an organization dedicated to preserving the American

way of life. Communism and its anti-Christian propaganda was a world force to be reckoned with, and an insidious growth inside this country as well. The liberals were pushing reconciliation down everyone's throats and gaining a strong foothold in the government. Radical left-wing organizations bent on the violent overthrow of the United States government and the elimination of Christianity were surfacing all over the place. Violent black organizations dedicated to destroying the Caucasian race were becoming common as well. Revolution was the key word. Unfortunately, strong forces inside the government were sympathetic to the liberal cause.

Most of the law enforcement arms of the government remained conservative; men and women drawn to this line of work tended to be patriotic. DePugh found a group called the Loyal Order of Mountain Men and thought they could be developed into a California contingent of the Minutemen.

In those days, Joan said, she had been an energetic, strong-willed conservative. She had been just about as radical as it was possible to be while still retaining a modicum of common sense. It didn't take long for her to become a key player within the organization.

DePugh traveled all over the country looking for right-wing causes to become involved with. One of those causes was the Florida-based resistance to the communist takeover of Cuba. DePugh's efforts down there drew the attention of the CIA.

Joan spoke freely and knowledgeably about the interaction between the CIA and the Minutemen. As a matter of fact, she said, the guns she would soon be turning over to Rabbit had been given to them by the CIA. The numbers on all the guns were cold; they couldn't be traced to any source, anywhere.

In the course of their relationship, the CIA, in collaboration with the local police, would give the Minutemen targets to go after. They were not given specific direction regarding lethal force, but common sense dictated that it was to be avoided. It was in their best interest to keep as low a profile as possible and not generate community hostility. When they carried out missions to disrupt meetings or destroy equipment, they never took credit or sought publicity.

Rabbit became so mesmerized by Joan's tale that he violated his own credo by asking questions. Fortunately, his questions came across as curiosity motivated by fascination, rather than appearing as though he were fishing or conducting an investigation.

"How did you avoid arrests?" he asked.

She laughed. She told him about a group within the Los Angeles Police Department called the Red Squad.

The hair stood up on the back of Rabbit's neck when he heard this. He knew this unit was not known outside the Department. As a matter of fact, it wasn't very well known within the Department. Rabbit had heard of the organization, but he'd never learned anything about it before joining the PDID. The Red Squad had actually been a precursor to the Public Disorder Intelligence Division that Rabbit now worked for.

Joan went on to explain how the Red Squad had been formed and how it had reported directly to Bill Parker, the legendary former Chief of Police who was one of Rabbit's idols. According to Joan, two men from the Red Squad were assigned to handle the Minutemen. In the event something went awry during one of their missions and it came to the attention of the police, these two detectives would be assigned to handle the investigation and report directly to Parker.

Rabbit reflected on something Harris had told him much earlier: there were two detectives in PDID who had done the original investigation into the Minutemen. He wondered if they were the same men Joan was talking about.

During one particular mission, an explosive device they had set went off prematurely, before Joan and the others were able to escape. She was thrown to the pavement and suffered a severe hip fracture, which caused her problems from that time forward. The investigation was closed as an unsolved. She formed a close relationship with one of the Red Squad detectives, but one day he fell off the radar.

She touched on a great many topics that DePugh had already discussed with Rabbit, giving her credibility. In some instances, she filled in gaps in his understanding of events that DePugh had left unexplained and that Rabbit had not questioned, because everything was on a need-to-know basis.

For example, she discussed the relationship between Hawthorne and DePugh. She was well aware of DePugh's clandestine meetings with Hawthorne's wife, and she knew that when Hawthorne learned about it, a meeting between him and DePugh had been arranged. DePugh had gone to the meeting location with Joan and another man. Joan was asked to wait downstairs while the two men went upstairs for the meeting. After a short time, Joan could hear an altercation involving the smashing of furniture. When DePugh and the other man reappeared, all three entered a vehicle and left the scene. That was the last time Hawthorne was seen alive.

That answered some questions that Rabbit had been harboring. It lent credibility to DePugh's fear of a reprisal from Hawthorne's family or the Loyal Order of Mountain Men. It also added to the pall that hung over Rabbit's mind like the humidity of a summer thunderstorm. Joan had filled him with a thousand new reasons to worry. His formerly insatiable appetite for information was waning, and with it, his curiosity about the guns that were his primary mission.

However, Joan would not let him off so easy. She apologized for boring him: "But I'm sure you're not interested in my life story. I'm sure you are more interested in the guns."

She went on to explain that she'd had the guns in storage for the past fifteen years. She received cash in the mail every month for the storage fees. There was never a note, nor a name or an address—only the cash.

She wished she could continue to be of assistance to Bob, but she was just no longer able to do it, as she was totally consumed by the tremendous responsibility of caring for her ill mother. Her greatest fear was that if ever the guns were discovered, she would go to prison, and perhaps her mother would as well, as this storage space had been rented under her mom's maiden name.

Joan knew if she were arrested, the police would use her mother's freedom as a bargaining chip to get her to roll over on Bob, the Minutemen, and all the patriots in the government who had been involved with the guns. An arrest would unquestionably result in the death of her mother. Joan told Rabbit that she just would not be able to live with that, and that she was resolved not to.

She asked Rabbit if he had access to a covered pickup truck or a van to transport the guns. Rabbit told her he did. Joan told him there were quite a few cases, and that the cases were very heavy. She had a very experienced and trusted member of the organization whom Bob had met in Leavenworth, and who would be helping with the job. It would take several trips to move everything. She preferred to spread the transfer out over several weeks in order to avoid attracting any unwanted attention.

She told him, "On the day of the move, we all need to be armed, just in case."

She then told him they would get together soon and begin the transfer.

With that Joan reached across the table, and with her palms turned up, she said, "Before you go now, give me your hands and let us pray." She began, "In the name of the Father, the Son, and the Holy Spirit, dear Almighty God, please help us in our battle against evil, and protect this young man from harm and help him accomplish his tasks, and may God bless America. Amen."

On the way out of the house, they stopped at the front door. Joan admonished Rabbit to be very careful.

"This is a very dangerous business that you have gotten into."

Rabbit could take care of himself, he assured her.

"I thought so, too—at one time."

She paused and solemnly began to relay a story: a few years ago, someone had done a drive-by shooting in an attempt to assassinate her on her own front porch. They had tried to make it look like a random shooting, but she knew exactly what it was about, and who had ordered it. She was hit twice, but her injuries were only flesh wounds, and they were taken care of by a doctor sympathetic to the cause, without the need for a hospital.

Rabbit asked why someone would have attempted to kill her, since she had not participated in any strike operations for a long time. Joan replied that it all went back to the guns. They wanted to make sure she would not be taken into custody and talk. That was why Rabbit, who had become close to DePugh and now knew about the guns, was in danger. She reminded him that he had to be vigilant, and urged him to arm himself and always to be ready.

Rabbit once more asked why a shooter would come for her after she had sat on the guns for so long without any problems.

She hesitated before answering and then simply said, "You will have to ask DePugh."

She led Rabbit out through the door and onto the porch. She pointed to a few small holes in the woodwork, which she said were stray bullet holes that she had never bothered to repair. She had left them there as a reminder never to relax her vigilance.

They shook hands, and Rabbit left with an entirely new respect and high regard for this kind lady.

Who knows how much knowledge Joan had about the Minutemen, LAPD Red Squad, and CIA connections, but based on the details she spoke about, it would appear that it was extensive. Joan had known DePugh for close to twenty years, and she was a tried and tested member of the Minutemen. He had for many years trusted her with the machine gun cache, which would have sent many people to federal prison if it had been discovered. Because of DePugh's record of past firearms convictions, he mostly likely would have been incarcerated for life.

Obviously, Joan had total trust in Rabbit, since he had been sent by DePugh, who ordered him to take possession of the guns. Joan's belief and purpose for joining the Minutemen was to be a first line of defense to fight the communists in the streets, should they ever attempt a takeover of America. She professed to be a loyal patriot and dedicated anti-Communist.

What the hell am I doing? Rabbit wondered. He was over-whelmed with the information he had just gathered. He knew Harris was waiting to hear from him, but he wasn't ready to talk to anyone about what he had just learned.

Instead, he made a dash back to Ercole's Bar in Manhattan Beach, where he sifted through Joan's words over and over again. At first he wanted to get drunk, but instead he had only a couple of beers while he sat in a corner by himself. He would have gone home, but he was afraid that Harris would be calling him every fifteen minutes looking for information about the guns.

Chapter 33
Death Trap

The next day, Harris was near convulsions. He was so angry, he found it hard to speak rationally. Rabbit half-expected to see foam spewing from every orifice on his face. Apparently this young smartass didn't realize that the entire free world was waiting breathlessly for information about his exploits.

"I'm being hammered by every son of a bitch in the Department who has any rank because I've been ordered to stay in your hip pocket, and you play hide and seek."

"I had to think about everything I learned so that I could put it down properly on the report."

"Bullshit! You were just screwing with my mind."

Rabbit knew he couldn't appease Harris with words, so he handed him the report. Harris snatched the report and began to peruse it. His mood changed rapidly. He glared at Rabbit and simply asked, "Is this straight stuff?"

Rabbit nodded in the affirmative.

Harris got up and walked off. He spoke softly over his shoulder, "I'll get back to you."

It didn't take long. Harris called that evening and set up another meeting first thing in the morning. When Rabbit said it would have to wait until he got off work at the airport, Harris told him to screw the airport. Rabbit reminded him that if this investigation were going to continue, he had to have the job, and right now he was in danger of losing it because of excessive absenteeism. That was a lie, but Harris had no way of knowing that it wasn't true, so he relented and agreed to meet him later in the day.

The meeting was scheduled to take place near Terminal Island, under the Henry Ford Bridge at the Red Witch Inn. They would need to discuss some very sensitive issues. As usual, Rabbit got there first. He was gingerly sipping on a burning hot cup of coffee while reading the *Los Angeles Times*. Policemen have an aversion to most of the trash written in the skewed stories of the ultra liberal *Times*, but it is really the only game in town. Besides, it is necessary to know what the other side is thinking.

When Harris arrived, he was more somber than he had been in a long time. Although there was no anger or recrimination in it, his demeanor was that of a professional about to deal with a subordinate.

"We have analyzed all the information in your last report, and it's all bullshit."

"What do you mean, bullshit?"

"This woman is obviously a psycho. She has dreamed up a lot of nonsense that is completely off the wall."

"She seemed like she had her shit together to me."

"I'm telling you, she's a crackpot," Harris said. "Are you a goddamned shrink? Who the hell do you think you are to determine if she's sane or not?"

"You've been trusting my judgment for years. How come all of a sudden I don't know what I'm talking about?"

"Look, Rabbit, this report has been examined by experts and it has been researched. None of that crap could have taken place. The lieutenant has studied the Minutemen extensively, and his expertise is matched by no one in the Department, and he considers this information bullshit."

Rabbit knew there was more to it, but there was no sense arguing. Besides, he was finally going to be out of this investigation.

"I suppose the investigation is off now."

Harris looked shocked that Rabbit would think like that.

"Are you out of your mind? We've got to get those guns."

Rabbit shook his head.

"Wait a minute! You just got through telling me that Joan is a psycho, and that she doesn't know what she's talking about, and now you want me to believe she has the guns?"

Harris hemmed and hawed. "We didn't say she didn't have the guns. We are merely saying she is making up a lot of nonsense to make herself look good to you."

"I don't see what I have to gain by talking to her anymore."

"Damn it, Rabbit, I'm telling you to get the guns, and I don't want to hear any more bullshit about it. Just do as you're told."

Rabbit was a little bit taken aback by Harris's aggressiveness. "I'll do what I can," he said.

"What you can do had better be getting the guns."

Rabbit was disappointed, but merely sighed. "Anything else?"

Harris cleared his throat. "Yes! No more written reports, especially regarding meetings with Joan."

Rabbit reacted strongly. "What do you mean no more reports?"

"You heard me. No more reports. We can't afford having them fall into the wrong hands."

"For all these years, nobody has worried about my reports falling into the wrong hands, but now it's a problem?"

"Think about it for a second. Suppose you got into a traffic accident and get knocked unconscious, and during the accident investigation some police officer or sergeant found your report. There's no telling what would happen to it, especially if it contained information like the last one."

"What about the reports when I did the surveillance of the Chavez compound? Would it have been all right if that report was found with my dead body?"

"Look, I have my orders, and now you have yours. I want a verbal report from you every day, but you are not to put anything in writing, you understand? Nothing in writing."

"Yeah, I understand. But I want a favor."

"I'll try."

"Find out about the shooting Joan told me about, the one where she got shot. There had to have been a report made on that one."

"Providing that it ever happened."

The veins were standing out on Rabbit's neck.

"If? Damn it, I saw the bullet holes in her porch. You've got to give me everything you can on her. I have to know exactly who I am dealing with."

Harris relented, "Okay, okay. I'll see what I can find." He extended his hand and Rabbit took it.

Rabbit looked into Harris's eyes and knew that this was not

his idea. It was obvious that Harris didn't agree with all of this, but he was the consummate good soldier. He was only carrying out his orders.

Rabbit had to ask, "Billy, tell me the truth. How much are the Feds involved in this?"

Harris shot back, "*Macht nichts aus.*"

"What do you mean, 'it doesn't matter'?"

"Don't ask questions like that," Harris said.

As Rabbit left, his uneasiness was growing by leaps and bounds. He knew the jargon Joan used had not come from reading books and newspapers. She referred to the former Chief of Police as Bill Parker. Not even cops who served during his tenure called him that. Maybe "Wild Bill" behind his back, but certainly nothing as informal as "Bill." Nor had her knowledge of the Red Squad come to her in a dream one night.

Why was the Department trying to stonewall him? For the past four years, he had been entrusted with more intelligence than any other policeman, yet it was apparent he was being lied to about this. Apparently Joan had opened the door to a very dark cellar, a door that was meant to remain closed for eternity. But why wasn't he taken into confidence? His loyalty to the Department bordered on fanaticism. What agenda had required him to be taken out of the loop?

The more he thought about it, the more his paranoia grew. For the past four years or so, he had been living on the brink of high anxiety. Every day was a roller coaster ride that caused his insides to shiver and the butterflies to dance gaily in the pit of his stomach. He lived every day on the edge. He had to plan every step he took so as not to be uncovered and probably whacked. At any moment he could get himself into a situation in which the Department would have to deny complicity and leave him to the wolves. There was even a risk that he might end up doing penitentiary time. He had become accustomed to this anxiety. It was a way of life.

This was very different, though. His mind was slowly filling with stark, overwhelming terror. The unanswerable questions pounded his brain until he was exhausted. He could not focus his mind on anything else.

The following day Harris contacted him again to check on his progress, or the lack of it. There was no progress, of course, but Harris was antsy. Obviously someone was pulling his string very early in the morning.

Rabbit asked him about the disposition of the guns once they were taken into custody. It was very simple to Harris—the guns would be booked into Property Division. Rabbit flipped out on that one.

"Property Division? What happens if DePugh or one of his soldiers comes to look at them? Do I send them over to the Parker Center? Or do I tell them they will have to wait until I check them out? Hell, I couldn't even get my own holster and six rounds of ammo released to me."

"We have no choice. We can't let those guns stay out there unprotected."

"What about me? If you take custody of those guns, I'll be out there alone, as always, and unprotected."

"It's out of my hands, Rabbit. The decision has already been made."

His terror increased. He tried vainly to get a grip on himself. How the hell was he going to fake this one?

Suddenly he got a call from DePugh, who wanted to know if he had taken possession of the guns. When he said no, DePugh pressed him to get them as quickly as possible. He couldn't help but wonder why in the hell DePugh was so anxious for him to take possession of these guns, which had been in storage for fifteen years.

Back with Harris for his daily update, Rabbit asked, "What about the shooting report at Joan's address?"

Harris was cool. "It must have been bullshit. I couldn't find anything on it."

Rabbit knew better than to take this any further. He was being stonewalled for some reason, and he could only figure that he had gone into an area where he didn't belong. He now felt as though he was a liability to both sides and operating completely on his own.

For the next week he received calls alternately from Harris and DePugh, each demanding to know when he was going to take possession of the guns. It almost appeared that DePugh was working for Harris or vice versa. Both friend and enemy were seeking the same goal, and he was caught in the middle.

Rabbit made up a number of excuses to avoid the inevitable. He dragged it out as long as he could before he finally made contact with Joan. He breathed a sigh of relief when she told him that she had a bad case of the flu.

As the days dragged on, DePugh and Harris became more insistent. Finally, Rabbit contacted Joan, and a tentative date was established to transfer the machine guns. Rabbit informed DePugh and Harris of the date, which made both of them happy. Once again, Rabbit reflected on how strange it was for both of these men to be hounding him for the same reason.

Harris set up another meeting, and he was very excited when they got together. He was like a kid who had brought in a brand-new play from the sidelines and was giving it to the quarterback. He handed Rabbit a roll of silver duct tape and instructed him to make two parallel lines running the length of the camper shell of his pickup. Harris said that if it was discovered, Rabbit could say that he was preparing to place a rack on the roof of the camper shell and that the tape would protect it from being scratched by the rack.

"But why am I putting tape on my vehicle?" Rabbit inquired.

"So the helicopter won't have any problem keeping you under surveillance."

"What helicopter?"

"A secure plan has been devised to make the arrest. After you and Joan have the guns in your truck, the bird will follow you to a secure location where there will be an absolute minimum of people, and then SWAT will pull you over and take possession of the guns."

Rabbit couldn't believe what he was hearing.

"Has everyone in Parker Center lost their mind? All we need is for me to pick up Joan and the ex-con she brings along to help me. We then go pick up the guns; I drive Joan and her friend back to her house, and then I bring the guns to you."

"No! I told you how it has to go down. We have to cover you in case something goes sideways."

"You have to cover me? Where the hell was the cover when I was confronted with the snake box back in Illinois? Where was the fuckin' cover when I was crawling around the Chavez compound with some armed psychos? Where was all the cover when I was traveling around the country with people who would have blown my head off in a heartbeat if they found out who I was? I don't need your fuckin' cover for this one."

"You don't understand. This is going to make great press for the Department when we take it down and make the arrests."

"If you make arrests, the only way you can make it stick is with my testimony. What about the deal we had at the very start of this assignment, that I would never have to testify ever, under any circumstances, because of the danger to me and my family?"

"The rules have changed. Arrests will be made, and you will have to testify."

"What do you mean the rules have changed? Nobody asked me if they could change the rules. I have a hell of a lot more at stake than anyone else."

"I had nothing to do with changing the rules. Decisions have been made at a much higher level than me."

"Listen to me, Billy. You and I know Joan and her ex-con are intelligent, savvy people. They know all about how police operations work. The second we are stopped and they see SWAT deployed in a secure position of advantage, they will know they have been set up and led into a SWAT trap. It will be crystal clear that I am the rat who gave them up. And in the blink of an eye, they will execute me on the spot, and then the firefight will be on. These are obsessed, dedicated revolutionaries who will be armed and will fight to their deaths. And to boot, one of them is an ex-convict who did time in Leavenworth and has no intention of ever going back."

Rabbit continued, "So what do you think about that? Do you think I am wrong? No, you don't. You know I am 100 percent right, and that I'm reading it exactly as it will go down."

Harris responded, "No. They will give up as soon as they see the overwhelming show of force. There is no way they will shoot it out."

Rabbit looked at Harris and shook his head in utter disbelief. He couldn't believe what he was hearing. Harris halfheartedly muttered that Rabbit's safety was foremost in the planning of the operation.

Rabbit thought for a second and then said, "Okay, let's say by some chance these people are not as smart as I think they are and they don't suspect me as the rat who set them up. Now what we have are the three of us sitting shoulder to shoulder in the cab of my truck, all armed with guns and ready for anything. Then a police car pulls us over, and suddenly there is a SWAT platoon with their M-16 rifles all over the place. The cops order us from the car, and then one of those infamous "furtive moves" happens, and it is interpreted by a young SWAT cop with his M-16 as the suspect going for a gun the cops knew he was carrying—as they were told that in the briefing from information I supplied them, that the suspects will all be armed and dangerous—and so the shooting begins.

"C'mon, Billy, we both worked the street long enough that we know all about the scenario of the armed suspect and the furtive move. Once we're pulled over, the cops have been given enough information—by me—to fire at the slightest wrong move."

Rabbit pressed on.

"This whole thing is being handled wrong. Those SWAT cops are putting together an assault that will look like the *Sands of Iwo Jima*, and you're telling me it's just for my safety? One way or another, this is working out to be my death warrant. This is an insane plan. Someone will not let me live long enough to go to court—that is, if I can somehow survive when the arrest operation goes down."

There was a very long silence. Both men just looked at each other.

Finally Rabbit broke the silence.

"Let's for a moment say that my hypotheses are wrong. What we do know is that Joan and her buddy are not going down without a fight. So they don't shoot me; instead they open fire on SWAT."

Rabbit reminded Harris of the time he'd gotten his ass beat at the Mouse Trap Saloon by following a stupid, ill-conceived plan. Being a good soldier, Rabbit didn't speak up about the plan until it was too late. "Well, that's not going to happen again. This time a screw-up guarantees a trip to the LA County morgue. What are the chances of anyone getting out of my truck alive after SWAT finishes their firepower demonstration? Who came up with this plan?"

The plan sounded like it had been designed by the Department's SIS—the Special Investigations Section, known by some as the death squad.

Harris tried to persuade Rabbit that he had to get a grip, that his scenarios were way off-base. "SWAT trains for this kind of operation, it's what they do."

Rabbit shot back that he had seen some of SWAT's great work, that he had been at East 54th Street in 1974 when SWAT fired thousands of rounds into the Symbionese Liberation Army's hideout before they finally burned it to the ground, killing the six SLA members.

"The SWAT boys don't subscribe to the same philosophy as Mother Teresa. This entire investigation has gotten way out of control. It's going to be my ass in the truck when this insane arrest operation goes down. No way can this work without a firefight. It's asking for suicide by cop. However you view this, it's just all wrong. I'm not faint of heart, but I just can't take part in this ambush."

"Yes, you can. You're just feeling the normal stress that goes with any major operation like this. Hell, I'm feeling it, too. We've gone too far to choke now. We've got to do this."

Rabbit shot back, "We? Detective Sergeant, just where is your ass going to be during the takedown? I realize you think I'm overly paranoid about the SWAT squad, so I got a great plan to fix that. When it's time to pick up the guns, I'll get you an airline uniform like mine, and then I'll tell Joan I'm bringing along a time trusted buddy that I work with to help her and her buddy pick up the heavy stuff that's in storage. What about that? Are you up for it?"

Harris scoffed, "That's goofy. I could never pull it off. For God's sake, quit making a big deal out of this. Just do it. You'll be okay."

"All right. If you won't do it, send another undercover sergeant from PDID with me in your place."

Harris said nothing. It was apparent all of this was wearing him down as well. Rabbit and Harris were in over their heads. They both sat silent, each fearing in his own way where this runaway train was going.

Harris left. Rabbit was in a state of total frenzy. He tried to sort things out, but the picture became more and more blurry. He believed without a doubt that if the police moved in while they were transporting the guns, a shootout would be inevitable.

Then it started to come together. In his paranoid state, he developed a scenario that was logical to him. No one could have known all that Joan knew about the CIA, LAPD, Red Squad, the operations of the Minutemen in Los Angeles, and DePugh's complicity in the disappearance of William Hawthorne. When Joan shared all those things with Rabbit in detail, both she and Rabbit became monumental liabilities to all concerned. The perfect solution would be for Joan, Rabbit, and the ex-con to die in a firefight with the police, taking to their graves the secrets of the past. Rabbit would probably get a hero's funeral for dying in the line of duty while trying to take down a dangerous white supremacist organization. Sadly, Joan and the ex-con would just die ignominiously, while the chief and SWAT would bask in glory.

Even if this scenario did not play out, Rabbit didn't have much longer to live anyway. If by the grace of God Rabbit made it through the SWAT operation, DePugh would never allow him to live long enough to appear before a grand jury. And without Rabbit's testimony, there was no case at all against DePugh.

Chapter 34
Last 24 Hours

It was 4:00 in the morning Los Angeles time, 6:00 a.m. in St. Louis. Rabbit's phone rang, jolting him from a deep sleep. It was DePugh. He told Rabbit to call him back as quickly as he could.

Rabbit quickly dressed and made his way to the phone booth down the street. He understood completely how it felt to be Pavlov's dog. It was a cold, damp, foggy night, and Rabbit was shivering.

DePugh answered on the first ring. It was apparent from the sound of his voice that he was angry. He said he'd spoken to Joan, and he wanted to know why the guns hadn't yet been moved. Joan had said she was ready and waiting for Rabbit to confirm the tentative date and time they had agreed upon, but Rabbit never called her back.

There was a long pause. DePugh asked Rabbit if he'd changed his mind about helping with the project. Rabbit said no, it just had been unusually busy at work, and it was difficult to schedule time off. After another long pause, DePugh asked Rabbit if something was wrong; he said Rabbit's voice sounded different than usual. Rabbit assured him everything was okay, it was just that he was standing outside talking on the telephone at 4:20 a.m. one block from the ocean. It was shrouded in heavy fog with a twenty mile an hour onshore breeze. He was chilled to the bone and still half-asleep.

DePugh said, "If you are with me, then you will do what I ask when I ask. Joan is getting nervous, and I don't like that. Everyone involved better understand, if this deal goes bad, there is going to be a heavy price to pay."

He told Rabbit that Joan was expecting him to call this morning to make a drop-dead time to get the guns. Rabbit wondered if there was a thinly veiled warning in DePugh's choice of words: "Drop dead."

DePugh abruptly ended the call, saying, "Just get it done now."

Rabbit knew the stall game was up. He had run out of wiggle room and had to do something, but he was out of ideas. This nightmare wasn't going away, it was only getting more intense. He started to wonder if Buddy and Charlie were right—maybe he had finally lost it.

Harris had confirmed what Rabbit had been thinking—it was out of their hands. For whatever reason, this four-year investigation had suddenly been seized by the command staff, and they were trying to dictate how it would go, despite not having a clue about how it worked.

Rabbit's next call was to Harris. "We got to have a meeting ASAP. The gun deal is going down. Meet me in two hours in the parking lot of the Venice Pier."

When Rabbit got off the phone, he hustled back to the apartment. Buddy had a pot of coffee going and was sitting at the kitchen table. Rabbit was happy for the coffee, but not so much to see Buddy.

When Rabbit asked him why he was up so early, Buddy answered, "What did you expect? You were crashing around in here in the dark like a madman at 4:00 a.m. I honestly thought Armageddon had arrived. Man, you look terrible. Seriously, are you okay? In all honesty, do you know what you are doing?"

Rabbit's answer was simply, "No, Buddy, I don't."

"You better get some help somewhere, my friend."

Rabbit went to his bedroom and closed the door. He always had a plan, and if it didn't work, he had a backup plan. That wasn't the case this time. As much as he wanted this to be over, he could not imagine how and when it would end. Certainly he could have never anticipated how the final twenty-four hours of this four-year investigation was about to play out.

At 6:00 a.m., he was at the Venice Pier. While Rabbit waited, his mind raced uncontrollably from one scrambled thought to another. He was aware that his shivering had become physically more noticeable. He hoped it was just the cold and fog and not something more. Maybe his coffee just needed another little shot of Jack.

Harris arrived. He didn't look too much better himself. It was apparent that the stress of this long investigation was taking its toll on both of them.

Rabbit told Harris he had been ordered to call Joan that morning and arrange to get the guns in the next twenty-four hours. He told Harris all the details of the urgent 4:00 a.m. call from DePugh. Harris said no problem, SWAT and the helicopter were on standby and could respond within two hours. They had all rehearsed the plan and were ready to go.

Rabbit again implored Harris to convince the brass to call off their plan. Rabbit told Harris their plan was wrong for a hundred reasons. Their objective was all about making a big splash in the headlines of the *LA Times* in order to get the chief some breathing room from the political left. He begged Harris to persuade the brass to let him make a smooth gun transfer with no interference. That would prove his ability and loyalty to DePugh. If the guns stayed safe with Rabbit and no arrests were made, DePugh would have one hundred percent absolute trust in him.

If the brass would give Rabbit until after Christmas before they closed out the investigation, Rabbit would go back to Missouri and spend Christmas with DePugh and his family. While there, he would do whatever he needed to do to learn the history of the guns, the individuals' names, and the agency that had supplied the guns. Once that information was obtained, then a major case would be made.

Rabbit pressed Harris, stressing that no detective as thorough and as accomplished as Harris was could possibly think this was the time to close the investigation. Was the plan for the investigation to culminate with the arrest of Joan and DePugh, letting the Feds off the hook? What kind of bullshit justice was that? This investigation should be about who supplied the guns, he said, not just who has them.

Rabbit continued, "And one more thing: why wasn't I included in the planning of the arrest? I've worked years in undercover operations and have always been involved in planning the takedown. No one is ever in a better position to know the threat level of the targets than me. How elementary is it that the arrest teams have the opportunity to see me in person so there are no identity mistakes made by the boys in SWAT with their M-16 rifles? There is something really wrong going on here, and you got to make them stop and rethink this."

Rabbit spoke uninterrupted for an hour. Unfortunately, he could see it had no effect at all. Harris just shook his head in obvious despair. He said the powers that be were dead set on the plan.

"You and I don't have a say in this anymore, Rabbit. It is way out of our hands, and it's too late anyway. Enough of this investigation has been shared with other units in the Department that your identity and involvement with the Minutemen is no longer secure. I'm really sorry for all this. It is not how I ever envisioned it would end. The arrests and seizure are going to go down. There is no stopping it."

Rabbit left the pier parking lot feeling like he had been run over and crushed by an eighteen-wheel semi truck. As he drove away, he considered an alternate plan: not telling anyone when he actually would meet with Joan. On his own, he could do the first truckload transfer of the guns and put them in a secure, alarmed self-storage unit that he had already located in anticipation of this eventuality.

As he contemplated this deception, he realized its folly. It would mean immediate termination, most likely arrest, and conviction on a host of federal firearm violations, including conspiracy to aid and abet possession and transfer of automatic weapons, as well as a host of other related charges. That plan, Rabbit decided, wasn't a good idea.

Promptly at 9:00 a.m., he called Joan and told her he would be available the next day at 10:00 a.m. to meet her and pick up what they had previously discussed. His thought was that at midday there would be a maximum amount of people walking and driving about the downtown streets, which would make it very difficult for SWAT to have a shooting party.

Joan agreed to the day and time. She said, "Be careful. There are people out there who wish us harm."

The beginning of the operation was now set in stone. Suddenly Rabbit was overcome with extreme guilt and nausea at the thought that it was he who would lead Joan into the police ambush and almost certain death.

Chapter 35
The Spy Master

Rabbit desperately needed help, and his last possible lifeline was Detective Sergeant John Paul Dodaine, his covert operations mentor. Dodaine was a master designer of cloak-and-dagger operations. If anyone could help him now, it would be John Paul.

Rabbit broke open the roll of quarters he kept in the glove box of his truck and one by one put them in the pay phone. He called every telephone number he had for John Paul. Finally, he made contact. After a brief conversation, John Paul agreed to meet him at the Sportsman Inn in Gardena where they used to meet informants years before when they were partners in the Vice squad. The meeting time was set for 1:00 p.m.

Rabbit arrived early for the meeting, as was his normal procedure. He parked across the street a half block away at a small neighborhood convenience market. The parking lot gave him excellent cover and an unobstructed view of the bar parking lot where he was going to meet John Paul.

He was now completely paranoid. He wondered if he could even trust John Paul. After spending a half hour watching the bar parking lot, he realized his paranoia was shutting down all the lights in his world. And besides that, he needed a drink. He drove his truck to the bar parking lot and went inside. He was nervous, but then, he was always nervous these days.

When John Paul arrived, he found Rabbit sitting in the end booth at the back corner of the bar, having a four-finger Jack Daniel's with very few rocks.

John Paul sat down, took one look at Rabbit, and said, "God-damn boy, you look like death warmed over."

Rabbit didn't care. The last thing on his mind was how he looked. He hadn't come here to meet John Paul for a job interview; he was desperate and afraid for his life.

John Paul was visibly disturbed by what he saw. Rabbit was a changed man. This was not the same young, energetic, fun-loving cop with the quick smile he had worked with years before. This was a stressed-out, beat-down, paranoid man who had aged twice his years since they had last worked together. His hair was graying and he had developed deep frown lines in his forehead. His fingernails had been bitten down halfway to the quick, and he squirmed about like a suspect in a secret police interrogation room waiting for the KGB.

John Paul began, "What the hell has happened to you?"

Rabbit had so much to say, he didn't know where to start. And when he finally did begin, he rambled all over the place—the conspiracies in PDID, the CIA, the overthrow of the US government, and the approaching Armageddon.

John Paul could see there was a disaster well in progress. In order to sort it all out, he would have to get Rabbit to settle down and tell the story in a way he could make sense of it. John Paul knew some parts of the investigation, as he had been the one who'd brought Rabbit to the attention of PDID in the beginning. He knew of the long hunt for the Minutemen's gun cache.

John Paul had worked PDID for ten years, directing covert operations. Then, when an investigation of his went upside down, he was out of the division—which was normal operating procedure for PDID. When something goes wrong, you will transfer out immediately to a faceless, generic assignment. You will remain silent or your career will be ground to dust.

Even though John Paul was no longer assigned to PDID, he remained silently part of it, and he had been around a long time. He knew the program well. Plus, he had a very strong personal relationship with someone very high up the ladder in the Department. It was also rumored that he was well connected with friends in US government intelligence.

The next two hours passed ever so slowly. It seemed like forever. Rabbit trusted John Paul—that is, as much as he could trust anyone. Rabbit laid out the events of the past four years, moving quickly over his assignment until he reached the contact point with DePugh and the Minutemen organization.

From that point on, he described the entire investigation in detail, slowly, step by step, including the known facts, his fears, and his premonitions of things to come. Rabbit recited the events in the manner of an expert witness on the stand. Finally, he had said all he had to say. For the first time in a very long time, he had told the whole truth, and he felt relief—a feeling he had forgotten long ago.

After a long pause, it was John Paul's turn. He began his questions, and there were many. Rabbit answered each one in the fullest detail. John Paul pressed hard with his questions, like a skilled attorney conducting a withering cross-examination, returning over and over to questions he had already asked. He was probing for any inconsistency in the answers that Rabbit had given. There were none.

Finally, the detective sergeant said nothing. He smoked his cigarette and stared at Rabbit in deep thought. John Paul had followed the investigation along by way of Harris, who had kept him informed. For an unknown reason, Harris owed his job to John Paul.

John Paul knew about the hunt for the elusive machine gun cache from back in the day when he had worked PDID. Now, what he had been told and what Rabbit was telling him were two very different accounts. Somebody was lying.

Focusing on the depth and severity of the stress symptoms that had overcome his old partner, John Paul noted Rabbit's inability to sit still and constantly looking about the bar. He could see Rabbit's jaw muscles continually tighten and flex when he was not speaking. He had apparently been grinding his teeth so much that the front ones were worn thin and had chipped to a ragged edge. In the course of his career John Paul had seen many stressed out operators, but he had never seen anything like this.

Rabbit patiently waited for the detective to speak. The only thing moving was the smoke drifting upward from John Paul's cigarette. At long last he took a final drag on it and snuffed it out in the dirty ashtray, which was filled with the butts of the other chain-smoked cigarettes he had burned during the last two hours.

John Paul surveyed the room slowly and then looked at Rabbit. He spoke in his quiet Southern manner, his voice so low it was barely audible. He told Rabbit he would help extricate him from the nightmare. To say it was going to be a difficult task and unimaginably stressful would be an enormous understatement. Everyone in on this—and there are many—outranked Rabbit. They were both inside the Department and out. He would have to face all of them by himself. These people would breathe fire, threaten termination and prosecution, and attack his credibility from every possible angle. He would go from a fair-haired boy to the enemy in a single tick of the clock. Rabbit's life and everything he had worked so long and hard for were unraveling at warp speed.

John Paul was concerned for everyone who had anything to do with the investigation. Obviously, it was out of control, and it had to end. The problem was how to accomplish that without doing immeasurable damage to everyone involved, including the Los Angeles Police Department. He would need to go to work on it immediately.

On the table in front of John Paul was a yellow legal pad on which he had written a few notes. He flipped to the last page, which was already pulled loose. He wrote at the top of the page "Statement of Facts," gave Rabbit his pen, and told him to sign his initials only at the bottom of the page by the "X." Far to the right of the "X" was a one-inch circle. He instructed Rabbit to press his right index finger in the circle. Rabbit complied, too overwhelmed from the past two hours to ask why.

John Paul advised Rabbit to get a motel room by the airport for the night, stay hidden, and get some sleep. He knew the next day would be a day from hell that Rabbit would never forget. He would need every bit of strength and courage he could muster.

He told Rabbit to call him at 6:00 a.m. If he did not answer, Rabbit was not to leave a message or speak to anyone else; he was to call back every thirty minutes until John Paul himself answered.

John Paul's parting comment to Rabbit was, "This meeting never took place."

It was just after 3:00 p.m. when Rabbit left the bar. He was desperate to find Charlie. More than ever he needed to talk to her. He looked everywhere. Hours passed. She was nowhere to be found. It was now late in the evening. He decided to disregard John Paul's advice to get a motel room. He was tired of living in rat holes and strange places. He really wanted more than anything to go to his little country cottage in the tree section of Manhattan Beach, although he knew that wasn't possible under the circumstances.

This would be a very long night. And as jacked up as he was, sleep would surely escape him. Harris would be badgering him, and he couldn't take it anymore. He knew he was on the edge. He needed to be alone to think this out.

He decided to hide from everyone, and he knew the place. He drove to the beach and parked. Leaving his truck, he walked three long city blocks to a desolate area of the beach at the north end of Manhattan by the Edison power plant. Nobody ever went there, not even the dog catcher. Rabbit knew that, because in happier days, that was where he had let his faithful Shepherd run free.

He sat tucked away, hidden back among the huge boulders, his heavy hooded jacket zipped up to keep him warm. As he watched the waves roll in and break on the beach, he tried again for the millionth time to make sense of the madness he found himself embroiled in.

How could this have happened? It was all impossible. It was absolutely the loneliest, darkest moment in his life. The night was pitch black, cold, and shrouded in thick fog. He had the feeling he was sitting somewhere on the moon, without another living soul around. He prayed for help. All he could think of was the two calls he had to make at sunrise, the first to John Paul and the second to Harris.

The next nine hours would seem like an eternity. He felt like an outlaw on the run. How could his career have taken him to this cold, dark place? He thought back to that proud moment at his academy graduation, how full of hope he had been, and how excited he had been to start his police career. Never could he have imagined this. If he had, he would have become the priest his father had wanted him to be.

Morning broke, which meant the moment of reckoning had arrived. The time had come to make those fateful phone calls. The nearest pay phone was the cold phone he used to communicate with DePugh. How ironic, he thought, that he would be more comfortable calling DePugh, whom he had come to know, than police headquarters.

It was exactly 6:00 a.m. when he phoned John Paul, who answered on the third ring. John Paul spoke at his normal low volume, barely audible. He said he had worked on the problem throughout the night. It was complicated. Because of those involved, he would need more time. John Paul assured him everything could be fixed. It would take another day to get final approval of the details of a modified plan that would placate the self-important masterminds who had crafted this ill-conceived plan. Those in charge were convinced their plan was in the best political interest of the chief, and serving those interests was their primary objective.

John Paul stressed to Rabbit that he would have to delay going forward with PDID's operation. "You must do whatever you need to do to stall it."

Rabbit was in a panic. He knew he didn't have any more time.

John Paul admonished him again, "Rabbit, most important of all, do not, under any circumstances, go near the guns."

The phone went dead. Rabbit knew his premonition of death was coming to pass.

Chapter 36
KMA-367

The time had come to make the most difficult call of his life. He dialed the pager number for Harris and waited for it to answer, then left his number. It seemed only a nanosecond passed between his hanging up and the sound of the phone ringing again.

Harris, enraged, barked, "Where the fuck are you? And what kind of shit are you pulling now?" Although he'd expected it, Rabbit didn't need to hear any of that.

Harris continued his rant. "This is goddamn D-Day. We've got an operation underway, and you're pulling some hide-and-seek bullshit!"

While Harris continued his tirade, a police helicopter and its pilot were sitting on the police helipad downtown, poised and ready to fly into action. SWAT had finished their briefing and were in their chase vehicles with their M-16s, standing ready to execute their plan of arrest and confiscate the guns. Command staff were assembled, exhilarated in anticipation of the pending bust.

The police radio inside Harris's car was crackling nonstop with inquiries and demands regarding Rabbit's whereabouts and the status of the operation. Harris's stomach was churning. He was filled with rage. He had long anticipated that this day would cinch his promotion to Lieutenant. Now it looked like he would fall back to earth as a clerk in Property Division.

Rabbit continued listening to Harris as he leaned against the telephone booth, holding onto it for dear life as if it were a life raft. He had the shakes. His knees felt like rubber, his mouth was as dry as the Gobi Desert, and his head felt as if it were going to explode. He felt his waistband for his gun, his only friend left. He pulled it from under his jacket and placed it on the metal shelf of the phone booth.

There was so much he wanted to say to Harris, but his brain was totally scrambled, and it was impossible to focus on a single thought. Besides, whatever he wanted to say, he had already said a thousand times. It no longer mattered. It was insignificant now.

He was tormented by the thought of Joan being killed and him surviving. He knew he would be as responsible for her death as would be the one who pulled the trigger, and he could not live with that.

Slowly, in a low voice, he muttered into the phone to Harris.

"Billy, please listen. I'm calling you to tell you it's all over. I'm finished. I can't go any farther with this. I'm sorry, I can't take part in destroying these people. They are going to die. You know that. The Feds who provided them the guns and the justification for this whole action are going to escape punishment, and that is the worst crime of all."

Harris shot back, "You're sorry? Are you completely crazy? You can't do this. Your career will be over. And that's not all—they'll give you a direct order to proceed with the operation, and if you don't, you're headed to trial board for insubordination and a guarantee you'll be fired. They will go to the District Attorney and get a felony filing on you for obstruction of justice and conspiracy.

"Listen, pal, this is big time stuff. For God's sake, get ahold of yourself. There are people from PDID, captains, commanders, bureau chiefs, and Chief Gates himself, and who knows who the fuck else. They are all expecting this to go down this morning. You gotta do this or we'll both go to the wall."

Harris waited. Stone silence at the other end of the phone. He was beside himself; he was having a meltdown in his disbelief that this was happening. It was his worst nightmare ever. How could this possibly have derailed? He thought he was going to have a stroke. His heart was pumping like the heart of a racehorse at the finish line of the Kentucky Derby. This was a disaster of major proportion. He wished he had been on the Titanic.

With unimaginable forces pulling in all directions at the same time, Rabbit's world imploded, sending him spinning blindly off into a massive black hole. He was lost. He was consumed by his stress-induced psychosis and had crossed the point of no return. It was like floating in the silence of deep space. In his mind all he could see was the sickening image of Joan lying on a cold, stainless steel table in the county morgue.

Harris still didn't get it. He yelled into the phone, "Goddamn it, Rabbit, do you fuckin' hear me? Where are you?"

Rabbit was standing in a glass phone booth, shaking. Lack of sleep, fear, and the cold had all taken their toll. His eyes closed tightly as his face pressed the cold, glass walls of the booth. It felt like an out-of-body experience. He could see the SWAT trap and his truck being pulled over by the police. Then suddenly there was movement, something happened, and the shooting started. Glass flying everywhere. There was the sound of bullets tearing into the truck and lots of screaming. There was a heavy, thick smoke, maybe from a smoke grenade. Then it stopped. The windows of the truck were all blown out. There was blood everywhere. He could see everyone in the truck slumped over—no movement, no more sound. Just silence and the horrible smell of death.

Harris screamed again into the phone, and that snapped Rabbit back to the moment. He desperately tried to put those thoughts into words, but it wasn't working.

Harris waited for what seemed like eternity, and then ever so faintly, he heard Rabbit trying to speak. His voice choked up and raspy, but unmistakably clear. After a hundred times, Harris finally comprehended Rabbit's fateful words.

"It's all over."

Rabbit dropped the telephone receiver. As it fell, it swung back and forth by the coiled stainless steel cord, banging into the glass.

Rabbit picked up his gun from the phone booth shelf, paused for a second, took a deep breath, and yanked open the door. He stepped out into the heavy fog and walked away.

Harris now clearly understood that the Minutemen investigation on which they had worked so hard on, for so long, was now finished—and his prize bird dog would never hunt again.

Chapter 37
Plan B

As ordered, Harris raced back to Police Headquarters, knowing the wrath of God awaited him. As he entered the office of PDID, sweat was pouring from his forehead. He was a physical wreck.

The secretary sitting at her desk looked up at him and nodded for him to go on in. There were a lot of anxious pissed off people waiting for him. As Harris walked past her, she winked and whispered *Good luck*.

Entering the squad room, he felt like a crippled gladiator without a sword, walking into the Roman Colosseum to engage a pride of hungry lions.

The squad room had been turned into a command post for this mission. There was the Bureau Chief, the Commander, several Captains and their assisting staff of the support units that had been assigned to this arrest operation.

The day before, he had envisioned all of these people would be waiting for him to lavish praise for the incredible job done well, but that was before the operation imploded. Now, instead of a celebration and high five's from everyone, the atmosphere was one of doom and gloom. It looked more like an angry lynch mob at the gallows, waiting for the arrival of the prisoner to be hung.

Several ranking detectives surrounded the PDID Captain, who was uncharacteristically waving his arms wildly. He looked more like a spectator at a football game than the ever-stoic captain of PDID. When he saw Harris, though, he stopped in his tracks. Exercising all the control he could muster to keep from exploding, and speaking through his clenched teeth, he ordered Harris to go into his office.

Harris promptly obliged, the Captain and the Bureau Chief two steps behind him. After they entered the room, the Captain slammed the door with such force that it nearly broke from the hinges.

The Captain, breathing fire like a beast of the inferno, hissed, "What the fuck happened out there with your golden boy?"

Harris had prepared as much as possible for this moment, which he'd known was coming. From the moment Rabbit dropped the phone in the telephone booth, he was well aware that it would be up to him to explain what went wrong—and to have a brilliant backup plan to keep from being thrown out of PDID and assigned to directing traffic at First Street and Spring for the rest of his time in the Department.

With his best effort, Harris calmly began, saying there was no way to know at that moment what caused Rabbit to break and walk away. Maybe he sold out to the Minutemen, or maybe he had some sort of a psychological malfunction. Whichever the case, this was not the time to focus on that—because the main objective of this entire investigation was to get the machine gun cache of the Minutemen.

Harris said that in every investigation he conducted, he always had a contingency plan in case a situation like this arose. He knew there would always be the possibility Rabbit might encounter some type of accident or other unforeseen issue that would prevent him from completing the investigation as originally planned.

Unfortunately, now that one of those issues had actually occurred, there was not a minute to lose, if PDID was going to make the weapon seizure without Rabbit.

Harris paused a brief moment to study the Captain and the Bureau Chief. It looked to him that his story was succeeding, so he continued on.

His back-up plan was to deploy SWAT to Joan's house and surround it. Once the SWAT team was securely in place, he would call Joan on the phone to announce that her house was surrounded by the police, and that if she failed to surrender immediately, the house would be tear-gassed with her aged, sickly mother inside.

Harris considered this plan foolproof, as Joan would never put her mother at any risk. He knew from the many conversations Rabbit had with Joan that her first and foremost concern was always for her mother.

Assuming the scenario would play out as he anticipated, Harris would then cuff Joan and her mother, separate them and offer Joan a deal. If she would take Harris to the gun cache, she and her mother would be released.

The Bureau Chief and the Captain left the office to discuss the merits of the plan and the probability of success. When both were satisfied with this Plan B, the Bureau Chief phoned the Chief to explain Harris's plan. The Chief gave his approval—and just like that, the Command Post was back in business, and Harris' Plan B was in motion.

##

Rabbit had no way to know what had been taking place since he and Harris had their last telephone conversation, but it was a safe bet that Harris and others were now hot on the hunt for him. He had not a minute to lose.

His first order of business was to return to the apartment that he shared with his friend Buddy to leave a short, cryptic note regarding his disappearance, in hopes that Buddy would make sense of it. In any event, it would, at the very least, give him warning that Harris and others would be coming to find Rabbit.

Next, he needed to grab some clothes, passport, all his cash and a few weapons—especially the fully automatic HK-91, as well as an improvised explosive device that he had spent time learning how to build and handle properly at the militia training camp in the San Bernardino desert. Rabbit knew that Harris and other detectives would soon search the apartment looking for any clues into Rabbit's unexplained behavior. Any illegal weapons or explosives found would result in Buddy's arrest, since the apartment and utilities were all in his name, and that would create a massive problem for him.

There was no way Rabbit would ever allow his good friend to go down for the sake of this bullshit investigation.

After all, Buddy never knew of the machine gun or the IED. He tolerated Rabbit's odd behavior because he loved him like a brother and believed Rabbit had succumbed to a spell that grew out of the silent, dark cult known as the Public Disorder Intelligence Division.

But the illegal weapon and explosives would have been infinitely more than Buddy would ever tolerate, and if he'd found out about them, Rabbit would have been out the door.

Rabbit secured all the things he wanted and was ready to go. With one last quick search of the apartment to make sure he had not left anything incriminating behind, he now realized what a terrible mistake it was getting Buddy involved by being his roommate. He felt terrible about that, but like so much of this nightmare, there was no way to undo any of it.

He had one more thing to do before leaving. As difficult as it was, he picked up his phone and placed a call to DePugh, for, he hoped, the last time. He'd created a cover story a long time ago, in the event something like this happened. Hopefully, the story would be convincing enough to give Rabbit a headstart for his hideout, before DePugh figured out that he was an agent of the government.

DePugh answered the phone. Something disastrous must have happened, Rabbit said. Joan wasn't answering her phone, and that wasn't like her. Rabbit acted panicked. He said he thought the Feds must be closing in for an arrest or something, and he had no intention of going to prison for any of this.

To Rabbit's astonishment, DePugh already knew something had gone awry. He told Rabbit not to panic, because that would lead to a mistake, and that was not acceptable. If this operation were to go haywire, a lot of people would go to jail. The critical task at hand, then, was to complete the gun transfer—at any cost.

Just like all the other times, DePugh directed Rabbit to go to the cold phone at Marine and Highland in Manhattan Beach. He would call him back in 30 minutes.

Rabbit got off the phone, now facing another quandary over what to do about DePugh's callback order.

After putting the last of his things in his truck and racing off from the apartment, Rabbit took a long, roundabout way to the cold phone. He had plenty of time, since he was already close to the phone location—and, besides, he needed a little time to think through his next move.

He parked his truck a block over from the phone booth and walked the final distance, in order to reconnoiter the area for any unusual activity. Everything appeared OK.

Before he had ample time to consider all that was so rapidly transpiring, the phone rang, startling him as if from a daze.

DePugh uncharacteristically spoke very fast, as time was of the essence. "Rabbit! You got to pull yourself together for the sake of our freedom and our organization. Now listen carefully to me."

Rabbit agreed, "I'm listening."

DePugh went on. "I just learned there is a snitch in one of our units in LA. Because of that, I hastily made some critical changes in the West Coast Operations in the last 24 hours. I cannot discuss any more of that with you now, but I have received information from a trusted source that something has been learned by the Feds regarding the guns. The situation is so bad I will never return to California again. I am now counting on you more than ever to help save the guns we have been sitting on for years."

Rabbit was stunned as DePugh continued, "Joan phoned just after midnight and was paranoid. She was sure she had seen plain-clothes cops patrolling her street, and, in a panic, she tried to contact you without success."

Rabbit responded, "You know I was working my job at the airport when she was trying to phone me. It was impossible for her to reach me. The plan she and I made was for me to contact her after my shift ended this morning."

Rabbit's mind raced. He wondered what could have spooked Joan this much.

Was it her paranoia? Or was there really something to it? Maybe the Feds were working a case and closing in on the guns. Or, even worse, was it another nutty inept move by Harris like the train station test? Only this time it would be to stake out Joan's house in an attempt to gather whatever information he could to help corroborate what Rabbit had been reporting.

Perhaps Harris had noticed something in Rabbit's attitude or demeanor that had aroused his concern about his loyalty to the investigation and decided to discern if his "Bird Dog" was straying to the other side.

DePugh snapped Rabbit back to the moment. "Don't worry about Joan," he said. "I got her calmed down. She was convinced the cops had surveillance in place and were about to spring an arrest. She was insistent on an earlier pickup out of concern for her ill mother's sake and the trauma it would cause her if the cops kicked the door down. I instructed her to call two former Leavenworth inmates that she knows and to make arrangements to transfer the guns as quick as possible."

Rabbit felt paralyzed. With one hand, he clenched the greasy pay phone pressed to his ear, and with the other, he squeezed the back of his neck. "So now where is Joan and where are the guns?" he asked, but as soon as he did, Rabbit realized that no answer to those questions would be satisfactory.

DePugh tactfully detailed the events that had occurred while Rabbit had been working his shift at the airport. He explained that the guns were already moved and reassured him that Joan was back home and that her part in the mission was finalized. At hearing this, Rabbit was relieved for her safety, but he was frustrated beyond belief that he had abandoned this epic mission to spare Joan from a deadly attack that, in fact, would never have occurred.

While Rabbit silently processed this information, DePugh continued. "Joan assisted in the first stage of the transfer of the guns from the storage unit at three o'clock this morning. It all was done without incident. The guns and explosives are in a moving truck that was heisted from a truck rental company. It is parked in a safe location per my instructions. I am now depending on your help for the next critical phase of the transfer."

DePugh instructed Rabbit to drive to the Los Angeles airport Parking Structure 3 and proceed to the second parking tier. The overhead structure would give him cover from any aerial surveillance that might be focused on him.

He was to slowly circle the parking deck until the contact man waved him down. He would be eating a hamburger, and his left hand would be wrapped in a yellow bandanna. Rabbit was to follow the man's orders from that point on, as if it was DePugh himself giving the order.

In ending the call, DePugh said, "Understand at this point there is no turning back without dire consequences."

Rabbit knew for his own well-being he had no choice but to reassure DePugh that he would explicitly follow his orders, just as he had sworn he would when he became a Minuteman. It was abundantly clear that DePugh's direction was not a request, but an order. Failure to follow it through would turn him into a hunted man, with a guaranteed trip to the morgue.

"I'll take care of it," Rabbit promised, as his mind raced.

Rabbit thought that if he followed DePugh's orders, maybe he could get the guns after all— or, at least know their whereabouts and deal with their seizure or destruction some other time. He knew there must be a better way to accomplish the objective without the carnage and mayhem that would result from the ill-conceived arrest plan the department was intent on executing.

The airport was only a short 20-minute drive from the phone booth in Manhattan Beach. Arriving at the airport, Rabbit did exactly as he had been instructed. After two circles around the parking deck, he saw the contact man leaning against a blue four-door Chevrolet.

Rabbit was taken aback. It was Walt, the ex-convict DePugh had done time with in Leavenworth—and the telephone man from the operation where they planted the cocaine and kiddie porn in the apartment.

And this time, Walt himself was clearly high on cocaine.

Being an alpha-male and ex-convict, Walt wasted no time on small talk and jumped right to the point: "You got a call from DePugh this morning and he told you he was no longer in charge of the West Coast, right? From this point on, I am the boss. You OK with that, or do you have a problem with it? If you or any Minutemen don't want to go along with the new program here, you can pack your bags and go back to Missouri with DePugh.

No one is going to get in our way now that we got the weapons. We are on a sacred mission."

Rabbit mumbled, "I got no problem with that."

Walt told Rabbit if he was on board with the new program, to leave his truck and get in the car. They had a long road trip ahead.

Rabbit said he had his automatic rifle in the truck and a few clothes and there was no way he was leaving those behind. Walt stared at Rabbit, after a long moment, told him to bring the stuff.

Rabbit got the rifle, a duffel bag, his .45 auto pistol, some ammo, and the IED, which he put on the backseat floor under a blanket. Then, they slowly drove out of the airport and proceeded east on Century Boulevard.

Across Los Angeles, 21 miles away, Harris' Plan B was in motion. SWAT stealthily made their way up the hill to Joan's house on the 400 block of Maltman Ave. They had the house surrounded, and, if this new plan failed, they were ready for a firefight.

A block away in an undercover police communication van was the SWAT commander, Harris, the PDID captain and a deputy district attorney for legal consultation.

After more than a decade of investigation, Harris finally made the call he hoped would make all the time and effort that went into this operation worthwhile. Joan, expecting a call from Rabbit or DePugh, answered to hear, "This is Detective Billy Harris of the Los Angeles Police Department. We have your house surrounded."

Harris then directed Joan and her mother to come out onto her front porch with their backs to the street and their hands raised. Failure to immediately comply would result in SWAT firing tear gas into her house.

The phone went dead. A long two minutes passed. Harris placed another call.

As the phone was ringing, the door opened. Joan, assisting her aging mother, stepped onto the porch and both raised their hands in compliance. The SWAT entrance team swarmed the porch and cuffed both Joan and her mother. Quickly and efficiently, other members of the team searched the house and secured the location.

Harris, now on the porch, had Joan and her mother separated and taken back into the house. Her mother was terrified and crying. Joan begged for her mother to be uncuffed.

The plan was playing out exactly as Harris anticipated it would. Joan was at his mercy.

But Harris knew that with each passing minute, the odds of his plan succeeding were rapidly diminishing. It would have been better to transport the two women downtown to police headquarters for a maximum interrogation effect, but there was no time for that.

Joan's frail mother was taken to the sewing room at the other end of the house, where the SWAT commander closed the blinds and left the door slightly ajar.

Harris began his interrogation of Joan in the front living room. "Joan, let me tell you why we are here. We know all about the gun cache. We know that you know about it, and we know that you have spent a couple of decades protecting it for the Minuteman cause and that you know where it is located."

Joan interrupted and defiantly responded, "That's ridiculous!

I have no idea what you are talking about!"

Harris paused and stared into Joan's eyes, and then, with melodrama, dropped a picture on the coffee table in front of Joan. It was a picture of Rabbit.

"You might recognize this man. He is an FBI agent. He was assigned to this gun investigation. Circumstances as they are, he has been directed to the East Coast to work a case that has National Security implications."

Joan sat handcuffed on the edge of her worn, green crushed velvet couch and stared in disbelief at the photo that Harris had dropped in front of her. Speechless, she began to tear up. It was as if she'd just gotten devastating news of her son being killed in combat.

At Joan's emotional reaction, Harris was speechless as well. He thought, "Was my golden boy that good that he convinced this old lady that he was the son she never had? Or was he so good that he had fooled me and turned his loyalty to the side that he swore to uphold?"

Either way, for that brief moment, Joan and Harris had something in common. And then, it passed, in the blink of an eye.

Harris shook it off and went on to say that the LAPD Bureau Chief wanted to commit neither the time nor the resources to continue this investigation. The Chief just wanted the guns off the street.

To that end, he explained, the police were prepared to grant immunity to both Joan and her mother, on the condition that Joan would reveal the location of the guns.

Joan could hear her mother crying and calling out to her from the room down the hall. It was a crushing heartache. She was devastated. This is what she feared more than anything in this world.

So, she told Harris that she would cooperate on three conditions. One, the District Attorney would have to put the grant of immunity to her and her mother in writing. Second, the cuffs would have to be removed from her mother immediately. And third, the written agreement was to be given to her attorney, who could be at her house within 30 minutes if she called him right away.

Ecstatic that his plan was working perfectly, Harris agreed. Out of the ashes, he'd managed to save his own ass. Maybe he would make lieutenant after all.

And now, for all he cared, fuck Rabbit.

What Harris didn't realize was that Joan's attorney was also a long-time loyal Minuteman.

After several calls between the District Attorney's office and Joan's attorney, the conditions were finalized. The agreement was handwritten and signed by Joan, her attorney and the deputy district attorney at the scene.

Once Joan's mother was released, she immediately left with Joan's attorney. The attorney drove down the hill one block to Sunset Boulevard, made a right turn, and stopped at the first phone booth.

He called DePugh.

"Bob, we got big trouble," the attorney told him. "The cops raided Joan's house and grabbed her and her mother. The good news is the cops didn't arrest them, and I managed to get them immunity for giving up the gun stash. The really bad news is: Rabbit is an FBI agent."

There was a huge gasp at the other end of the phone, followed by DePugh shouting, "No, No! This is far more than bad news.

It needs to be fixed immediately. Walt is with the rat right now moving the guns. I got to get a hold of him."

With that, the phone slammed down. Once again, Harris had made a monumental mistake in his blind ambition.

Harris, Joan, the SWAT team and a large LAPD equipment truck departed the house for the gun cache.

Directed by Joan, the caravan made its way from the 5 Freeway and to the 101, heading west into the Valley and finally exiting at Van Nuys Boulevard. It was a long, tedious ride, and Harris was getting nervous.

His mind raced back, remembering that Rabbit once said the guns had been stored somewhere in Downtown Los Angeles. But then again, there had been so much information, some of which was as yet unconfirmed, that maybe he was just confused.

In any event, he was becoming more anxious by the minute. He took a deep breath and tried to recompose during the journey, which would take over an hour.

After several turns, they arrived at a self-storage unit far away from the main area of Van Nuys. Joan directed them to #150, whose door was secured by a combination lock. She spun the dial and opened it.

She was about to raise the door when Harris told her to step aside. He wanted to be the one to roll up the metal door and to be the first into the room containing the long sought-after Minuteman machine gun cache.

He raised the door, making a great clattering noise, and there, in the center of the large storage bin, were two boxes of beaten-up World War II semi-automatic M1 carbines—*completely legal*. The rifles could be purchased at almost any Army Surplus store for a few dollars each. The street value of the guns was negligible.

Harris stared in disbelief, lost for words. Now he was furious. He realized the kind old lady Joan and DePugh had had their own contingency plan for something like this, and they had once again thwarted the government agents.

Chapter 38
The Reckoning

Rabbit and Walt made their way Southbound on the 405 toward the rendezvous in Torrance, where the truck with the weapons had been parked. Walt was obviously more preoccupied than he'd been several months earlier during their first operation—and Rabbit found this unsettling.

After several miles of quiet tension, Rabbit broke the silence.

"Hey man, I am freaking out by all the last-minute changes. I want to know where we are going and what the plan is, otherwise you can count me out. If need be, I'll jump out of this fucking car and hitchhike off into the sunset. I am not going to jail over some bullshit I am kept in the total dark about."

Walt continued driving and calmly responded, "Dude, you need to take it easy."

He went on for a long time: "Here's what's going down. The original plan to transfer the guns was unexpectedly aborted by DePugh at the last minute. DePugh told me on the phone late last night that he found out there is a snitch in one of the groups in LA, and the rat has told the Feds about the guns. That is what necessitated the last minute change of plans. Even though Joan couldn't get a hold of you last night to help, DePugh insisted that you remain in on the transfer. He said at this point you are the only one in LA that he completely trusts and that's good enough for me. I don't know anyone in LA that I have that much trust in and I need another hand to help with this operation.

"DePugh wants the guns moved far from Los Angeles. He no longer trusts and has lost all confidence in the LA organization. It has been compromised by snitches and agents provocateurs. He wants the guns in a safe location near San Diego. That is where I come in."

It turns out that for years, Walt had been in charge of a large militia in that area, with a detailed plan for a series of attacks on National Guard armories, where they would seize arms and equipment to be used in an upcoming consummate race war.

"We have been planning a revolution for years," Walt continued. "We have studied the insurrections throughout the U.S. to learn the catalyst that ignited them, and how they were contained by the government. Based on what we learned, we have designed the most lethal and devastating riot of all time. It will make the 1965 LA riots look like child's play. To accomplish our objective, we need a substantial amount of automatic weapons and explosives to attack and overwhelm any resistance at the armories."

So that's what they needed DePugh's arsenal for. Once they'd taken control of the armories, they would seize newer and more lethal war equipment that they would need when they engaged the Army that the government would deploy to reestablish order.

Rabbit sat listening in disbelief. DePugh would never go along with that plan. How would Walt get away with such a crazy scheme?

"Of course, I knew that DePugh would never go along with

our plan," Walt admitted. "So, I made up a story that convinced him that we would always be loyal to him and dedicated to the Minutemen cause. I assured him that the most secure place for the weapons would be to transfer them to my unit, and he went for it."

So Walt wasn't a Minuteman—or even close to one—nor did he believe in their objectives!

DePugh had envisioned small, armed groups of patriots ready to defend the freedoms of the country against a left-wing takeover of the constitutional government that was of the people, by the people and for the people. But Walt, on the other hand, was simply an anarchist, hell-bent on creating mayhem.

DePugh had been totally deceived. His and Walt's philosophies were as different as night and day! This maniac was a serious threat to society.

Trying to better understand the diabolical logic of Walt, Rabbit asked, "At some point you must have believed in the Minutemen. What caused you to change your mind? Maybe I've overlooked something in their program."

Walt looked over at Rabbit several times before he let loose with his answer. "DePugh is a true believer, but his vision is a fucking fantasy. Somehow, he believes that he and his band of Minutemen can save the country. It ain't ever going to happen. I never bought into it, even after all the years of discussing his philosophy while we were doing time in Leavenworth. Here is a cold undisputed fact: The White race has been totally fucked up by the left wing Jew-controlled, Black-loving system that runs this country.

"I and a lot of others have paid a huge price behind it. I am a pissed-off White man who is tired of riding in the back of the bus.

My divine mission in life is to burn this whole shithouse to ashes. It is time for this fucking system that hijacked the government from the White Anglo-Saxons who created this country to pay up."

Before Rabbit could even begin to figure out how to respond, Walt continued, "The only reason I am risking my life in this weapons deal is because I know what my guys in San Diego are going to do. I did time with most of them in the joint, and I know they don't believe in DePugh's fantasy, either. All they want are the weapons, and now we have him convinced we are one hundred percent with him.

"What we are going to do is to launch an all out guerrilla war, killing as many Jews and Blacks along the way as possible."

Walt then looked over at Rabbit once again, sizing him up a little too closely for Rabbit's comfort. "You seem to be a smart boy, and I don't think you really believe in DePugh's pipe dream either," he said, "That is why I am OK with you being a part of this operation in moving the weapons. But listen to me real close, if you rat on any of this to DePugh or anybody, you will be in the fucking morgue before the sun comes up. I can guarantee you that. You got any questions on any of this?"

Rabbit surprised Walt by responding, in fact, with a question. "How do you think you can start a riot as big as you imagine no matter how many weapons you have?"

Walt answered in a very calm voice. The bluster was gone, but his intensity was still focused like a laser beam.

"We live in a totally divided society," he said, "There are many underlying tensions from all the injustice, and those issues we can build on and exploit to our maximum benefit. We have widespread support. White people have had it with all the affirmative action bullshit, and they are waiting for someone to step up and light the fuse of the revolution."

Without pause, he also added: "And I am the one to do that."

Rabbit decided to continue probing. After all, he was trapped with Walt for a few hours anyway—and if he had accepted everything that Walt said at face value too easily without challenging him as he had in the past, Walt would know something was up.

"I understand all that, but you still didn't answer my question. How do you intend to make this mega-riot happen?"

Rabbit could tell that Walt was pretty pleased with himself. At this point, each time Rabbit fished for information ended up becoming just another opportunity for Walt to boast.

As a smirk began to emerge on Walt's face, he explained that he didn't have enough time to lay out all the details. He would, however, give Rabbit a thumbnail sketch: With the help of some cops who were loyal members of their organization and had helped finalize some of the details of the plan they'd designed in prison, they were going to set up some very realistic-looking traffic stops late at night. Their members, dressed in cop uniforms, would stop Black motorists, shoot them, and then speed off.

Walt seemed pretty confident that if they could repeat that several times—making sure there were witnesses at every stop— hoards of Blacks would be in the streets, burning and looting the city, within 24 hours of the first shooting. With cops overwhelmed trying to stop the riot, Walt's militia would have their snipers go after politicians and judges on their "kill list."

By this point, Walt was no longer trying to hide his smugness.

His face was plastered with a full-on grin, stretching from one ear to the other.

"It will be total mayhem," Walt said, almost with a giggle, "There is no way the system can handle this type of calamity. The news networks will spread the event like gasoline on a fire. As the news is broadcast across the country, assholes in city after city will start rioting. Then, when law and order totally collapse, other like-minded White militias will follow our lead and go into action, shooting looters. Cops and National Guard soldiers won't even respond to duty, because they'll be at home trying to protect their wives and children. Anarchy will be rampant, and the system will implode. From the ashes, White militias will take control, and a new system will rise. The Blacks, the Jews, and bleeding-heart liberals will be gone forever."

To Rabbit, this madman's plan—if it worked— sounded like Armageddon. He was at a loss for words when Walt asked him what he thought.

Rabbit paused for a moment and then said, "Sounds like you boys did a pretty thorough job putting this together. Now, what is the plan for the guns and other equipment on the truck that you got from Joan's storage unit?"

Walt wasn't about to put all of his cards on the table just yet. He said he would lay out that plan when they got to the cargo truck rendezvous in Torrance.

An hour after leaving the airport, Walt and Rabbit exited the freeway at Torrance Boulevard by the large Alpine Village complex. The weekly outdoor swap meet was underway in its huge parking lot. As always the case, the lot was overflowing with vendors and shoppers. Traffic on the surrounding streets was busy, affording adequate cover for what they had to do in the cargo area of the truck. No one would pay any special attention to them or to the truck. It just looked like another vendor organizing his sale merchandise.

The driver had already arrived and was waiting at the curbside. He was young, maybe in his early 30s. He was six-feet tall and very neatly dressed, with a cropped haircut and a well-disciplined demeanor and spoke in a military fashion. He'd parked the truck under a large overgrown tree and raised the hood of the truck as if there were a mechanical issue with the motor.

Walt parked the car directly behind the rental truck, further blocking the view of any passersby.

When the three men rolled up the metal door in the rear, Rabbit was impressed with the number of boxes. Most of them were rifle boxes. Others had "Danger: Explosives" printed on the side in large, red letters. There were a lot of ammunition cans and wooden grenade boxes, too.

As Rabbit noted, the truck had been loaded in a hurry. It was totally disorganized. Several of the boxes had fallen over, and M16 rifles from one of the spilled cases were strewn about the floor.

Walt told Rabbit to be on the lookout for anyone who looked like a cop. He and the driver loaded two of the M16s and laid them on the floor at the rear of the truck in the event the cops did show up and there was a firefight.

Walt then sprung into action, directing the rearrangement of the boxes in a much more precise manner. Rifles were to be stacked in a horseshoe configuration, from floor to ceiling up against the sides and the wall adjacent to the truck's cab. The explosives, ammunitions and other boxes of material were to be placed in the center. And once everything was securely tied in place, the driver was to wire the detonator to the C-4 explosives and tape it to the boxes marked with red lettering "Danger: Explosives."

It was like déjà vu for Rabbit, remembering that time he'd been forced to drive up north to the Cesar Chavez compound with Easton and his men Gary and Greg. Without thinking, he exclaimed, "What the fuck are you two doing wiring this truck into a bomb?"

Walt told Rabbit not to worry. "The kid doing the wiring is a military bomb expert. This is just a precaution. As soon as he is done, you and me are going on a little road trip down south."

Rabbit said, "Listen, man, we've already been through this. Where the fuck are we going?"

And with that, Rabbit finally had his answer: to the Yaqui Pass in the Anza-Borrego Desert, where one of Walt's men would be waiting. "He'll take over for you so you can head back to the LA airport and get your truck," Walt said.

It would be a three- or four-hour drive down the freeway to Highway 78 and out to Julian, where they'd stop for fuel, get something to eat, and call DePugh to assure him that all was going according to plan.

It all sounded OK to Rabbit—except for the bomb. That was a major problem that made no sense, even when Walt tried to reassure him that the bomb was just a precaution.

Knowing that Walt was going to be the one to drive the truck wasn't much comfort to Rabbit, especially since he was going to have to drive the car and stay off to Walt's left side three or four cars back the whole way. If for any reason the cops were to try to stop the truck, he'd have to run interference, making an erratic lane change into them as if he hadn't seen them, entangling himself with the cops while Walt—and the truck—could continue down to the next exit.

"I'll park the truck in an open area, walk away and trigger the remote firing mechanism, blowing the truck and guns into a million pieces," Walt explained. "All that will happen to you is maybe a ticket for an unsafe lane change."

Rabbit argued, "That is absolutely crazy. Have the soldier boy follow you and crash into the cops. I am not doing that."

Walt shot back, "Listen motherfucker, you don't have a choice. Soldier boy has to get his ass back to his base, and you committed to do this; so whether you like it or not, this is how it's going down. This is serious shit. If I get caught with this stuff, it'll be lights out for me 'cause they would send me back to prison forever. I did 16 hard years for killing a cop, and as much as I enjoyed shooting the motherfucker dead, it was a steep price to pay. So do exactly as I say or your ass is dead."

This was all very bad news. Rabbit didn't like any of it; and with each turn of events, it all kept getting worse.

Rabbit thought that when he'd told Harris he was finished, the operation would be over. But somehow, as always, the operation carried on—only now he had no support of any kind. He wondered if this monster would ever die.

Rabbit grunted, "OK I got it. Now how about you quit being so fucking aggressive toward me? And another thing, would you mind if I put my own automatic rifle and shit in the back of the truck in case I need to do your crazy crash-into-the-cop-car plan? That way I don't get busted for possession of an automatic weapon when they search my car after the crash?"

A bit more civil now, Walt simply said, "Go ahead and do it. We got to get going."

The truck left the parking lot with Walt driving and Rabbit following in the car. They entered the freeway and began their journey to the rendezvous in the Yaqui Pass.

The hours on the road seemed like an eternity, and a fierce late March rainstorm that had started slowed them down even more.

While stopped in Julian, Walt went outside in the cold rain to the pay phone. Walt was soaking wet, but it didn't seem to bother him. He spread his coins out on the wet metal tray and called DePugh's number. The phone was busy. Walt waited a few minutes and retried the number, but it was still busy.

He asked Rabbit what number he had for DePugh, but it was the same as Walt had dialed. He decided to call Joan. Her phone rang and rang, but no answer. Walt asked Rabbit what number he had for Joan, but Rabbit once again repeated the same number that Walt had.

Walt tried DePugh one more time. Again, the phone rang and rang, but this time, someone finally answered. Walt asked to speak to DePugh, and after a brief conversation, he said, "I got it, I'll take care of it"—and, with that, he hung up the phone.

Walt appeared to be very disturbed, his face contorted and frozen stiff. Rabbit asked if everything was OK. Walt just said, "Yeah."

His curt answer was even more foreboding than the dark sky and the eerie, low-hanging cloud cover that shrouded the surrounding mountains. But Rabbit couldn't dwell on it because they had to get moving, as the road from Julian to Anza-Borrego was very narrow and dangerous to travel in the rain—and even more so after dark.

So, they set off on the final leg of their journey. For the next seven miles, they rounded one hairpin turn after another, the highway signs warning of dangerous curves, steep grades and flash floods. The creek running next to the road had swollen from the pouring rain and was now a raging river.

The two vehicles moved no more than 20 miles per hour through the narrow, twisting, turning road into the remote mountain desert.

For miles, there was no sign of life. There were no buildings, no lights, no cars...nothing but emptiness. Finally, they came upon a very old, tiny sign with lettering so small that it was almost unreadable. They could barely make out that it read "Tamarisk Grove Yaqui Pass" and pointed to an even smaller road on the left.

Rabbit had driven this road many years before and remembered it to be mountainous and remote, with lots of sharp turns. A plan to bring this madness to an end once and for all started to emerge in his head. Maybe at some curve in the road, he might be able to drive full speed into the rear of the truck and push it off a cliff, causing the bomb to go off, blowing up the guns and the asshole Walt to oblivion. The only downside was that he might get blown up in the process.

He knew he needed to come up with a better plan.

Rabbit continued following the truck, passing the Tamarisk Campground. His mind raced, and his thoughts began to resemble the very twists and turns of the road he was traveling. As he reflected on where he was going and where he had been, he realized that he was so deep down the rabbit hole, he no longer knew the difference between up and down, light and dark, right and wrong.

Whatever was going to happen, he knew the end was near. He could feel it.

As they closed in on the rendezvous, and with time almost out, Rabbit thought about the police officer who'd been killed by this psychopath. He wondered if the policeman had a family, and, if so, how much pain and suffering they endured over his killing.

Feeling alone and desperate in the fog of the moment, he hoped the policeman was there in spirit with him.

Walt was driving the truck up the steep grade at a snail's pace. He strained to see out the windshield, with the wipers going full speed in the heavy rain. Spotting no approaching headlights, he decided to stop.

Walt pulled the truck off the road onto a wide berm and shut the lights off. He looked into the side view mirrors and saw Rabbit a few car lengths back. He opened his lunch bucket and removed his .45 Colt semi-automatic pistol from it.

As he got out of the truck, he pressed the gun tightly to his pant leg and, with his other hand, tried to shield his eyes from the rain and bright headlights of Rabbit's car. He motioned for him to shut them off.

As he slowly walked from the cab, he stayed pressed to the side of the truck and whispered to himself, "Fucking FBI agent."

Rabbit stopped a full car length back from the truck. He rolled the window down and called out, "Why are we stopping?" He didn't see the gun, but he instinctively knew this was all wrong.

He kept the high beams on Walt.

For a long moment, time seemed frozen. Then suddenly Rabbit jammed the car into reverse and pushed the gas pedal to the floor.

In that split second, Walt crouched down into a combat shooting position and opened fire on Rabbit's car. Several rounds hit the hood, and a few more missed. Then, three rounds smashed through the windshield toward the steering wheel.

Rabbit dove down onto the seat for cover as the car erratically sped backward. It uncontrollably careened off the road, crashed into a guardrail, and then slid across the road and came to rest in the dirt embankment, now crossways to the road.

The engine died. The shooting had stopped.

Rabbit rose up just enough to see that Walt was at the back of the truck with the metal roll up door opened, picking up one of the loaded M16 rifles. Rabbit could also see his own duffel bag with his gun and IED, right next to Walt.

As Walt turned toward Rabbit with the rifle, Rabbit grabbed the trigger device of the IED from his coat pocket and pressed the trigger switch. Nothing happened. He pushed it again. Still nothing. He frantically banged it on the steering wheel and then raised the trigger device to the open window and pressed the switch again. This time, the signal was sent.

Then came the blast, followed instantaneously by a second, more powerful one. A massive shock wave rocked the car. Chunks of metal and all sort of debris went flying through the air. The flash was brilliant—a white-hot fireball followed by a cloud of heavy smoke. Then, there was dead silence.

Deafened from the blast and disoriented, Rabbit sat up and

peered out of the blown-out car windows. All that he could see were a million small, unrecognizable pieces of debris from the truck scattered about. It was surreal.

The force of the blast, coupled with the rain-soaked earth, caused part of the berm where Walt had parked the truck to break away, sending what was left of the truck plunging down the steep wall of the canyon, disappearing into the abyss.

Walt was gone, the guns were gone, and the truck was gone.

At long last, the mission was finally over.

The End

Epilogue 1

Joan and her mother vanished.

DePugh never returned to Los Angeles.

Detective Sergeant Billy Harris was promoted to Lieutenant.

Charlie's attempt to deliver Rabbit's police pistol to him left her with the dubious distinction of being the sole individual arrested for a firearm violation in the entire operation.

Disillusioned and stripped of emotion, she retreated to a reclusive life in the country and assumed a new identity.

Rabbit never received the promotion to detective.

Rabbit did receive his police pension—however, the price he paid, "was not worth it."

Epilogue 2

After lengthy investigations into its secret activities and rogue operations, the Los Angeles Police Department's Public Disorder Intelligence Division was ordered shut down and disbanded in January of 1983.

APPENDIX

Rabbit / Bird Dog 757 .... Undercover Police Officer
Charlie .... Dancer/entrepreneur, Rabbit's "wife"
Buddy Brown .... Rabbit's close friend and roommate
Grasshopper .... Rabbit's biker connection and buddy
Isidro .... Rabbit's guide in Ecuador jungle

Chief Gates .... L.A. Chief of Police
Captain James (Doc) Docherty .... Friend and mentor
Captain Green .... Administrative Vice / Nelson's CO
Lt. Danny Shih .... Administrative Vice
Sergeant Allen .... Novice special ops sgt.
Det-Lt Ralph Weyant .... Rabbit's ex-father-in-law
Det Sgt John Paul Dodaine .... Rabbit's vice partner
Det-Sgt Billy Harris .... Rabbit's Control Officer
Det-Sgt Doug Nelson .... Vice Supervisor (Venice Division)
Det Steve Martinez .... Special undercover ops
Det Terry Silva .... Special undercover ops
Peter Keller .... Special operations instructor

Robert DePugh .... Leader of the Minutemen
Rev. John Harrell ..... Leader of Christian Patriots Defense League
Shelton .... Leader of United Klans of America

William Hawthorne.....Leader of Loyal Order of Mountain Men
Joan Becker.............. DePugh's most trusted member in L.A.
Walter Ritlin....................................Close friend of DePugh
Walt.. Ex-con friend of DePugh
John Dolan.. Minutemen scout
Peter Ferris...................................... "the Pizza Man"
Harry Moran...................................... "the Squirrel"
Mike Shuster ....Radical anti-bussing group
Easton ....Member of Posse Comitatus
Gary and Greg........................ Members of Posse Comitatus
Charlie Bellows..... Pilot of plane for Chavez Compound Op.
Karlin ....Right wing extremist
Shank ....Ex-con / major drug dealer

David Poiry